This book is due on the last date stamped below.
Failure to return books on the date due may result
in assessment of overdue fees.

APR 1 4 2001	MAY 1 6 2012
APR 1 4 REC'D	MAY 0 2 REC'D
NOV 0 3 2005	
MAY 0 5 2008	
MAY 0 5 REC'D	
OCT 2 7 REC'D	
MAY 1 4 2009	
MAY 0 4 REC'D	
DEC 1 6 2010	
DEC 0 8 REC'D	
FINES	.50 per day

D0971171

SYLVIA PLATH

A BIOGRAPHY

Linda Wagner-Martin

Simon and Schuster

New York   London   Toronto   Sydney   Tokyo

Contents

CONTENTS

Preface

Sylvia Plath's *Collected Poems* won the Pulitzer Prize for Poetry in 1982, nearly twenty years after her death on February 11, 1963. This was a rare event: the Pulitzer is almost never given posthumously. But the poems Plath wrote in the last five years of her life, leading to those she wrote during 1962, the year of her *Ariel* poems, were so distinctive—such virtuoso performances in technique, such spellbinding expressions of emotion —that the Pulitzer jury could award the prize to no other book.

Plath would have relished both the prize and the reasons it was given. She believed in her poetry, and she knew her craft thoroughly. In her poems, she wrote about the crucial issues of her life, but she made expert art from those issues. She voiced anger as well as hope; she spoke of sorrow as well as joy. She wrote scathingly about people of whom she disapproved and about the husband who angered her. She wrote peacefully, with a calm lyricism, about her children and their daily activities. And she wrote politically: Plath cared intensely about the arms race, nuclear power, and people's injustice to others.

Plath was a feminist, in a broad sense of the term: she never undervalued herself or her work. She insisted that she be recognized as the talented writer she was even while her children were infants and she was spending more time as a mother and a wife than as a writer. She sought out women as friends and mentors and long admired the writing of Virginia Woolf, Marianne Moore, Stevie Smith, Elizabeth Bishop, and Anne Sexton. Yet, product of the American fifties that she was, Plath knew that, because she was a woman writer, her work would be judged by standards different from those used to judge the work of male writers. She knew that becoming successful would be difficult, if she were to remain true to her artistic convictions and to her own poetic voice. That knowledge angered her, as did other circumstances of her life in 1962, when the pressures of caring for an ancient house and two children in diapers seemed relentless. Her "October" poems, written in part to release that anger, formed the heart of *Ariel*, the first book published after her death. There were a great many other fine poems from the 1960s; some were published in other posthumous collections, *Crossing the Water* and *Winter Trees*; others did not appear until *The Collected Poems* in 1981. Even the so-called *Collected Poems* is not complete, and it is possible that other of Plath's poems will be found.

Although her writing in the final year of her life has gained the most attention, Plath wrote well from early in her career. She considered herself a professional writer beginning in 1950, when at the age of seventeen, she published nine pieces of writing in *Seventeen*, *The Christian Science Monitor*, and *The Boston Globe*, all for payment. In college, her publications appeared in *Harper's*, *The Atlantic*, the *Monitor*, *Mademoiselle*, and *Seventeen*, as well as campus magazines. Several years out of college she was appearing as well in British magazines, and had added *The New Yorker*, *Kenyon Review*, *The Nation*, *Partisan Review*, *Ladies' Home Journal*, and other American journals to her credits. Her first poetry collection was chosen the alternate to the winner of the prestigious Yale Younger Poets book competition. In 1960 this revised collection, *The Colossus and Other Poems*, was published in England. It appeared in 1962 in the United States. In 1961 *The New Yorker* gave Plath a "first reading" contract, which meant that that magazine chose first from all her new work and paid her for the privilege. In early 1963, her novel *The Bell Jar* was published in England.

This biography emphasizes Plath's identity as a writer. Her

life was shaped by her ambition to be a writer, and the consequences of her important personal choices are clear in her work.
Because much of the life of a writer appears in one way or
another in the work, I have used every known fragment of
Plath's writing, the manuscripts and work sheets of her poetry
and fiction, her journals, and her correspondence. Most of these
materials are now housed at either the Lilly Library at Indiana
University, Bloomington, or the Rare Book Room at Smith College. At the estate's mandate, one group of Plath's papers at
Smith has been sealed until the year 2013; another is closed until
after the deaths of both her mother and her younger brother.
Publication of the Plath materials in these libraries is controlled
by Ted Hughes, Plath's husband, from whom she was estranged
at the time of her suicide.

Unfortunately, the draft of her last novel, *Double Exposure*,
"disappeared somewhere around 1970," in Ted Hughes's words.
And, as he explained in his 1982 introduction to *The Journals of
Sylvia Plath*, a collection which is less complete than its title
suggests, "Two more notebooks [the journals] survived for a
while, maroon-backed ledgers like the '57–'59 volume, and continued the record from late '59 to within three days of her death.
The last of these contained entries for several months, and I
destroyed it because I did not want her children to have to read
it (in those days I regarded forgetfulness as an essential part of
survival). The other disappeared." The "other" notebook is, of
course, the one that would chart Plath's life during the period
of her greatest accomplishment as a poet, the fall of 1962 when
she wrote many of the poems that would comprise *Ariel*.

So far as possible, I have used available materials in these
collections as well as those held privately by Plath's friends. I
am grateful for access to this wealth of information, and to the
more than two hundred people who agreed to be interviewed or
otherwise helped so graciously and with such keen interest in
Sylvia Plath and her work. The notes include a complete listing
of sources, personal and published. As is his usual practice, Ted
Hughes would not allow interviews.

When I began researching this biography in 1982, I contacted
Olwyn Hughes, who is literary executor of the Sylvia Plath
estate. Olwyn was initially cooperative, and helped me in my

research by answering questions herself and referring me to others who could be of assistance, As Olwyn read the later chapters of the book, however, and particularly after she read a draft of the manuscript in 1986, her cooperation diminished substantially. Olwyn wrote me at great length, usually in argument with my views about the life and development of Plath. Ted Hughes responded to a reading of the manuscript in draft form in 1986 with suggestions for changes that filled fifteen pages and would have meant a deletion of more than 15,000 words.

Of necessity I continued to correspond with Olwyn Hughes in order to obtain permission to quote at length from Plath's works. But on every occasion Olwyn objected to the manuscript, frequently citing Ted Hughes's comments (although, as mentioned earlier, Ted Hughes refused to be interviewed directly for the book). I did make many changes in response to these comments. However, the requests for changes continued, and I concluded that permissions would be granted only if I agreed to change the manuscript to reflect the Hugheses' points of view. When I realized that this tactic would continue indefinitely, I had to end my attempt to gain permission to quote at length if I was ever to publish this book. As a result of this circumstance, I have had to limit quotations. Consequently, this biography contains less of Plath's writing than I had intended. The alternative would have been to agree to suggestions that would have changed the point of view of this book appreciably.

December 10, 1986   Linda Wagner-Martin
East Lansing, Michigan

Special thanks to Andrea Wagner, Sarah Fryer, Marcellette Williams, Cathy N. Davidson, Clarissa Roche, Elizabeth Compton, Jo Hollingsworth, Margaret Petrak, Ruth Tiffany Barnhouse, Karen Williams, Cheryl Vossekuil, Betty Uphaus, Emily Toth, Elaine Markson, Fred Eckman, Alan M. Hollingsworth, Howard O. Brogan, Sam S. Baskett, and the National Endowment for the Humanities, American Council of Learned Societies, and the Michigan State University AURI grants program. My editor, Bob Bender, is responsible in good part for whatever grace the book achieves.

1
Childhood

1932-40

"The Center of a Tender Universe"

f her early childhood was not idyllic, it came close. Sylvia
Plath was the daughter of loving and highly educated
parents. Born October 27, 1932, in Robinson Memorial
Hospital in the Jamaica Plain section of Boston, Massachusetts, she was the first child of Otto and Aurelia
Schober Plath. Weighing eight-and-a-half pounds at
birth, although she was supposedly three weeks early, Sylvia
became a sturdy child. She was bright, too, eager for information about anything, and she loved food, the sea, being read to,
and attention.

In the Plaths' first house in Jamaica Plain, near the Arnold
Arboretum which her father loved, the family led a simple life.
Their energies were devoted to work and family. Otto, Professor
of Entomology at Boston University, did his professional writing
at home. Quite withdrawn from the daily life of the family, he
loved his daughter deeply and insisted she be treated as a unique
personality. Reminiscent of Bronson Alcott's involvement with
his children's education, Otto urged his wife to read books on
education—among them Froebel's *Education of Man* and writings
about Maria Montessori's life and work. His urging was hardly
necessary: Aurelia Plath prepared for motherhood with her cus-

tomary diligence, reading, as she said, "all the books available on child rearing." She had taken a number of courses in psychology, and the Plaths often discussed theories of child psychology.

As a result, Sylvia was one of the few infants born during the 1930s to be fed on demand, although her mother sometimes pretended to be as rigid about feeding schedules as most of her neighbors were. Aurelia did encourage an early bedtime for Sylvia, between 7:00 and 8:00 P.M. She wanted time free so that she could help Otto with his research. Otto and Aurelia feared having a "spoiled" or unmanageable child, but both Plaths had great confidence in their abilities to rear children.

When Sylvia was six months old, Otto held her up to a rope tied to the porch awning and saw—as he had predicted—that her feet grasped the rope in the same way her hands did. Although her father occasionally experimented with Sylvia, more often the baby was the responsibility of her mother. Sylvia was rocked and sung to, and Aurelia systematically and energetically recited poems and rhymes to her. Whenever Sivvy, as Sylvia was called, cried, she was picked up and held.

The Plaths believed in a natural, healthy existence for their daughter. She was fed well and often. She weighed ten pounds at one month and thirty-one pounds at two years. She was frequently taken to the ocean, which she loved from an early age, and she was as frequently sunned. Aurelia wrote in Sylvia's baby book—crowded with notes and observations—that during the first spring of Sivvy's life she lay in the sun daily, and sometimes twice daily, so that by summer, only eight months old, she was deeply tanned. According to Aurelia, the baby walked alone at ten-and-a-half months and said four or five recognizable words even before that time.

Her mind was as active as her body. One of her early games was asking her mother for "a many"—seeds, beans, small objects all alike—from which she made patterns and designs.

Sylvia looked much like her mother. She had prominent cheek bones, wide features, and a gentle, alert expression. She also had her father's ruddy complexion, straightforward stare, and tall, slender body structure. As a child she wore her hair in short curls, with a ribbon around the crown of her head tied in a bow to the side. Her dark eyes sparkled. The energy fairly sparked from her, and she was consistently adventurous. No wonder Aurelia spent hours taking her on walks and telling her stories. And in a household where one parent studied and wrote at home, the natural exuberance of a restless child could be enervating.

Aurelia was adept at making up stories, and Sylvia was responsive. She had a delightful and fantastic sense of humor, which showed in the stories she told and in the jokes she played on her parents and grandparents. She would hide her grandfather's pipe in a large rubber plant and call it a pipe tree. She spun long stories about Sunshine School, her kindergarten, and about favorite times at her grandparents' house in Winthrop, Massachusetts. The house fronted on a bay of the Atlantic Ocean. Even before she was a year old, Sylvia was creeping on the sand, wading, being carried into the blue-green waves. One of her first memories was crawling out on the sandy edge of the water, heading into those waves, and being saved from exploring right into the ocean by her mother's firm hold on one foot. She was already the curious, daring Sylvia she would be later in her life.

She may well have learned those traits from both her parents. Her father, Otto Plath, had struggled to reach goals through a life that was neither easy nor predictable. Born on April 13, 1885, in the town of Grabow (or Grabowo) in the Polish Corridor, he was the oldest of six children of German parents, Theodore and Ernestine Kottke Plath. His grandparents went to America and settled on a small farm in Watertown, Wisconsin. They then offered to house Otto, their bright grandson, if he wanted to attend small Northwestern College in that city. Otto went to Wisconsin by way of New York City, spending a year there to improve his English. He attended adult education classes, promoting himself from one grade to the next when he felt he knew the vocabulary and accent of the grade level he was then studying. (He already spoke fluent German, Polish, and French.) After that year in New York, when he also worked in an uncle's combination food and liquor store, he began school at Northwestern, majoring in classical languages.

Unfortunately, Otto's grandparents expected him to become

a Lutheran minister, as most Northwestern students did. For them, such a vocation justified going to college. Otto, however, had also studied philosophy and science, particularly the work of Charles Darwin. He was filled with doubts, and when he found that Darwin's writings were forbidden at the seminary he changed his vocation to education. He seemed genuinely surprised when his grandparents grew angry and accused him of breaking their trust. The anger was permanent. Otto's name was stricken from the family Bible. Even later, when his own parents had come to America, Otto saw them infrequently. By the time of his marriage to Aurelia, he had not seen his relatives for years. His education had cost him dearly.

From 1912 to 1914, Plath was a teaching fellow in German at the University of California. He did some graduate work at the University of Washington and then moved east. From 1915 to 1918, and again from 1921 to 1923, he was an instructor in modern languages at M.I.T. During the 1920–21 academic year, he was an assistant in zoology at Johns Hopkins University, but he left there to begin graduate work at Harvard. Somewhere between 1914 and 1920, Otto Plath married a woman named Lydia, with whom he lived for about a year.

Once in the graduate program at Harvard, Plath taught in the Boston area most of the time. In 1922 he became an instructor in German at Boston University. In 1925 he received his Master of Science degree and in 1926 began teaching biology in addition to German at Boston University. When he received his Sc.D. in Entomology in 1928, his appointment at Boston became permanent. His years as a student had been marked by poverty and self-discipline. He was forty-three when he received the doctorate and nearly forty-seven when he and Aurelia Schober were married. If not a driven man, he certainly was diligent and conscientious. It also seems clear that he thought of himself first and foremost as a college professor and a scholar, rather than as a husband and a father.

Aurelia Schober shared Otto's traits of perseverance and ambition. Born in 1906, her life was somewhat easier because of her parents' ambition and love for her, but she too had known early privation. Both her parents were Austrian immigrants. Everyone in the Schober family worked hard; money was never plentiful. When Aurelia started elementary school, she spoke only German. Other children made fun of her, and she in turn was sometimes punished at home for repeating idiomatic English phrases like "shut up." Bright and serious, the oldest Schober child remained something of a misfit among her American peers. At fourteen she began working in the pubic library; throughout her college years she worked as a typist and secretary.

Aurelia met Otto Plath when she was his student in a Middle-High German class at Boston University. Twenty-one years younger than he, she was then teaching German and English at Brookline High School, as well as studying for her M.A. degree. A tall, thin, pretty woman with piercing deep-set eyes and strong features, her eager manner complemented an obvious intelligence. She feared being known as "a green stocking": Aurelia had been salutatorian of her high school graduating class and valedictorian of her college class. Raised as a Catholic, as an undergraduate she had broken with the Church because of what she thought of as repressive and controlling ideology. By the time she met Otto, a Protestant who had already been married, she was a practicing Methodist.

Herself given to serious study and quantities of reading, Aurelia admired Otto's knowledge and position, and perhaps his striking blue eyes and handsome profile. Aurelia and Otto first began to see each other socially in 1930, when they spent weekends hiking in the Arnold Arboretum, the Blue Hills, and the Fells Reservation. They already shared interests in languages and science and soon developed others. Otto brought to Aurelia the worlds of entomology and ornithology; she encouraged him to enjoy theater and literature. Together they planned to work on projects such as the evolution of parental care in the animal kingdom, subjects that combined their interests.

Over Christmas vacation in 1931, Otto Plath and Aurelia Schober—with Mrs. Schober as chaperone—drove to Reno, Nevada, where Otto got a divorce from his first wife. Then he and Aurelia were married in Carson City, Nevada, and she resigned her teaching position. Within the year, Sylvia was born. In a somewhat chilling incident, Otto called for a son, two and a half years "from now." Remarkably, their son Warren was born April 27, 1935, only two hours off schedule. Professor

Plath was greeted by his colleagues as "the man who gets what he wants when he wants it."

Even with two children, the Plath family life revolved around Otto and his scholarship. Aurelia referred to the first year of their marriage as "the year of The Book." Otto was then revising his dissertation into a book manuscript, which was published in 1934 as *Bumblebees and Their Ways*. Dedicated to his major professor at Harvard, the study quickly became a landmark contribution to the field. Then came "the year of The Chapter," the section entitled "Insect Societies" for *A Handbook of Social Psychology*, published in 1935.

The close working relationship between Otto Plath and his young wife is evident in her description of the completion of the chapter project:

> We worked together on this; my husband outlined the sections, listing authors and their texts to be used as reference (there were sixty-nine authors), and I did the reading and note-taking along the lines he indicated, writing the first draft. After that he took over, rewriting and adding his own notes. Then he handed the manuscript to me to put into final form for the printer. By this time I felt I had had an intensive and fascinating course in entomology.

It should be noted that during this busy time, Aurelia also had a baby and a home to keep. She was clearly a versatile and adaptable woman, one who did not mind hard work.

But from some of her comments about the marriage, one senses that Aurelia was not completely prepared for the experience of living with Otto Plath. For example, "At the end of my first year of marriage, I realized that if I wanted a peaceful home —and I did—I would simply have to become more submissive, although it was not my nature to be so." Aurelia had envisioned running a warm and open house, filled with Otto's students and fellow faculty members. But it became evident that Plath felt that his future professional standing depended on publications; he concentrated on writing and did not encourage entertaining. When Aurelia wanted to invite friends for dinner, she did so on the nights her husband taught evening classes. That in itself caused little problem. The problem lay in the fact that Otto wrote on the dining room table, so she had no place to serve meals. Aurelia's strategy was to draw a careful diagram of the position of each book and paper, remove them for the meal, and then replace them before Plath returned, according to her drawing.

Entertaining diminished during the third year of their marriage when Aurelia was pregnant with their second child. Sylvia was nearly two, an energetic and active child. She was sometimes disruptive at home, but she benefited from the constant attention of her maternal grandparents.

The Schobers lived on Point Shirley in Winthrop, Massachusetts. Their house at 892 Shirley Street was a haven for Sylvia. Grampy and Grammy Schober, as Sylvia called them, maintained a traditional Austrian household—orderly, warm, and highly literate. They were full of genuine interest in their own three children and in Sylvia, their first grandchild. Grammy Schober, whose first name was the same as Sylvia's mother's, had graduated from the Vienna schools with fourth-highest grades in the city, and she had been chosen to present a bouquet to Emperor Franz Josef on a parade holiday. She was a talented musician, and her letters show that she was a generous, practical woman who wrote fluently in English.

Frank Schober, Sr., spoke and read Italian, French, German, and English. A bright boy who ranked highest in his class, he faced hardship when his mother died, and he left Austria with an Italian couple who had taken an interest in him. He lived, successively, in Italy, France, and England before coming to the United States and working as an accountant. Grampy was Sylvia's special love, as she was his. ("He worshiped her," Aurelia said.) He took her on long walks. He swam with her and taught her to enjoy the ocean. He teased her and coaxed her back to good humor after she had been punished. The Schobers' home was where Sylvia went when her mother needed to work on Otto's writing and also when Aurelia was in the hospital giving birth to Warren in the spring of 1935.

Despite her closeness to her grandparents and the hours of preparation for the new baby's birth, Sylvia reacted angrily to her brother. She felt rage at his invasion of her territory. As she recalled much later, "A baby. I hated babies. I who for two and a half years had been the center of a tender universe felt the axis wrench and a polar chill immobilize my bones. I would be a bystander. . . ." She may have been, but she was also an outright trouble-maker. Whenever her mother fed Warren, Sivvy became her most demanding. Special toys were purchased for her. Scarcely three, she read letters arranged into words, sometimes in newspapers. She built replicas of structures such as the Taj Mahal with blocks. Her mother recalled that—before three —Sylvia read the STOP sign on the corner as "pots." And at the same time she dug holes under the fence and crawled away to freedom.

The Schober house continued to be a refuge. Sylvia asked to go there much of the summer following Warren's birth, and Aurelia took the children there to live during the extremely hot summer of 1936. Plath's memory of the house shows the protective quality it had taken on for her. "The road I knew curved into the waves with the ocean on one side, the bay on the other; and my grandmother's house, halfway out, faced east, full of red sun and sea lights." As fantasy-like as the mermaids she believed in as a child, the Schobers' was truly a *safe* house, the place where Sylvia was petted and coddled, no matter what the circumstances were at her own home.

Another part of her fantasy as a child was that the sea would always protect her. The Schober house was a haven partly because of its location on the ocean edge. All the family loved the sea. They would spread blankets on the shore and picnic there, their entertainment the movement and changing colors of the water. That the grandparents' telephone number also suggested the sea (it was Ocean 1212-W, which Sylvia used as the title of a late essay) created for her a fusion of her family and the sea itself.

The sea was also a place she could be alone, walking carefully along the beach, gauging the limits of the water's reach. She was curious about sea and plant life and loved to explore with her grandfather. In his casual way, he would let Sylvia play in his garden. She would dig, hoe, prune and harvest the flowers and vegetables he grew. She played nurse to starfish which had lost arms, begging empty jam jars from her grandmother and filling them with water.

Sylvia's time with the Schobers increased during the mid-1930s. Not only was her brother sickly, but Otto had begun suffering from an undiagnosed illness. Aurelia's energies had to be devoted to her infant and her increasingly debilitated husband, but she worked hard to give Sylvia special times. The child loved movies and her art class at the Boston Museum of Fine Arts. Despite her love for her grandparents, her hurt at being sent away from her own home to their house seems clear in letters written during the spring of 1938. Sylvia was five-and-a-half, and she was living at the Schobers' because Warren was ill.

Aurelia wrote her daughter letters, telling her she was lucky to be able to live with her grandparents. She also wrote instructive letters, sending Sylvia pictures to color or directions to read and follow. She reminded her to behave, to stay within the lines when she colored, and to do her best at all times. And once Sylvia started school, there was even more admonition: "I am so proud of the fine coloring you are doing. Try to write as nicely as you color. Try to *write* words instead of *printing* them." From these letters, one might conclude that staying within the lines was more important than any other part of a child's development.

During the fall of 1936 the Plaths bought a house on Johnson Avenue in Winthrop Center, near the Schobers' home on Point Shirley. Sylvia's childhood was now lived within a true extended family. The Schober family included Aurelia Plath's sister Dorothy ("Dot"), younger than she by five years, and Frank, Jr., her handsome younger brother who was only thirteen years older than Sylvia. She idolized her young uncle who played tag, carried her piggy-back, and later let her help him and his fiancée build a sailboat. One of her childhood highlights was being flower girl in Frank's wedding, but exposure to chicken pox almost prevented her from participating. When one small spot appeared the day before the wedding, Sylvia convinced her family that it was only a pimple. The day of the ceremony she marched as proudly down the aisle as if she were the bride. The next day, however, she was blanketed with the pox.

Sylvia's early childhood alternated between her feeling lonely (which she was even at the Schobers' house) and being the center of attention. Because she was afraid of being abandoned, she learned to develop the language skills that won her parents' attention. She talked early, she spoke in complete sentences, she had a large vocabulary, she made up rhymes and stories, and she "read"—and, later, wrote. But she also misbehaved sometimes: she ran away, locked herself in rooms, and had temper tantrums.

Her father, the dominant parent, much preferred a "good" daughter. He praised Sylvia's intellectual and verbal accomplishments and was more at ease with his daughter as she grew older than when she was a child. Otto saw his role in the family as mentor, financial manager, and adviser. He shopped for groceries (often on Saturdays, when he could find bargains before the Sunday closings), but he preferred to eat his meals without the children. He created experiments for them as they were growing, but he seldom read to them or took them for walks.

One of the things Otto did enjoy with Sylvia was discussing his day. She met him in the hallway as he came in. Sometimes he brought her a treat. After dinner, while Aurelia bathed Warren or sat with him as he went to sleep, Sylvia watched her father correct papers. The red ink marks fascinated her. Otto's approach to raising his children was to involve them in *his* life, rather than becoming a part of their lives. In some ways, he treated Sylvia as if she were a miniature wife. The situation was complex. Because Sylvia saw how much time Aurelia spent with Warren, she campaigned diligently for her father's attention. One of her tactics was making Warren look younger than he was —she pinched him or kicked him under the table to make him cry. In contrast, "Sivvy" was capable, energetic, happy, and, by implication, better loved.

In the spring of 1937, the Freeman family moved into the neighborhood. Sylvia's friendship with David, six months her senior, and Ruth, a year younger, made her less dependent on her family. Sometimes Warren tagged along but more often the three older children played in one yard or the other or, often, in the Freeman home. Plath's friendship with Ruth would continue past their college years.

Mrs. Freeman tried to help Aurelia. The constraints of having Otto working at home, a practice that increased as his health declined, were more and more obvious. Aurelia found the natural noise of two small children in the house unbearable sometimes, and she took them to the ocean, the Arboretum, her parents' home, and the Freemans' whenever she could. They made these outings if Warren was in good health, but he suffered from food allergies, and he was subject to bronchial pneumonia as well as asthma. Or the children stayed in the upstairs play-room and told stories about Mixie Blackshort (Warren's crea-tion), or heard tales read by Aurelia from Robert Louis Stevenson, Kenneth Grahame, and A. A. Milne. Poems by Eu-gene Field, limericks, rhymes, and poems from *Sung Under the Silver Umbrella* were later supplemented with Dr. Seuss books and Tolkien's *The Hobbit*.

It was fairly common for Sylvia and Warren to be sick simul-taneously and, when they were, Aurelia put the two of them into the twin beds in her room and entertained them with sur-prises while they listened to the radio. For the children, "being sick" at the Plaths' was a pleasant, attention-getting experience.

Otto Plath's illness, which dominated the family's life in the late 1930s, had begun in 1936, the year after Warren was born. Otto suspected that he had cancer. A close friend had died of lung cancer and Plath had vowed never to undergo such trauma. Even when he realized that he was seriously ill, he did not go to a doctor. Countless arguments with his wife had no effect. It was the summer of 1940 before Otto admitted that he needed medical help.

During the four previous years, he had managed to teach his classes, but hardly with the brilliance he had been known for earlier. Plath was a sociologist as well as a scientist; he prided himself on keeping his students interested, thinking about rela-tionships as well as facts. Early in a course, he tested his stu-dents' assumptions by skinning and cooking a rat, which he then ate, to prove that most human reactions are learned. Why eat one kind of animal and not another? But once he became ill, Otto could no longer teach with such dedication. He relied on Aurelia to do much of his work. She kept his class notes current, found bibliography for his research, graded papers, and—with his help—corrected graduate theses. Once he returned home from campus, Otto visibly collapsed. He lived in his study and often ate meals there. He withdrew from the normal life of the family almost entirely.

Perhaps for twenty minutes in the evening he would be strong enough to see the children. Then Sylvia and Warren would show off. They discussed what they had learned that day, recited poems, made up stories, performed. Hardly a normal interchange, this kind of session created the image of father as critic, judge, someone to be pleased. It robbed the children of the chance to know their father in the way they knew Grampy Schober or to see him as a loving and supportive parent.

Growing up in this kind of household prepared the Plath children for performance-oriented schoolrooms, and excelling at school became an extension of normal behavior for them. Academic success was second-nature, but so far as personal development was concerned, their family experience was disastrous. Under Otto's careful eye, rewards were given for exceptional achievement. When Sylvia gave up taking piano lessons, there was a hint of failure in her explanation that she was "never very good." Doing things for the fun of doing them was less important than doing them because she could do them better than most people. It was a lesson that could end only in defeat and deprivation.

When she started school, Sylvia was her most excitable. She was a bit frightened to be leaving her mother but thrilled to be a part of other children's lives. Aurelia walked her to the Sunshine School, a private kindergarten close to home. Sivvy looked around with her wide-eyed calm, smiled, and told her mother sternly that she could go back home. She was genuinely at ease at school. For years she had watched children walk past her house, and she had played school with the Freemans and with Warren. Now she was eager to prove how good and how bright she was in the real setting.

Sivvy's straight-A record in the Winthrop schools indicates that she was both motivated and gifted, and suggests that her friendships with other children helped her survive the increasingly confusing circumstances at home. She played "Superman" games with David Freeman and listened to both that serial and "The Shadow" on the radio. She traded playing cards at recess, played marbles and dodgeball, jumped rope, and led an imaginative life with other children. Hungry for the knowledge that both her parents valued, she poured her energy into achieving grades that her father and mother would praise. If her effort in school was not so precocious as her preschool achievements had been, that was perhaps better for her psyche. After all, this was the child who, when scarcely more than a toddler, had learned the polysyllabic Latin name for an insect so that she could pronounce it glibly when Otto "tested" her in public.

One of the more memorable episodes from Plath's first year in school was the September 21, 1938, hurricane. She recalled the near-hysteria of the adults and her own trauma at being in a situation that even her parents could not control. She worried most about the Schober house, built directly beside the ocean, but her primary reaction was curiosity. She described being "pale and elated" waiting for the storm to hit and, after it had, "The wreckage the next day was literally all one could wish." Even though there was a dead shark in her grandparents' flower bed, their sea wall had held. When Plath re-created this memory in her poems "Point Shirley" and "The Disquieting Muses," she focused on two separate parts of the experience. In the first poem, Grammy is the heroine creating order in the aftermath of the hurricane, as she sweeps up debris with her broom and dustpan. In the second poem, however, the children are frightened as they watch the twelve windows in their father's study belly in "Like bubbles about to break." Nothing helps. Although their mother makes Ovaltine and sings about the nightmare winds ("Thor is angry: boom boom boom! / Thor is angry; we don't care!") the children do not sing along. They are tense, locked into a situation that provokes both their fear and the anxiety they sense around them. Sylvia sensed that there were many things about the world that her parents could not, finally, control, and her growing fears about her father were only reinforced by the near-doom the hurricane had created.

Even at age eight, Sylvia could see that her father was becoming a different person. His continuous tiredness, his short temper, his almost complete withdrawal from the family's life left her lonely and abandoned. As Otto grew more and more weary from the long battle with illness, Sylvia was less often welcome in his study. One can imagine the confusion in her mind as she received the conflicting messages: Otto loved his children, yes, but he loved them best when they were absent.

Despite all Aurelia's attention, Otto's condition grew worse. By 1940 it was grave and when, that summer, he injured his toe and inflammation and gangrene set in, a doctor was finally called. The diagnosis was not cancer but diabetes mellitus, a treatable ailment. But by this time the disease was far advanced, and on October 12, 1940, Otto's leg was amputated at the thigh. Aurelia explained the operation to Warren and Sylvia as a means of saving their father's life. They discussed the prosthesis and how Otto would learn to walk with it. Sylvia remained silent. Finally, with studied calm, she asked, "When he buys shoes, Mummy, will he have to buy a *pair?*"

Late on November 5, Otto Plath died of an embolus in his lung. Hospitalization practices were such that he had been kept nearly immobile after his surgery, and this postoperative care led to his death. He was only fifty-five.

Aurelia waited until the next morning to tell the children. When she told Warren, he hugged her and said he was glad she was so young and healthy. By that time, in the adjoining room, Sylvia had no doubt guessed the worst. When she was told, she only said dully, "I'll never speak to God again." Then she pulled the covers over her head and insisted she was going to school, which she did.

The position of a bereaved young child is complicated. The center of sympathy and attention, the child has had no earlier experience with death, no knowledge of what behavior is expected. In the case of the Plath children, their mother confused them by showing little grief herself. (She remembered having felt lost at seeing her mother cry during her own childhood, and was trying to spare Sylvia and Warren that fear.) But without Aurelia's grief to witness and respond to, the Plath children had no model for their mourning. Neither did they have an opportunity to mourn: Aurelia decided that Otto's appearance in the casket was so forbidding that she did not let the children see him. They did not attend the funeral or the burial. Much later, Sylvia showed great anger toward Aurelia, accusing her of having felt no grief at Otto's death. There is, in fact, some suggestion that Sylvia was disoriented enough by her father's death, or the circumstances surrounding it, that she wished to die herself —or so she later told friends.

One of the most frightening immediate reactions to Otto's death was a quick reversal in the family's financial position. Otto was not entitled to a pension from Boston University, so the only financial resource the family had was an insurance policy, and much of it went for Otto's medical expenses. After Aurelia spent $375 for a burial plot, she had little money left. She quickly returned to teaching high school languages. For a position that paid $25 a week, she left home at 5:30 A.M. to commute to Braintree High School, where she taught three classes of German and two of Spanish each day, in a post that was considered part-time. Her own health problems worsened and by the next year her duodenal ulcer, which had developed during the last two years of Otto's life, became serious. Warren and Sylvia were also frequently sick. The week after their father's death, in fact, they got measles, followed by pneumonia for Warren and sinusitis for Sylvia. The next summer, both children had tonsillectomies.

Financial worry increased within the Schober family too when, a few days after Otto's funeral, Frank Schober, Sr., lost his job with the Dorothy Muriel Corporation because of management changes. Then he was told that some eye problems from macular degeneration would steadily worsen, so he left accounting completely and took a job as *maître d'hôtel* at the Brookline Country Club.

As the older child, Sylvia felt responsible for much of the financial worry her family was experiencing, and she also feared further change. Her reaction to Otto's death was a natural one —an overwhelming fear of losing the parent who was left. When she came home from school on the day she learned of Otto's death, she brought a note for Aurelia to sign. It promised that her mother would never remarry. Aurelia willingly signed the note, unthinkingly reinforcing Sylvia's sense that she was herself an adult. Always central in the life of her family, Sylvia expected events to revolve around her.

Losing Otto, then, made Sylvia heavily dependent on her mother. Her later fiction showed that shifting alliance, from the father as head of the family to the mother as the source of all support and love. No wonder Sylvia was fearful about her standing with her mother: she had in the past been judged more critically, she felt, by Aurelia than by Otto. It was her mother's letters that urged her to be better, to do more difficult things, to try to excel.

One of the interesting patterns in Sylvia's writing about her parents is that she consistently described Otto's death in terms of the *child*'s loss. Her attention remained on the child as she comes to understand absence and on the child as different, as an outsider, because of the absence of a parent. "You will be aware of an absence, presently," she wrote in a late poem to her own son, after her husband was no longer living with her and the children. In her powerful story "Among the Bumblebees," written in 1952 for a Smith College English class, she created the picture of a daughter bereft after the death of her father.

The story opens with the Biblical-sounding "*In the beginning* there was Alice Denway's father, tossing her up in the air until the breath caught in her throat, and catching her and holding her in a huge bear hug." From that initial comforting image of the father as protector, in control whether he is in the ocean or on campus, Plath describes his descent into illness and death. In the closing scene when the child Alice monitors the weak pulsing of his heart, she realizes that he is about to die, that he has forgotten her as he has withdrawn into the "core of himself." She has already lost the powerful parent who had earlier made her feel as if, with him, "she could face the doomsday of the world."

Once her father was dead, Sylvia was less sure about her place in the world, about her mother's ability to care for her—about her very existence. But she continued to benefit from the love of her strong mother and the Schober family, as well. Her father's death may have struck like a hurricane, but the efforts of her extended family helped her rebuild her young, promising life.

2
Adolescence
1940-47

"Once I Was Ordinary"

For a time after Otto's death, Sylvia and Warren had a great deal of attention. They no longer had to share Aurelia's energy with an ailing husband, and they gained the care of their grandparents as well. When Aurelia went back to teaching, the Schobers moved in with the Plaths at 892 Johnson Avenue, putting their own house up for sale.

The emotional fabric of the new family was quite different. The family before had been characterized by order and control, with Otto Plath the unquestioned patriarchal head of the household. Now it was less formally organized; authority was divided. Aurelia made decisions but she was still, in her mid-thirties, a relatively young daughter and she relied on her parents' opinions. She was happy within a traditional framework. In effect, Sylvia and Warren had moved back in time at least part of a generation. The household norm became that of their European grandparents as often as it was that of their mother. There are indications that Aurelia was often tired beyond endurance, and that she needed whatever help her family could provide.

Mrs. Schober became particularly influential. Not only was she at home all day, to be with the children and to cook and clean, she was also the licensed driver. Aurelia Plath would not learn to drive for a dozen more years, so the family car, a second-hand Plymouth, belonged to her mother. After some investment losses during the 1920s, Frank had turned control of the family finances over to his wife. The Plath–Schober household gradually became a matriarchy. The change was confusing for Sylvia; she had spent her younger days identifying with her father and grandfather, even preferring zippers on clothes instead of buttons, and now she was surrounded by women's things and women's attitudes.

For the Plath–Schober family—certainly for Sylvia—1942 was the year of decision. It was the year that the family moved inland. It is significant that in Sylvia's recollections, her father's death and the move to Wellesley came at the same time. In fact, she was eight when her father died in 1940 and nearly ten when the family moved away from Winthrop in 1942. She writes in *The Bell Jar* that she was happiest before she was nine. With psychological accuracy rather than factual correctness, Plath the writer fuses many events, any one of which might have created apprehension for a child: her father's death, her mother's being away from home teaching, her grandparents' coming to live with them, her mother's illnesses, the war, and the move to Wellesley away from the school and the two homes—the Schobers' as well as the Plaths'—that had been most familiar to her.

One of the reasons for the move to Wellesley was that Aurelia had been offered a position at Boston University. In a course in Medical Secretarial Procedures, which she created, she taught methods of interviewing patients, the nomenclature of disease, procedures for handling insurance forms, case histories, and office maintenance. The move was also meant to benefit the family's health—Mrs. Schober's arthritis and the children's sinus problems would be better inland. Moving to Wellesley also located the Plaths in an elite upper-middle-class suburb, where education was valued and where Wellesley College might provide a good education for Sylvia.

Soon after they moved, however, Aurelia experienced a frightening gastric hemorrhage. She was hospitalized three weeks in the winter of 1943 and, despite the Schobers' loving care for the children, Sylvia was terribly afraid her mother would not return from the hospital. Her letters to Aurelia during her hospitalization show clearly that she thought if she were "good," her mother would return. She lists her "good-girl" behavior: she has practiced the piano, she has bought a homecoming present for Aurelia, she has walked to school with Warren and "defended" him from his schoolmates.

In July of 1943 Aurelia had a second hemorrhage. This time she arranged for Sylvia to spend a month at Scout camp, and for Warren to spend the time with Aunt Dot. Sylvia, not yet eleven, had never been away from family before. She wrote to Aurelia that she missed her terribly. And on July 18, nearly two weeks into her month's stay, she feels very sorry for herself: "*All* the girls in my tent are going home tomorrow so I feel left out. I didn't get a letter from you yesterday, I hope you are all right. . . ." Many of Sylvia's letters are full of bravado. Others include news she knows will please her family—that she has been frugal, conscientious, and that she has been writing. Sometimes this kind of pleasing is combined with accounts of the prodigious amounts of food she has eaten. Perhaps she is trying to gain weight; more likely she is trying to justify the cost of going to camp. Money seems to have been a constant concern, with amounts spent itemized and discussed ("I have washed: 2 pairs of socks, 1 face cloth, 1 jersey, and 1 pair of pants. I have spent about 45¢ on laundry, about 20¢ on fruit"). Near the time of her return, she wrote her mother that there have been great changes in her "caracter" and that she hopes they can go to bed at the same time some night so that she can share her camp stories with Aurelia.

The Plath and Schober families had moved to 26 Elmwood Road in Wellesley, a house described in Sylvia's photo abum as "our little white house" and "our cozy white house." Compared to many of the larger homes in the neighborhood, the house might have seemed smaller than it was. With its center entrance, it had a living room to the right, dining room to the left, a kitchen, a bedroom, and a screened-in porch downstairs, and two large bedrooms and a bath upstairs. Built on a half-acre corner lot edged with trees, it was comparable to many of the houses in the Wellesley Fells division. Sylvia often read and wrote perched in the branches of the apple tree in the front yard.

While it was smaller than their Winthrop house, 26 Elmwood Road provided adequate space for the family of five. The living room was large enough for the upright piano; the dining room served as the family gathering place, its walls decorated with the children's artwork. The only problem with the home, from Sylvia's point of view, was the fact that her mother shared her bedroom. The larger of the two upstairs rooms, Sylvia's was furnished with her grandmother's antique desk,* a vanity, chairs, a wooden storage trunk, and twin beds. It was, in fact, larger than her friends' bedrooms, larger than the Plath living room. Nevertheless, careful as her mother was to use the room "for sleeping purposes only," the situation was far from ideal. And it continued from the time they moved into the house in 1942 until Warren left for Exeter in 1949. Whenever he was gone, Aurelia slept in his room. For a child who already felt keen pressure to perform, to excel in everything she did, sharing a room with a parent was probably not easy.

Exciting as moving to Wellesley may have been for the family as a whole, the children had reservations about the change. They loved their Johnson Avenue house, especially the large enclosed porch, which Otto had used as his study. The house had been the scene of many of her school triumphs, and it is the house she lamented leaving in her poem "Let the Rain Fall Gently," written when she was fifteen.

After five years of being inseparable from her friends David and Ruth Freeman, Sylvia hated to leave them. She also hated the fact that when she moved to Wellesley, she had to repeat fifth grade. Her mother was no doubt right in deciding that Sylvia was too young (almost two years younger than students in the sixth grade would be) to go into sixth grade in Wellesley. The more relaxed fifth-grade schedule allowed Sylvia to become a star Girl Scout, earning eleven badges in that single year.

Photographs from the early 1940s show Sylvia as tall and attractive, her dark blonde hair worn in long braids with fluffy bangs. Her legginess was as noticeable as her toothiness, and each gave her a sense of being a little oversized. She was more shy in Wellesley than she had been in Winthrop. She spent

---

* Nearly twenty years later, from England, Sylvia wrote that she hoped someday to be able to afford having "Grammy's" desk sent over for Frieda, her daughter, to use.

much of her time reading books and writing extra book reports, forty of them. There are some signs that Sylvia was already creating the ideal "Wellesley self," who appeared confident, happy, poised, excited by life. She was a child robbed of her beloved sea and shore, separated from her best friends, and frightened by her mother's serious illnesses, but she did as she was told and got all *A*'s in school, despite being the "new girl."

War darkened 1942 and 1943. For a family as committed to their country as the Schobers and Plaths were, following evening war news on the radio was imperative. The radio voice that could not be interrupted spread its pall of anxiety over the household, especially because young Frank was a lieutenant in the Medical Corps abroad. Sylvia had vivid memories of wartime paper drives, blackouts, rationing.

Life at 26 Elmwood Road eventually stabilized. Aurelia's health improved, and she felt more confident about teaching college. Her program at Boston University became so successful that she taught there for the next twenty-nine years, teaching one course in shorthand and transcription to make her position full-time. Throughout her teaching years, Aurelia usually returned home before the children. When they came home from school, as a rule, both Aurelias were there to welcome them: their mother the college teacher and their grandmother, whom Sylvia described as "Viennese . . . Victorian" at work in the kitchen, humming and thumping bread dough.

Despite the loss of her father, Sylvia's childhood in Wellesley seemed rich in many ways. She accumulated pets—Mowgli, a tiger alley cat, parakeets, and a tame squirrel. She rode her bike on Wellesley's wide sidewalks, exploring the Hunnewell fields and tennis courts, Morse's pond just two blocks away, and Lake Waban. She and Betsy Powley, her new best friend, were intrigued by the woods at the edge of a new subdivision, and sometimes built huts of fern there on summer days.

For all her studious bent, Sylvia was more of an outdoor girl than an indoor one. She responded honestly to weather, hating the cold, opening out into the sunlight as if she drew physical nourishment from it. Sun was as important to her as the sea had been, and even though her yard was shady she managed to sunbathe much of the spring and summer.

After her two years at Marshall Perrin Elementary School, with nearly perfect grades and a reputation for excellence, Sylvia entered the Alice L. Phillips Junior High for her seventh, eighth, and ninth grades. The dull red-brick building was located near the center of town, not far from the Unitarian Church where Aurelia Plath taught a weekly Sunday School class. Sylvia was a serious, intelligent student, interested in achievement and recognition, dutiful about working hard. She was comfortable with older people as well as classmates, and some of her own friends came from associations of her mother's.

Aurelia had moved to Wellesley partly because several of her friends from Boston University lived there. Long before Otto's death, Margaret Brace, wife of novelist Gerald Brace, and Mildred Norton, the mother of Sylvia's friend Perry and his brother, Dick, had made special efforts to befriend Aurelia, suspecting that her marriage was not an easy one. Both wives of Boston University professors and well-educated and competent themselves, they were important to Aurelia's sense of herself as a professional woman. The three women maintained their relationship through university groups and through the church.

The Nortons lived in Wellesley Hills and belonged to the Unitarian Church; the Braces lived near them for several years until they moved to the suburb of Belmont. The families who were acquainted through Boston University—the Schoonovers, the Despoteses, the Andrewses, along with the Braces, the Nortons, and the Plaths—were drawn together partly because their children were close in age. At gatherings such as picnics or Christmas parties, the Brace and Norton boys played word games, anagrams, board games, and conundrums with Sally Andrews, Poppy Despotes, and Sylvia. The friendships of these children—most of them academically talented, all destined to attend good schools on scholarships—created an important world for Sylvia. They reinforced goals her mother was establishing for her and for Warren.

Aurelia was particularly close to Mildred Norton. Sylvia and Warren called Mrs. Norton "Aunt Mildred," and the three Norton boys called Mrs. Plath "Aunt Aurelia." As the families spent time together, the children gradually became good friends.

Even if Aurelia Plath had had no friendships of her own to

maintain, she probably would have cultivated the association of the faculty group. Much of her life was motivated by finding what would be best for her children. Whom should they know? What should they learn to do? The Plath family spent hours during these years at the small branch library near Elmwood Road. Aurelia still read aloud to the children (*The Yearling* and *Johnny Tremain* were the last books she read before their own reading speeds made them want to read for themselves). Sundays meant services at the Unitarian Church, where both children received perfect-attendance medals each year. Every Christmas, Sylvia found a diary in her stocking, and from the time the children were born, Aurelia put what little extra money there was into a "book fund" for them, believing, as she wrote in an unpublished memoir, "We had no money, save for essentials. Through education we could, however, build a priceless inner life!"

During Sylvia's junior high years, Aurelia began taking the family to plays and concerts. When Sylvia was in seventh grade, they saw *The Tempest* with Vera Zorina and Canada Lee at the Colonial Theater in Boston. Both children had read the entire play (when Mrs. Plath gave Warren *Lamb's Tales from Shakespeare*, he insisted on reading the full version, as Sylvia had). Sylvia's fascination with Ariel, Miranda, and Caliban, then, dated from January of 1945. *The Tempest* is not a play she read in school, but the father-daughter relationship, the reunion, the ocean, and the androgynous powers of Ariel made the story especially germane to a young girl fashioning her adolescent self-image.

That April the family heard the Gordon String Quartet at the Isabella Stewart Gardner Museum in Boston. A few days later, Sylvia went to help out at the Nortons'—cleaning and cooking for "Uncle Bill" and the three boys, Dick, Perry, and little David—while Mildred was in bed with severe influenza. At home, however, Sylvia seldom did housework or cooking. Grammy Schober reigned in those departments, so Sylvia was free for piano lessons, reading, writing, drawing, playing with friends, jumping rope, riding bikes, and drinking Cokes at the local Howard Johnson's.

Sylvia's seventh grade year, 1944–45, saw her receiving all A's once again, except for a first-term B in sewing. At the June 20

Awards Assembly, she was given the Wellesley Award, as the outstanding student in seventh grade. She also received two commendation cards from her English teacher, and two Honor Certificates for extra book reports.

The year 1945 saw her first publications in *The Phillipian*, a slick-covered junior-high magazine. As a seventh grader, she wrote about nature and moods ("The Spring Parade," "March," "Rain"), still deeply in the sentimental tradition of her first published poem, about crickets and fireflies, which appeared when she was eight-and-a-half, in the *Boston Sunday Herald*. A few months after that publication she had won a $1 prize for a drawing of a woman in a hat. Writing and drawing were important pastimes for Sylvia but she seemed unsure of her friends' reactions to them, and often justified them in terms of possible payment, or publication, or both. Even when she was a child, just enjoying an activity was not enough reason for spending time on it.

During junior high, Sylvia made posters and drawings and often sketched in pastels and ink. As a younger child, she had hidden drawings under her mother's napkins at the dinner table. Now she illustrated her own writing, designed paper dolls and their clothes, and made intricate wrapping paper. Her special occasion cards (labeled "Plathmark" on the back) were prized by her family, especially her grandfather, who carried her artwork in his wallet until the paper was worn through.

She also wrote a great deal—diary entries, fiction, and poetry. During the summer of 1945 she kept a meticulous diary of her weeks on Cape Cod at Camp Helen Storrow with Betsy Powley. In rounded, perfectly spelled words she described fellow campers, duties, nights around campfires, and her gratefulness for being at the camp. The flair for journalism which was obvious during high school and college first appeared now and pointed to her real gifts in objective writing. In her early poems, Sylvia used some varied rhyme and stanza arrangements but her poems and stories are what one might expect from a gifted adolescent.

Some of her most interesting writing appears in her letters home from summer camp. Illustrated with stick drawings, they show Sylvia's old concerns about being good, saving money, and eating a lot ("Lunch—two bowls of vegetable soup, loads of peanut butter, 4 pieces of coffee cake, chocolate cake and marshmallow sauce, 3 cups of milk . . . Supper—Haddock, 19 carrots, lettuce and tomato, cucumber, punch, 2 potatoes, 4 slices of watermelon"), but she also wrote about camp personnel, the neatness of her room, and her improvement in swimming. The note of economy recurs when she mentions to Aurelia that she was able to buy Kleenex for only 15¢, and wonders whether her mother would like her to buy an extra box to bring home, if she were allowed to do so.

By 1946, Sylvia and Betsy Powley were joined in camp by Ruthie Freeman, Sylvia's Winthrop friend, and the three of them bet nickels to see who could avoid swearing. Sylvia was known as "Siv" this year. She spent money a bit more casually and wrote more descriptive letters. One of her triumphs at camp was imitating Frank Sinatra in the camp variety show (though Betsy did the actual singing), but otherwise the two weeks away were comparatively unpleasant: the campers got ptomaine poisoning from bad fish; she had an infected toenail and a cold and missed five days of swimming; and she never mastered what she called the "horrid" art of diving.

Following Sylvia's July camp, Aurelia took the children to Loungeway farm, the home of a friend in Oxford, Maine, so they could experience farm life. The profile of Sylvia that emerges from these years is of an adolescent dutiful about enjoying the benefits her mother provided. At every turn, she is given vacations, lessons, books, art supplies. But the gifts are not without responsibilities: having such advantages will enable her to excel in even more ways, and her family will be even more proud of her in turn. She wrote in her 1946 diary, after a poem by Sara Teasdale ("Late October") which she copied onto the page, "What I wouldn't give to be able to write like this!"

Sylvia's eighth and ninth grades were as full of accomplishment and as directed toward writing as seventh grade had been. And it is just as well that she continued to succeed academically. Her social life, which she—like the rest of the girls at Alice L. Phillips—considered of supreme importance, was not flourishing. Tall and gangly, Sylvia had a hearty, talkative manner that was the opposite of flirtatious. Most boys were a little afraid of her and, because she was not popular with boys, girls did not want her friendship either. Sylvia might list girls as friends, but she had only one person to eat lunch with during ninth grade, another girl who felt just as left out of things as Sylvia did.

The relationship that saved her pride to a certain extent during these junior high years began during her ninth grade. Phil McCurdy had come home on the bus with Warren one day after school. He had just moved to Wellesley with his young mother and her new husband and was adrift—emotionally and socially. His home two blocks away on Durant Street seemed less welcoming than did the Plaths', where both Aurelia Plath and Sylvia were kind to the handsome and talented seventh grader. Gradually, he came to visit Sylvia instead of Warren. They took long walks, sketched, talked, and shared confidences. In befriending Phil, Sylvia was showing the side that made her a reliable babysitter, friend, teacher, a genuine and loyal confidant.

Phil taught her to play tennis, a sport he loved, and they biked together. He encouraged her to be more aggressive. At his urging, she ran for class secretary and, though she lost, had a good time with her elaborate campaign. Losing did not enhance her shaky self-image much, and she wrote in her scrapbook, "Perhaps I was doomed always to be on the outside."

Most of Sylvia's activities during eighth and ninth grades were those of the smart loner—making announcements over the school's PA system, making posters, writing and publishing in *The Phillipian*. "Fireside Reveries," one of her ninth-grade poems, describes the poet as a solitary daydreamer who may become a writer of some importance. Another poem, "Sea Symphony," borrows from Sara Teasdale's lush imagery to describe Sylvia's love of the ocean, just as "Interlude" describes "Slender, silver birches clad in plumes of misty green." Her poem "Adolescence" boasts in its opening, "I was not born to love one man/ And him alone"; and foreshadows one of her primary worries during her school years, whether she would date.

Sylvia's graduation from the ninth grade at Alice Phillips was a triumph. She again won the Wellesley Award for outstanding student (this time her prize was a copy of Cleanth Brooks and Robert Penn Warren's *Understanding Poetry*, the Bible of poetry

explication at midcentury). She also received a unique commendation card for having all *A*'s in academic subjects during
her three years at the school, and another for perfect punctual-
ity. Then Sylvia was given a sixth academic letter, an award
never before given, for "being the only pupil in the history of
the school who had earned enough credits for a sixth letter." She
also won a certificate for a drawing (first place in a Carnegie
Institute contest) and Honorable Mention from the National
Scholastic Literary Contest.

Throughout these years, Sylvia had worked incredibly hard,
dedicating herself to getting the grades she knew her mother
expected. Early in junior high, Sylvia had scored near 160 on an
IQ test. Aurelia had taught her to type so her work would
always be neat. Sylvia had also become more clothes conscious,
wearing with pride what new clothes her mother could afford
for her and those she could buy herself with money she earned
babysitting for neighbors' children.

Yet for all the marks of maturity, Sylvia would often revert to
the fears that had surfaced after her father's death. Near the end
of her junior high years, her mother was offered the position of
Dean of Women at Northeastern University in Boston. Such an
administrative post would have meant an increase in prestige as
well as money; it would also have provided a way for Mrs. Plath
to use her remarkable talents in dealing with people. But when
Aurelia talked with her children about making the change, and
pointed out that the job would require more of her time, Sylvia
responded angrily, "For your self-aggrandisement you would
make us complete orphans!" Aurelia declined the job offer. The
sense of dependence and the narcissism that were to mark, and
sometimes ruin, Sylvia's relationships in the future clearly orig-
inated in her childhood fear of abandonment. That fear would
surface unexpectedly—and always detrimentally—in the years
ahead.

3
Bradford High School

1947-50

"The Rich Junk of Life"

When Sylvia entered Gamaliel Bradford High School (now Wellesley High) in September of 1947, she was a tall, slim fourteen-year-old girl of five feet eight inches, weighing 119 pounds. With the long arms and legs inherited from both her parents, she was a competent basketball player but, despite the efforts of Mrs. Gulliette Ferguson's "dance assemblies," she would never be more than an average dancer. She was a good deal more likely to be writing scripts for variety shows than to be singing and dancing in them. Sivvy—for all the cuddliness of her nickname—was not one of the 1940s blondes who tried out for cheerleading and swooned on the arm of the star quarterback. She would have liked that role, however, and one of the ambitions of her high school years was to date as much—and with as many different boys—as possible. During early high school, unfortunately, boys who knew her were awed by her brains, her competence, even her swingy, sunny manner. She was simply too much for them. That she was not part of the right social group was also a problem. Wellesley was an extremely wealthy suburb, and the Plath family circumstances were never other than modest.

At sailing camp in Oak Bluffs, Massachusetts, the summer before starting high school, Sylvia had tried to create a new personality for herself. She used the nickname Sherry, one of what would be many pseudonyms, and had "tons" of fun "without any of the old restrictions." Her aim was to be something more daring, more fun-loving, than the serious junior high student she had been.

But the new Sherry was every bit as competitive as the old Sylvia. She recounted to her mother triumphs in English class: her essay was better than even Perry Norton's, and classmate John Pollard praised her work as well. She eventually dated both boys, but not often during tenth grade. Sylvia's sophomore year was not very social, though Pollard took her to the Prom in the spring and Perry Norton was her date for several other school dances. Aside from playing guard on the girls' junior varsity basketball team and having tennis dates with Phil McCurdy, Sylvia devoted most of her energies to school work.

The staff at Bradford High was superior. Sylvia was particularly challenged by Wilbury Crockett, the English teacher she had for all three years there. A select group of twenty sophomores were called the "Crocketeers," the equivalent of today's advanced placement track. During tenth grade, the group studied American literature; during eleventh, British; and during twelfth, world literature, especially Greek, Russian, and German. Crockett, who had begun teaching at Bradford in 1944, tried to bring literature and writing into his students' lives. Reading Hemingway, Eliot, Frost, Dickinson, Faulkner, Hardy, Lawrence, Yeats, Joyce, Woolf, Dylan Thomas, much Shakespeare, Plato, Greek drama, Mann, and Dostoevsky's *Notes from the Underground* and *Crime and Punishment*, the Crocketeers formed a tight-knit group during their school years. They also acquired what their teacher called a "life library," because he suggested that they buy the books they read, some forty each year.

Mr. Crockett balanced class discussion with private conferences and writing assignments, so that each student would have a chance to excel in some area. Sylvia excelled in all. She and the other students wrote four 5,000 word essays or term papers a year, instead of taking tests; they then presented their essays to their classmates. They were taught to have convictions about what they wrote.

Crockett thought Sylvia was an extremely well-adjusted, vibrant, outgoing, and brilliant student, always interested in what she read, always willing to talk about her feelings. She had "joy, bounce, and lovely enthusiasms." Her intensity sparked the class; Crockett wondered whether she ever relaxed. She read with great maturity but was tolerant of the views of other students, even those not at her level. "She was reacting constantly" to what was going on in class, recalls Crockett. One day she rescued the class after a boy who was a fine student but a stutterer broke down in tears. While the class stared in horror at the sobbing student, Sylvia picked up the discussion, speaking directly to Crockett, and by the end of the class the boy was once again able to become involved. Crockett was repeatedly indebted to "Miss Plath."

Maintaining stiff standards of quality for these gifted students, the young Crockett modeled his classes on college courses (he also taught at Wellesley College and Connecticut College at times). He believed that formal relationships aided high quality work, so he called his students "Mr." and "Miss." Despite the formality in class, Sylvia often visited Crockett at home, usually meeting also with his wife, a children's librarian who always welcomed students. They would sit in the back yard under pine trees or in the living room by a fire and discuss—or continue discussing—either Sylvia's writing or what had been introduced in class.

Crockett recalls that Sylvia played down her accomplishments. She would say things like "I know this isn't very good," "This isn't my best," "I know this doesn't measure up." But she had confidence in her own judgment and was not afraid to disagree with Crockett. (Sometimes, when he made suggestions, she would say simply, "No, I don't think so.") Whatever her reaction, Sylvia knew why she had come. She would park her bike out in front of his house purposefully, intent on not wasting his time with what he might consider frivolous talk.

One of the most important things Crockett's class did for Sylvia was to make her aware of social conditions in the outside

44

world. Crockett made connections: if the class read Thomas Mann, he discussed current politics in Germany. One of the requirements for his course was that each student contribute a dollar a month to CARE, from earned money rather than allowances. He also arranged international pen pals, and from 1947 through 1952 Sylvia corresponded with Hans Neupert, a German student. In these letters, as in her journals, she discussed the atomic bomb, the Korean War and its atrocities, the peace movement, and other events on the international scene. Some of her creative writing in high school also dealt with political themes: strikers on the labor front, being an American, the responsibilities of moral political action. Even as a high school student Sylvia thought of herself as a political person.

As part of Crockett's attempt to integrate study with life, he took groups of students biking through Europe and England during the summer. Sylvia and her close friends Perry Norton and Phil McCurdy could not afford a summer abroad; the fifteen to twenty students who did go were the target of Sylvia's envy. The closest she came to the Crockett summer program was writing about it when she was editor of *The Bradford*, the school newspaper.

The Crocketeers were not just excellent students. Some of them produced and acted in plays; others edited the paper and yearbook; and they all wrote and submitted their writing to magazines and newspapers in order to accumulate the rejection slips Crockett required. And they played jokes. In April Sylvia and some other students woke Crockett at 2:00 A.M. (the day following his scolding them because they had never seen a sunrise) and took him for a lakeside cookout breakfast, promising him worse punishment if he ever again criticized their habits.

Sometimes, however, Sylvia's laughter was more frenetic than amused, Crockett thought, and he wondered whether she was able to relax enough to enjoy life. Would she ever give up her aim of always being the best? Would she ever mature enough to realize the impossibility of that? Crockett's method of teaching was to make students care passionately about what they were doing, but his tactics were not without humor, and behind his businesslike manner was a world of love. Sylvia's need to excel came not from Crockett, nor from any other of her teachers; it came from herself and, of course, from her mother. It was unconsciously connected with her natural need to be loved. From early childhood, she had learned that her parents' love depended on her achievements.

Crockett's classroom influenced Sylvia in other ways. It made her conscious of religion and the power of differing religious beliefs. It made her see that she was part of what Crockett called the "privileged community" of Wellesley. As part of that elite world, she had responsibilities beyond her own self-satisfaction. The life she chose to lead should take account of this responsibility.

Sylvia shared in many of Wellesley's privileges but others were closed to her. She was not completely accepted in the high school. She did not have as many clothes as some of her classmates, nor were hers always the right ones. She had no car and did not learn to drive until several years after her friends had licenses. She had seldom been out-of-state. Her family rarely went on vacations or even ate meals out. She recalled what a thrill it was to pick up Mr. Schober on Sundays at the Braintree Country Club and be offered a meal there. Like the rest of her family, Sylvia appreciated good food but she felt disadvantaged knowing it was being provided only because she was an employee's grandchild. Later in life Sylvia would mention her mother's "threadbare financial situation" and that, as a result, she "could not travel, vacation, go to summer school, etc."

Sylvia also came to realize that her only route to a good college education was through scholarships. In Wellesley, a "good" college was an Ivy League or Seven Sister school. Any public institution was considered inferior. Her financial situation did not make Sylvia poor, but it did undermine her sense of self during the years at high school and, later, college because she was surrounded with comparatively wealthy friends. Sorting out values was difficult, especially when her own family cared a great deal for material things. As she later lamented to a college friend, "Why the hell wasn't I born with a whole place setting of sterling silver in my mouth?"

Worries about money surfaced often in Sylvia's journals and diaries. She didn't need Crockett's encouragement to submit her writing for publication. She was already doing that, hoping for extra income. For a girl who babysat, 50¢ a line for poems was royal payment. Sylvia sent her work to places that she knew paid well—*Seventeen, The Christian Science Monitor, The Atlantic, Mademoiselle.*

Sylvia submitted material from her sophomore year in high school on, and by her senior year she had accumulated sixty or seventy rejection slips. But she also had acceptances from *Seventeen, The Christian Science Monitor,* and *The Boston Globe.* Her news stories in the latter paid $15 each, as much as the short story she had sold to *Seventeen.* In all, Plath's earnings for nine acceptances during her senior year totaled $63.50. Even more important, she was succeeding in a professional market while she was still a high school student.

Despite this success, Sylvia wrote in her diary during that senior year, "Never never never will I reach the perfection I long for with all my soul—my paintings, my poems, my stories." Whatever she tried, it had to be done perfectly. Sylvia's idealization of herself, of her talents and capabilities, pushed her to try to excel in everything. When she did not or could not, the less-than-perfect results depressed her seriously.

Excelling in high school meant long days of hard work. A typical day from Sylvia's sophomore year ran up to sixteen hours. Taking the bus to school; going to English and second-year Latin, physical education or orchestra; lunch; French, geometry, and art; and then basketball practice for nearly two hours, taking the late bus home in time for dinner. After the evening meal she began the hours of homework. Sylvia kept her straight-*A* record throughout high school but the record was not earned without strain. Many of her diary entries mention sore throats, high fevers, long bouts with minor but debilitating illness. She took a rigorous academic schedule and worked as well in the school orchestra, on decoration committees for dances, and on the school paper.

What she worked hardest at, however, was being accepted socially. In the fall of her junior year, she was asked to join Sub-Debs, a sorority. That invitation helped her feel as if she belonged, and then the dating that she thought was crucial to her maturity started in earnest. She asked Perry Norton to the fall

Sub-Deb dance and John Pollard to the Christmas party. There were reciprocal dates; in fact she mentioned a dozen different boys in her diary under the heading "1948–49—Boys Gone Out With." She even tallied everything:

Boys asked by me   4
Dates requested   19 (7 turned down)
Dates gone on in all   12 + 4 = 16

Sylvia's obvious delight in the improvement in her dating situation shows in her flippant tone (one list titled "Boys who asked and were unlucky") and her "List of excuses for unwanted dates," which included "TB or cancer" and the note that she had turned communist and no longer associated with wealthy boys.

Sylvia dated, or at least flirted with, nearly forty boys during her last two years in high school. Her diaries suggest that all this activity—her long awaited popularity—was not simply fun. Schoolgirls of the 1940s and 1950s, including Sylvia Plath, had their sights set on marriage. The list Sylvia kept of her dates during the summer of 1949, between her junior and senior years at high school, shows how conscious she was of a boy's origins —the prep school or college he attended, the relative status of his family.

During the summer of 1949, she swam, went to stock car races, went dancing, motorcycled, and took day-long trips to Cape Cod with a dozen different boys. Late that summer she met John Hall, the first date who, in her words, made her feel "confident and joyful," and they dated steadily before he left for Williams College that fall. With John she played tennis, went for long walks and drives, climbed the local tower—which must have been an ordeal for Sylvia, who was afraid of heights— danced, and visited friends on the Cape, driving their Jeep along the beaches. "Say fun!" is the caption under Sylvia's photo of the Jeep, written with an ebullience new to the usually serious girl.

Sylvia's popularity seemed to calm her, and she was able to give up taking the sleeping pills that had become routine. In late September she began dating Bob Riedeman, a sophomore botany major at the University of New Hampshire. Blond and musically talented, Riedeman dated Sylvia seriously for over a year although she continued to write to Hall and visited the Williams campus that fall. Most of Christmas break she spent with Riedeman—seeing movies, going to supper, skating, and dancing. They spent Christmas and New Year's Eves at the Plaths', listening to records, especially "Put Another Nickel In." They found ways to escape to the Riedeman family car for long sessions of intense talking and necking, serious about their love for each other. Sylvia once asked Bob what he was "building" for her life.

Sylvia spent several weekends at the University of New Hampshire, including the February Snow Circus carnival. On the weekend of Bob's birthday in May, she took the bus to New Hampshire to give him a surprise party, carrying for his present three records ("These Foolish Things," "I'll Remember April," and "That's a Plenty") and money for dinner out. Riedeman took Sylvia to the prom, to graduation activities, and to early summer events, but he left for two months at a forest service camp in Wyoming in mid-June 1950. Sylvia gave him Housman's *A Shropshire Lad* as a going-away present.

Her other friendships with boys like Perry Norton and Phil McCurdy continued through high school. She sometimes dated Perry, but he often thought of her as a sister. Whenever they did go out, Perry was nervous around the highly competitive girl. Usually Perry and Sylvia were confidants, taking long walks and talking endlessly about their adolescent problems. She did that, too, with McCurdy, including in their conversations discussions of menstruation and masturbation as well as religion, ambition, art, and nature. Phil was an excellent science student, and with him Sylvia was willing to play the role of pupil.

In all her relationships, Sylvia seemed to be divided. While she was usually affable with Riedeman, there were times when she let him know that she did not appreciate his being better at some things than she was (as when she called him Dick Button at the skating rink). The dominant element of Sylvia's personality during high school was her need for control. She didn't like surprises; anything unexpected unnerved her. Sylvia liked life to be predictable. When it wasn't, she became involved in work, or depressed, or ill. She also showed a less agreeable side to her mother and her family during these later high school years, turning more often to girlfriends like Mary Ventura and Patsy O'Neill. On the surface, however, Sylvia remained the dutiful achiever, needing the attention her accomplishments brought as reassurance that she was the perfect American girl.

What the perfect American girl was one could discover in the pages of the 1950s teen and women's magazines. According to the media, a woman should be a wife and probably a mother. If there was time, then she might do volunteer work, but she was not expected to be a professional. In a decade when the average marriage age for women had fallen to 20.3, the lowest ever recorded in the U.S., Sylvia did not plan to be an unmarried career woman. To choose not to marry would be to label herself *unfeminine*. Throughout high school, Sylvia examined boys as possible future husbands. Part of her closeness to Perry Norton stemmed from her conviction that the Norton boys would make wonderful husbands.

Typical of the message Plath and other young women received during the late 1940s and early 1950s was a 1949 Listerine advertisement. Featured in *Ladies' Home Journal* as well as *Seventeen* and *Mademoiselle*, the ad shows three pretty women wearing graduation caps and gowns. Two of the three are prominently displaying engagement rings. The caption for the ad reads, "One Course They Didn't Teach Her" and the opening line identifies "her" as "Dora": "Even though it was Graduation Day Dora felt a little pang of loneliness. What was the diploma compared to those precious sparkling rings that Babs and Beth were wearing?" The message was clear, *The only happy woman was the married woman*.

A corollary to this emphasis was the culture's concern over sex and virginity, another issue that worried Plath as she was growing up. Her reputation at Bradford was that of a good girl, one who had not had sex. But she had done her share of necking and petting. The midcentury code of morality was entirely negative—nice girls didn't have sex. It was a delicate balance, for a girl to appear "normal"—i.e. sensual—and yet remain a virgin. According to the magazines, women were supposed to enjoy sex, but with just one lifetime partner. Doris Day's naive allure became the ideal, just as Farnham and Lundberg's *Modern*

Woman: The Lost Sex became the 1950s guide to satisfying relationships. Thoroughly Freudian, *Modern Woman* stated that women would find sexual satisfaction only through motherhood. It was a commonly held opinion, and during the Fifties the birth rate rose with such speed—the peak of the "Baby Boom"—that the nation's population grew more than 18% in that decade.

Sylvia had grown up with these attitudes and with the embodiment of them all—*The Ladies' Home Journal*. When she came home from school, she devoured that magazine. Several years later, when she lived in England, she frequently asked Aurelia to send her back copies. As her unpublished short fiction shows clearly, she often wrote stories aimed at that market (Ted Hughes recalls that she wrote for either *The New Yorker* or *Ladies' Home Journal*, "the two alternating according to her mood"). Somehow, the latter magazine epitomized the American woman's ideal life, and Sylvia was never certain that she did not want to live that life. Her early conditioning to live exactly as her mother directed and to please her parents in order to win their love was almost impossible to shake.

Her high school fiction reflects the pressure she felt from those cultural ideals. Much of her writing is concerned with women's lives and the choices women make. Even at fifteen and sixteen Sylvia saw herself as outside the mainstream of society, and she worried about being out there. Whether she felt guilty (why did she want to be different from other women? from her mother?) or rebellious, she hid her feelings except in her writing. Throughout her life, Sylvia's writing expressed feelings she did not allow herself to admit otherwise.

In "The Dark River," a 1949 story, the striking older woman protagonist tells the young female listener of having given up the man who loved her so that she could lead her own life. Her final parting from him is defiant, described by Plath as a triumph:

> It was good to run. As her feet thudded over the gravel path, the blood pounded in her ears and drowned out the sound of the river, which still echoed in her brain. Something pent up inside her broke, free and wild. Her hair flew out behind her as she ran. . . .

Generally, Plath's stories from this period depict a girl or woman protagonist desperate for a lover, yet here a broken romance is the climactic event. Young as she was, Sylvia was exploring women's lives in considerable dimension.

Much of her early fiction concerns the conflict between some "ideal" woman—virginal or married, a good daughter or wife—and the slightly suspect "career woman." The continuing character in Sylvia's stories is the girl who must choose between roles, sometimes an overachiever and usually alienated from life around her. Other poems and stories reflect her growing suspicion of her family's values, her mistrust of her mother's advice. Much of her writing is already complex and ambivalent. The story "East Wind," for example, presents Miss Minton, a single woman who is lured through city streets by an elfin child, almost to her death. Here the water imagery that Sylvia often used to depict security becomes the place of suicide. Ostensibly, Miss Minton is chasing her hat in the strong wind of the title, but the chase brings her to a river bridge:

> She reached out over the railing, and there was the water down below. Way, way down the dark surface of the river leered up at her. If she leaned just a little farther, just a little . . . there would be no more apartment, no more ugly brown cloak, no more. . . . The wind would bear her up. She would be floating on the wind; light as a feather she would be caught and tossed up, up. For one breathless exultant moment she leaned out, her eyes shining. She laughed giddily. She was going to. . . .

But with a shift in the wind, Minton leaves her fantasy and goes home, forgetting the episode and, Plath suggests, losing as well those moments of clarity that the elf had made possible. "Sane" survival has also meant a kind of loss.

In senior year Sylvia continued her writing, submitting to magazines, and being undisturbed at rejections. It was a year of French III, art, biology, English, and American history with Mr. Upham, who wrote on her final report, "You are what makes teaching worthwhile." It was also a year of leadership in the Unitarian Church's youth group and membership in the United World Federalists, a club to promote world peace.

The most important event of her senior year was her decision to attend Smith College. She wrote, "I know my whole life will be different because of my choice." (Her choice was either to live at home and go to Wellesley College, or to use a number of scholarships and go to Northampton.) Attending Smith, however glamorous, meant increased financial worry for both Sylvia and her mother. Scholarships were given for one year only, so each spring was a trial while various awards were announced. For her freshman year, Sylvia had a $450 scholarship from the local Smith Club and an $850 scholarship from the Olive Higgins Prouty fellowship fund at Smith. Mrs. Prouty, the well-known author of *Stella Dallas*, the novel and radio serial, as well as other novels, became one of Sylvia's lifelong benefactors and friends. She lived in Brookline, Massachusetts, and befriended Aurelia and Warren as well as Sylvia.

At her high school graduation, Sylvia was recognized for winning the *Boston Globe* contest (first prize for a news story and honorable mention for a poem) and for winning top prize in *The Atlantic Monthly* Scholastic contest for fiction. The uneasiness of her hard-won popularity, however, showed in the school paper's Class Prophecy on June 6, 1950. There Sylvia appears, intent and serious-minded, "explaining her theory of relativity to Pat O'Neill who is listening, as always, with the patience of Job."

The triumph of Sylvia's graduation from Bradford High was, in some ways, foreshadowed by her earlier essay, "Childhood Fears," a writing assignment for Crockett's English class. According to the essay, Sylvia had never been afraid of anything but, knowing that she should have some fears to be normal, she chose carpet sweepers (for noise) and opening umbrellas (for motion). Later, she described the way she and her friend Ruthie Freeman talked themselves into being afraid of escalators and subways, of circular stairs and cut-out steps, of people hiding in closets, and of dreams (the girls studied dreams with a book from the Freeman attic). The impertinence of Sylvia's essay suggests that she had experienced a childhood that was generally peaceful and secure and that, at fifteen, she felt in control of her life. But a careful reader might have noticed that her flippant essay did not mention the various losses and worries she had actually known: her fear of change, worries about money, her father's death, academic pressure. Whether Sylvia was a fearless high school student, the remainder of her school years would not be carefree.

4
Beginning
Smith College

1950-51

"Blameless as Daylight"

n the summer of 1950, with her characteristic discipline, Sylvia began keeping a serious journal. In it she described scenes from dates and summer jobs and meditated about issues important to her—the Korean War, the "decline" of America, people's inhumanity to each other, her identity, whether she could become the writer she now dreamed of being.

Her thoughts about what it means to be a writer, to depersonalize feelings so that they can be recorded, take up much of this summer journal. Her obsession with this one subject suggests that she was not comfortable with her ambition. Sometimes she felt that she was being opportunistic because she wrote about the people in her life, boyfriends included: "At home on my desk is the best story I've ever written. How can I tell Bob [Riedeman] that my happiness streams from having wrenched a piece out of my life, a piece of hurt and beauty, and transformed it to typewritten words on paper? How can he know I am justifying my life, my keen emotion, my feeling, by turning it into print?"

Had Sylvia made this entry public, perhaps someone would have assured her that her ambitions, her emotions, needed no justification. But whenever she wrote, she expressed a need to be "justified," to be reassured that this activity was acceptable. From the first her private journals seemed to contradict the picture of confident mastery she was adept at projecting.

Her summer journals include a moving passage about Mary Ventura, her friend who had moved from Wellesley to Natick during their senior year. Always looking for role models, Sylvia admired the more experienced girl, whom she described as "something vital, an artist's model, life. . . . Mary is me . . . with her I can be honest." Aside from Phil McCurdy and Mary Ventura, there were few people Sylvia felt she could be herself with. In the course of her life, her deepest friendships were with people with whom she could show a frankness that was often discouraged in "polite" society.

Plath's journal relates other summer events. She and Warren had full-time jobs at Lookout Farm, a truck farm where fruits and vegetables were raised for the city markets. Every morning they biked as far as Wellesley College where they caught rides with other workers. It was a long day of hard labor, setting out strawberry plants, cutting asparagus, weeding corn. What was satisfying to Sylvia was that she could do the work and that she was accepted by her coworkers. (Almost accepted. There was one day when the boys in the group planned to throw her into the washtub, but Warren stood them off.) Sylvia's hunger to know people led to her romanticizing the farm workers, as in her poem "Bitter Strawberries" and an essay, "The Rewards of a New England Summer," both of which were published that fall in *The Christian Science Monitor*.

There was a sexual dimension to the farm experience as well. Ilo, a Latvian immigrant, was working there before going to New York to start a career as an artist. He had been studying art in Munich. Sylvia's interest in drawing led to friendship, but she was frightened when Ilo French-kissed her and she realized how attracted to him she was. One of her college stories, called "The Estonian" and, in a second version, "The Latvian," describes that attraction. So too does "Den of Lions," which she wrote about another summer date, and which was published. The tension between fear of the sexual and fascination with it gave these stories a sensuality, which she also caught in "A Day in June," a story about adolescent girls. Her journal, however, presented a much more caustic Sylvia, who described dating as "this game of searching for a mate, of testing, trying." She wrote with wicked humor about "the strong smell of masculinity which creates the ideal medium for me to exist in," but she also described, perceptively, the real sexual conflicts she endured: "I have too much conscience injected in me to break customs without disastrous effects; I can only lean enviously against the boundary and hate, hate, hate the boys who dispel sexual hunger freely . . . and be whole, while I drag out from date to date in soggy desire, always unfulfilled. The whole thing sickens me." She ironically called herself "the American virgin, dressed to seduce. . . . We go on dates, we play around, and if we're nice girls, we demur at a certain point."

The wry candor of Plath's journals did not show in any of her published writing from these years. In August of 1950, as she was about to enter Smith, *Seventeen* published "And Summer Will Not Come Again." Based on Sylvia's tennis court dates of the summer before, the story is about a high school girl who falls for the college boy who coaches her, only to discover that he already has a girlfriend. The story established her reputation as a writer at Smith, but it was less important in itself than as the impetus for her five-year friendship with Ed Cohen, a Chicagoan who wrote to her after he read the story.

A student at Roosevelt University, a small, politically radical liberal arts school, Cohen introduced himself as a former University of Chicago student who wanted to be a psychiatrist but would never have the patience to go to medical school, a "cynical idealist" who was impressed with Sylvia's writing. Four years older than she, Cohen came through even in his first letter as a comparative "man of the world." He smoked, he had recently broken off with a live-in fiancée, and he had temporarily dropped out of college so that he could live in a way he considered more full. He was, in fact, about to vacation in Mexico, a statement that was more alluring than he could have known to the little-traveled New England girl.

There were letters from Cohen on August 8 and 19, and one on August 25 from the Hotel Belpra in Mexico City. Once back in Chicago, Cohen wrote—usually in the middle of the night (and for Sylvia, who needed ten hours of sleep a night, his writing habits were as exotic as his vacations)—every week in September. Each letter, single-spaced, ran from four to ten pages. All Cohen's letters were candid, troubling accounts of his alienation from society; all attempted to involve Sylvia in his life. Cohen and Sylvia were soon corresponding the way she and Phil McCurdy had always talked—openly and with an element of self-dramatization that might, given the right circumstances, topple over into fiction.

Much of Cohen's correspondence had to do with sex. He recommended that Sylvia read Walter Benton's *This Is My Beloved*, a book of graphic sexual poetry popular at the time. He frequently advised her about her own sexual behavior ("I not only did not advocate promiscuity, I think I very specifically said the person who indulges in it is likely to be unhappy").

Cynical humor dotted Cohen's letters, and Plath frequently borrowed his epigrams: "It is quite true that women grow up faster than men do; however, they never seem to grow up quite as far." "Life might be simpler if we were born in pairs." "Those who believe in God are mental cowards; those who devote their lives to his service are physical cowards as well." "The meek shall inherit the earth—but how long will they stay that way?"

An important element in their correspondence was their shared disgust with the Korean War. Cohen described the "state of terror" he and his friends lived in, because of the draft, and wrote about coming home from Mexico only to hear Truman "telling me that after all this living, I'm going to die in Korea. Why? WHYWHYWHY? I want to know what the hell it's all about. I'm damned if I intend to stop living for a lot of fancy slogans." In other letters, he described the way his friends and he felt about the draft and about war. On September 21, he wrote that Sylvia's antiwar letter—a letter she had recently sent him—which he called "a powerful document," had helped him to change the views of several friends from prowar to antiwar.

In quality as well as quantity, Cohen's letters impressed Sylvia. In many ways, the two were kindred spirits, and she recognized this from her first letter. She wrote in a style that was, for her, new and tough. With Hemingway-like abruptness, she wrote, "My father is dead; my mother teaches. I have a kid brother." About her job at Lookout Farm, "I'm up at 6, in bed by 9, and very grimy in between. But I just smile when my white collar acquaintances look at me with unbelieving dismay as I tell them about soaking my hands in bleach to get them clean."

Plath showed her own satiric vein in her August 11 letter, calling herself "a red-blooded American girl (Do I hear strains of the national anthem in the background?). . . . I'm sarcastic, skeptical and sometimes callous because I'm still afraid of letting myself be hurt. There's that very vulnerable core in me which every egoist has." She told Cohen she was not religious, scornful of a salvation that is "spooned out to those too spineless to think for themselves." She too saw herself as alienated and told Cohen that, for a girl, alienation was worse because boys were always trying to categorize her as brainless, never realizing "the CHAOS that seethes beneath my exterior. As for the Who am I? What am I? angle . . . that will preoccupy me till the day I die."

The subject of greatest interest to both of them was their shared disaffection from society. Writing as the McCarthy hysteria was reaching its peak, Sylvia was furious about the reaction to dissenters: "You're a Communist nowadays if you sign peace appeals. Ed, people don't seem to see that this negative Anti-Communist attitude is destroying all the freedom of thought we've ever had. . . . Everything they don't agree with is Communist." Like her early poem "Youth's Appeal for Peace," with its imagery of apocalypse, and the essay she wrote with Perry Norton, which appeared in *The Christian Science Monitor* in March of 1950, Plath's view was that pacifism would solve the world's problems.

There was a core of idealism to Sylvia's often stubborn character, and her anger usually flared when her ideals were not respected. She believed in truth and honor as more than platitudes, and she was far from being a materialist, no matter how much she yearned for good clothes, records, and books. She also looked for people's spiritual dimensions, although, since she had been reared on Unitarian optimism, she believed people could determine their own future. Individual will was more important than the quality of a person's belief in God. "Knowledge" was often the path to spiritual growth, even if that knowledge was not primarily religious. In Sylvia's household, "character" was the mark of an accomplished person, and any one could reach his or her goals through self-betterment. Sylvia carried this personal belief into her dealings with other people, and she grew impatient when her friends were less than perfect. Nearly all her friends commented on her tendency to become disillusioned with people, and they observed that she had the same idealistic expectations for herself.

In fact, the most noticeable trait of Sylvia's personality in 1950, as she entered college, was the relentless demand she made on herself. Anything less than complete success in all areas was failure to her. Now that she had achieved such successes as her academic record, her admission to Smith, even her social life, she might have been ready to believe in her own abilities and talent. But Sylvia was not. She was still apprehensive, and as the move to Smith grew closer, her journal filled with her fears.

Complicating the issue was Sylvia's rejection of the prevailing mode of femininity. She wrote in one journal entry, "Spare me from cooking three meals a day—spare me from the relentless cage of routine and rote." Instead, she wished for freedom, power, the means to achieve whatever she desired: "I think I would like to call myself 'The girl who wanted to be God.' " And in a later entry: "I love freedom. I deplore constrictions and limitations. . . . I am I—I am powerful."

On September 27, 1950, Sylvia took with her to Smith her fears, complete with her self-contradictory image as the responsible intellectual and the daring woman who insisted on living fully. She was intent on realizing potential, including her sexual potential. Yet the admonition she put foremost—with characteristic guilt at her good fortune—was to prove herself worthy of the $1300 in scholarship money.

The self-imposed pressure was intense. Sylvia's letters from Smith, one written only a few hours after she arrived, show her nervousness about being there. "I've so much work to do." "Just now the schoolwork seems endless. . . . I don't see how girls can play bridge in the livingroom all night. For these first months, I'm going to study every chance I get. I'll be amazed if I get one A." The steady litany of exhaustion in these letters home suggests either that Plath was defeated before she began, or that she felt bound to convince her family of the incredible work ahead.

Part of Sylvia's uneasiness stemmed from the fact that—at Smith as in Wellesley—she felt that she was an outsider. Both Smith and Wellesley radiated well-kept serenity, expensive serenity. Wellesley's exclusive shopping districts and the mammoth stone castle that serves as its Town Hall surrounded Sylvia with the marks and the privileges of wealth. In a somewhat understated manner, the Smith campus gave the same impression. Immaculate lawns and parks surrounded Paradise Pond; the women lived in thirty-five houses that served as dormitories. Sylvia lived in Haven House, one of the frame residences along wide, tree-lined Elm Street. She was given a single room on the third floor. Considering her need for a great deal of sleep, such a room should have been ideal.

At first she was ecstatic at having forty-eight girls as housemates. As she wrote to Aurelia, "Girls are a new world for me. I should have some fascinating times learning about the creatures. Gosh, to live in a house with 48 kids my own age—what a life!" The next day in another letter home she announced somewhat prematurely, "I've gotten along with everyone in the house. It's good to see more faces familiar to me. . . . The food here is fabulous. I love everybody. If only I can unobtrusively do well in all my courses and get enough sleep, I should be tops. I'm so happy . . . I keep muttering, 'I'M A SMITH GIRL NOW.' "

But there were hints that Sylvia was not quite right for Haven. Comments about her constant studying hurt her feelings, and there was a time after Thanksgiving when she was afraid to go downstairs and mix with her housemates. She went out on blind dates, but few of the men she went out with called her again. She did not play bridge. Her clothes were not casual enough. Her attitudes were too conventional for her to be a rebel, and too rebellious for her to be part of the mainstream. Her discomfort occurred despite the fact that Haven was less homogeneous than some of the Smith houses, which were conservative and discriminatory. The women in Haven at that time were independent, even idiosyncratic; and most of them were willing to judge their fellow women on merits other than the number of cashmere sweaters they owned.

Hoping to be bright "unobtrusively," she worried herself into the customary sinus ailments before she had been at school a month, and in mid-October she was in the infirmary. Buried under tests and papers, a week before her eighteenth birthday, she wrote, "I get a little frightened when I think of life slipping through my fingers like water—so fast that I have little time to stop running. I have to keep on like the White Queen to stay in the same place." "All I'm trying to do is keep my head above water. . . . If only I'm good enough to deserve all this!"

A parallel fear seemed to be her anonymity on the campus of several thousand talented women: "God, who am I? . . . Girls, girls everywhere, reading books. Intent faces, flesh pink, white, yellow. And I sit here without identity. . . . If I rest, if I think inward, I go mad. There is so much, and I am torn in different directions, pulled thin, taut against horizons too distant for me to reach." Plath's utter, and unreasonable, hopelessness could not be alleviated by kind words; she shut herself off from cheering up. She was reassured only by A's on assignments and by boys calling her for dates.

During the Smith years and afterward, what Sylvia wrote in letters to her mother was often quite different from what she wrote in her journal. To Aurelia, she seldom complained, or if she did, it was for effect, with what seemed to be self-mocking humor. In her journals, however, Sylvia was often bitter. Nothing she did pleased her; no accomplishment was enough. She and Aurelia had different expectations. Sylvia wanted everything. Aurelia was satisfied if her daughter made good grades. She reminded Sylvia that thankfulness should be her basic attitude. Sylvia, burned-out and depressed, found it hard to consider herself lucky.

Sylvia's academic life at Smith was similar to that in high school. She had courses in European history, botany, painting, English, French literature, and physical education. She managed a low-B average in the last; in each of the other courses she carried an A or an $A-$ average, except for English where Mr. Madiera, her instructor, persisted in giving her B's. He did give her the highest mark on a research paper on Thomas Mann and a long critical analysis of Edith Sitwell's poetry so she ended the year with a *B+* average. This uncomfortable situation in English kept Sylvia from declaring the major she had planned, and she thought seriously about majoring in art.

The aim of the Smith curriculum, a source of pride for its 200 faculty members, was truly liberal learning. Smith women took a five-course load both freshman and sophomore years, choosing from courses in the sciences, history or government, philosophy or religion or language, and art, music or creative writing. During their last two years, they specialized, doing intensive work in courses or opting for an honors program in which they took seminars ("units") and wrote theses. Sylvia's favorite course during her first year was Mrs. Koffka's European history. Koffka was an imposing woman with gray hair, piercing eyes, great enthusiasm, and a somewhat difficult accent. Sylvia later ranked Koffka's influence on her with that of Wilbury Crockett. She enjoyed Koffka's integrative approach to history, and she wrote a paper on Darwin, Marx, and Wagner for the class.

Both botany and painting were laboratory classes, worth six credits instead of the usual three. Sylvia spent twenty-four hours a week in class, including Saturday sessions, and devoted many evenings to finishing art projects. Because she had so little time during the day to study, she spent other evenings in the Neilson Library's comfortable reading room. Furnished with couches and chairs, elegant paintings and tapestries, this room became an important hide-away for her. When she studied there, instead of in her room, her housemates could not call her a grind.

School was Sylvia's first priority (letters home include strategies for getting better grades, such as inviting Mr. Madiera and his wife for dinner), but she worried almost as much about her social life. Ann Davidow, a Chicagoan, became Sylvia's best friend and arranged several blind dates for her. Ann and Sylvia were each fascinated by religion, and spent long hours talking about it. They planned to room together their sophomore year, and Sylvia felt lost when Ann did not return to Smith in January. Ann had felt inadequate to the workload, and had become increasingly depressed during fall term. Minor frustrations such as her inability to type loomed large. Sylvia was supportive, even to the point of typing one of Ann's longer English papers for her. Ann's foundering self-confidence was a drain on Sylvia's as well. If her closest friend couldn't cope, how well could she?

Separated from Ann, Sylvia spent time with Sydney Webber, a history major who also took English courses, and Enid Epstein, an art major who had also published in *Seventeen*. Epstein's work and Sylvia's had been placed on the College Hall bulletin board when school had opened, which was where Enid and Sylvia met. The next few years, they worked together on Press Board, the college's public relations division; for time spent writing press releases, women received salaries. Enid eventually became president of the Board and was, therefore, Sylvia's boss. Sylvia, always outwardly affable, usually chose to be close friends only with people who shared her academic strengths and ambitions.

She broke that pattern, though, when her search for a sophomore-year roommate led her to exuberant Marcia Brown, a sociology major. Marcia had many friends and often went out with the other women in Haven; by contrast, Sylvia studied unless she had a date who would pay the costs of going somewhere. Marcia provided Sylvia with a bridge to other housemates. Sylvia also had fun with Marcia. They talked nonstop, giggled, accepted each other's personalities and loved them. One of Marcia's gifts was to bring out Sylvia's strengths, and Marcia said in turn that she never talked so well as with Sylvia. Even as a listener, her Wellesley friend was intense and compelling.

Sylvia's most exciting experiences during her first years at Smith—traveling and working on the Cape during the summer, visiting New York—occurred with Marcia and, often, because of Marcia. The short, brown-haired girl was Sylvia's opposite in many ways besides appearance: she was direct and forthright, independent, and unconcerned about what people would say, or about what she should be doing.

During her years at Smith, Sylvia and Ed Cohen continued their correspondence, which was valuable to Sylvia both emotionally and sexually. For example, one of Cohen's 1950 letters describes different kinds of orgasms. For a virgin freshman girl, such explicit information was hard to come by. Sylvia also considered Cohen her "double," her soul mate. He was a rebel; he was a would-be writer. Politics continued to be a refrain in their correspondence. Plath meditated on political themes in her journal, too. Much of this interest occurred when she was upset about her own life, as if she could legitimately show anger about international subjects when it was difficult for her to express anger about her more personal concerns—or too upsetting for her family. The political and personal came together most notably when Wilbury Crockett was called before the Wellesley town board to explain his political beliefs. (He was a pacifist.) Plath was deeply offended.

In her journals and in letters to Cohen, Sylvia showed a nihilism that few other people saw.

Life is loneliness, despite all the opiates, despite the false grinning faces we all wear. And when at last you find someone to whom you feel you can pour out your soul, you stop in shock at the words you utter—they are so rusty, so ugly, so meaningless and feeble from being kept in the small cramped dark inside you so long. Yes, there is joy, fulfillment and companionship—but the loneliness of the soul in its appalling self-consciousness is horrible and overpowering.

Part of her anger came from her sense of being limited, of having to choose between marriage and a career. She wanted both. She did not want to be a "meek" Christian wife. She wondered what Lillian Hellman, Willa Cather, and Virginia Woolf were like as women. Like them, Sylvia knew even at eighteen that her writing meant a great deal to her. She believed that the only immortality would exist through her writing ("I think I will be snuffed out. Black is sleep; black is a fainting spell; and black is death"). She asked repeatedly, "What is my life for and what am I going to do with it? I don't know and I'm afraid."

Most college freshmen show some confusion about the future, but few express such deep and unremitting anger. Plath's rage and her resulting depression were more likely the product of her childhood years of loss and perceived abandonment, emotions always hidden—so that her anger did not upset her mother—or disguised—so that she could remain safely within the pleasant family circle. Like a small child, Sylvia usually expected great happiness in the future. She was repeatedly disappointed. Nothing could have met her exuberant expectations.

Part of Sylvia's anxiety stemmed from financial worries. An accounting she gave of her expenses during the 1950–51 year shows how carefully she watched even small amounts of money: $270 covered food and room, art supplies, books; $15 for the year's entertainment, and $50 for clothes. She wrote to Warren in a humorous poem that she had "nuffin' " to wear and her closet was "grungy." She did not even walk along Green Street, where the clothing shops were. Aurelia's health was poor, and with Warren now at Exeter both children could have used more money for clothes, entertainment, and travel. Sylvia worried often about her mother. She took a job with Press Board, making $20 a month for spending several hours each day writing press releases for Smith. She also sold stockings in her dormitory. In some ways, a new source of pressure was added once Sylvia learned that her Smith scholarship was funded by Olive Higgins Prouty. At the suggestion of Mary Mensel, Smith's scholarship counselor, Sylvia wrote to Mrs. Prouty and thanked her. Thus began a relationship that was to be important to Sylvia throughout her life. Mrs. Prouty invited Sylvia to tea, and from then on, Sylvia felt great pressure to maintain the reputation she had with her patron. Typical of her complex relationships with supportive older women—including her mother—Sylvia alternated between gratitude for Mrs. Prouty's help and anger at what she saw as her benefactor's influence on her life.

Throughout freshman year Sylvia's social situation remained unsettled. She was planning to break off with Bob Riedeman, now a junior at University of New Hampshire, although she invited him to Smith for a fall weekend and saw him over Thanksgiving. Part of her challenge at Smith, as she saw it, was to make a good "catch." Smith was the hub of a wheel that radiated out to many men's colleges within reasonable commuting distance. Fall mixers with men's colleges were a regular part of the Smith calendar. But Sylvia saw herself as a giantess, five feet nine inches tall and weighing 137 pounds, and a scholarship student as well. She convinced herself she was doomed to be a wallflower, as described so well in her story "Initiation," and so she was willing to date anyone who asked her out. One of her blind dates, a twenty-five-year-old disabled veteran, took her on a long walk and suggested they have sex. Sylvia wrote about the date to her mother, wondering naively whether she should see the man again. But in her journal, she described the experience —his moving her hand along his penis, her disgusted yet curious reaction. Her description of the "soft, writhing flesh" foreshadows the scene in *The Bell Jar* in which Buddy Willard proudly shows her his penis; as does her anger at the double standard: in the journal she exclaims, "I hate you. Damn you. Just because you're a boy. Just because you're never worried about having babies!"

Evidently Sylvia did not see him again. But she wanted a boyfriend as much as she wanted good grades, and she often put the two together, "I know I am capable of getting good marks; I know I am capable of attracting males." These were parallel ambitions for many women in the Fifties, and Sylvia equated having acceptable dates with stability. As she complained in November of 1950, "I need someone real, who will be right for me now, here, and soon. Until then I'm lost. I think I am mad at times."

Because this was the situation as she saw it, she grew desperate to have a boyfriend who would impress her Haven friends. When Dick Norton, the oldest son of the family friends and Perry's older brother, wrote her on January 20, 1951, inviting her to Yale, Sylvia was beside herself with excitement. She even spent $1.75 to have her hair done. Dick had stopped in at the Plaths' during Christmas week, when he was out running, and the invitation grew from the conversation he and Sylvia had had then. Blond, tall, handsome, with an engaging, wide-eyed expression, Dick was a senior science student who had been accepted to Harvard Medical School.

Despite his greater age, Norton seemed unsure of his role with Sylvia. 'Dear Cousin," his letter began. He asked to be remembered to "Aunt Aurelia," and in a postscript told Sylvia that she could share his letters with her mother.

Sylvia had never been to Yale. Going as Dick's date and getting to spend some time with her good friend Perry, who was a freshman there, pleased her. Uncharacteristically, she did not mention the weekend to her mother until afterwards, although her mother probably knew about it. Then Sylvia pretended Dick was just being nice and showing her around. Her enthusiasm for him was boundless; she thought he knew everything. She promised herself that she would study science on her own so that she could understand him. She didn't tell Aurelia that he had asked her to the Yale prom, but she did tell her that they had missed the last train to Northampton by "one fatal minute" so that she was late getting back to Smith and was confined to campus for a week.

Norton's letters before the big prom date were both distant and literary. He sent Sylvia some excerpts from Sherwood Anderson's novel *Poor White*, mentioning that he had been to the Yale library to see exhibits from the manuscript collections of Gertrude Stein, Alfred Stieglitz, and Sinclair Lewis. He called Sylvia "artist" and signed himself "scientist" but his letters were calculated to impress her with his versatility. The prom itself was a fairy-tale date, with Sylvia carrying a black purse and wearing a white formal and crinoline, silver sandals, and a fur (all but the dress borrowed from housemates). She wrote to Cohen that she felt like Cinderella. After they stayed out till 3:30 the night of the dance, walking all around campus to the hill behind the Chemistry Building, Norton finally kissed her. Then they composed a joint letter to "Dear Aunt Aurelia." Dated March 10, the letter—which was mostly from Dick— described the dance, their getting in late, and a telegram from Brenda Marshall, another family friend from Wellesley, wishing them much happiness on their big weekend.

If Sylvia felt hemmed in by the "family" nature of this romance, she didn't express any reservations. Dick remained the most exciting, smartest, best-looking boy she knew. But her pride took a blow the very next weekend when Norton turned up at Smith as the prom date of Jane Anderson, another Wellesley girl a year older than Sylvia. Jane had invited him earlier, but his error—in Sylvia's view—was that he didn't let her know he was coming to Smith, for whatever reason. He left a letter at Haven telling Sylvia that he was on campus. Sylvia was enraged.

Luckily for Norton, spring break came and he drove to Florida to spend time with his grandparents there before driving them back to Massachusetts. His letters to Sylvia from Florida opened "Dear Beauty and Kindness" and talked about trying to find a place to have "a houseparty weekend" in later spring. Furious as

Sylvia had been about his date with Jane, she evidently had not conveyed her anger to Dick. The tone of his relatively noncommittal letters did not change; they were filled with messages to Aunt Aurelia and assumptions that, of course, Sylvia would be glad to see him, whenever he appeared.

Sylvia's own spring break was unexpectedly eventful. Late in March, just after Cohen had written her that he had broken his second engagement, he appeared in Northampton. He had borrowed his parents' car on the pretense of visiting some relatives in Detroit, which he did briefly, but then he continued nonstop to Massachusetts. In bad emotional shape, he felt that he needed to see Sylvia; she had become his alter ego as he had become hers. Unshaven and tired, he had been driving for over thirty hours. Their meeting at Haven House was nothing like either of them had expected.

Sylvia had been waiting for a ride home, so she drove with Cohen instead—a largely silent trip as the two loquacious correspondents, who wrote easily about everything from existentialism to sexuality, felt that they were each in the presence of a stranger. Perhaps both were frightened. Once at 26 Elmwood Road, Sylvia curtly introduced Ed to her mother, from outside the house, and then dismissed him. Aurelia was horrified at Sylvia's lack of manners: the man from Chicago was clearly in need of hospitality, not to mention food and sleep. Ed himself was furious at Sylvia's disdainful treatment. He turned around and kept driving, only to have a head-on collision in Ohio, but he was not badly hurt.

Spring break was limbo for Sylvia. She was angry about Norton's treatment of her and angry that Cohen had simply appeared at Smith without advance notice. Spontaneity was not, and could never be, one of Sylvia's traits. She needed time to prepare herself for any experience. She could already see that what most college women expected from men was not what she wanted. Most women echoed what Mrs. Norton had told Sylvia, "Girls look for infinite security; boys look for a mate. Both look for different things." Security was not a priority to Sylvia. In her journal, she commented, "I am at odds. I dislike being a girl, because as such I must come to realize that I cannot be a man. In other words, I must pour my energies through the direction and force of my mate. My only free act is choosing or refusing that mate." She spent her week at home taking stock, barraged by letters form Norton and Ed, the first organizing her life for her, the second analyzing her "incredibly rude" behavior. At the end of the week, she wrote in her journal,

> would marriage sap my creative energy and annihilate my desire for written and pictorial expression . . . or would I if I married achieve a fuller expression in art as well as in the creation of children? Am I strong enough to do both well? . . . That is the crux of the matter, and I hope to steel myself for the test . . . as frightened as I am.

With relief, she went back to Smith and Marcia.

But as soon as she was back at Smith, Dick came for a weekend. They succeeded in missing nearly every meal as they walked and talked together. Sylvia was sick by the time Dick left and was sure the "sweet wonderman," as she called him to her mother, would not want to see her again. But he reappeared April 28 to help her decorate for the Haven dance that night, even though she had invited Bob Humphrey, a friend from Wellesley, to the dance itself. After decorating, Sylvia had one of her sinus colds and was too sick to go anywhere.

As the term ended, Sylvia worried about examinations. She wrote Aurelia, "as I look ahead I see only an accelerated work-pattern until the day I drop into the grave." *Seventeen* published her "Den of Lions" as the third-place winner in a fiction contest, with a prize of $100. In April Sylvia and Marcia Brown applied for summer babysitting jobs on the Cape, so they could be together and, more directly, so Sylvia could be near Norton, whose summer job waiting tables was in Brewster. Sylvia planned to ask for Mondays off because that was Dick's day off.

She went to Yale May 10 to 12, "the best weekend yet," for a dance, a production of Thornton Wilder's *The Skin of Our Teeth*, and a beach picnic at Sachem's with beer, hot dogs, and volleyball. Then she and Dick read Hemingway aloud on the beach for hours. Although Sylvia enjoyed her dates with Dick Norton, his "older cousin" attitude confused her, and she wrote to her mother about it.

As the year ended, Sylvia finished her exams and then packed to drive home with Norton on June 3. He and Perry were about to leave for a bike trip to Maine, but he asked her to come to Class Day and his Yale graduation with his family. She spent the night at the Nortons' because they were leaving early. (Mildred Norton was up at 5 A.M., packing a picnic lunch for the day and cleaning house; then she made a hot breakfast.) One wonders whether Sylvia remembered her own stint as househelper when Mildred had the flu, or "Cousin Dick's" first letter to her in 1943, when they both were home with colds. Then fourteen, Norton wrote that he had found Otto Plath's book on bees and was reading it to help pass the time. Yale graduation with "Aunt Mildred" and "Uncle Bill" was the high point of a long family friendship.

As Sylvia and Mrs. Norton went to bed that night in New Haven after the graduation and a visit to an amusement park, Dick called to say he was leaving the next day for Arizona with friends. Then he would go to Brewster, and after his summer job he was taking a Western trip to see other friends. His peremptory announcements may have been in retaliation for Sylvia's taking his father's side in a family argument earlier in the day, but, whatever the reason, Sylvia resented his making these curt announcements of plans to be away from her. She had taken her summer job to be near him.

His plans also renewed her frequent worries about money. Dick had gone to Florida during spring break, he and Perry had just taken a trip to Maine, and now he was going to Arizona. In contrast, she stayed in Wellesley and mowed the grass. She had already complained to her mother about having to work all summer; she was tired. At Smith, she had gone five months without a menstrual period, and she had written hardly anything all year. In a letter home, she said,

I wish I didn't have to work all summer, just so I can work the rest of the year. The Theory of the Leisure Class is fine only so long as you're a member of the aristocracy. When you aren't a member of the nobility, you might as well revolt and institute a classless state. (Your reply, I suppose, will be to count my blessings.)

Back in Wellesley, with Dick gone and Marcia in New Jersey, Sylvia was faced with the ever-widening difference between what she wanted for herself and what everyone else—including her family and boyfriends—seemed to think was appropriate for her. It was a time of depressing recognition.

5

Conquering Smith

1951-52

"Eating the Fingers of Wisdom"

Sylvia's letters home from the Mayo household during the summer of 1951 were one long cry for help. She had no idea what to do with three children, for whom she was expected to cook, clean, make beds, entertain, and get up at night. The radical expansion of what "babysitting" had meant in Wellesley almost capsized her. Joey, the baby girl, was two; Penny, four; Freddie, seven. Dr. Mayo and his wife entertained a great deal. They needed Sylvia, in addition to their part-time cook, to handle family activities.

Just outside Sylvia's window was a beautiful beach. She quickly learned to get the children to the beach as often as possible. After two weeks of this, Marcia Brown came to do similar work for a nearby family, and things improved immensely. Both girls, however, were bothered by their heavy responsibilities.

Part of Sylvia's initial upset was in reaction to an even cooler tone in Dick Norton's letters. In his June 21 note, which opened "Dear Sister-Cousin," he described a "big sisterish" waitress who was helping him improve his dancing. He asked Sylvia to come to Brewster in early July, but she decided not to go—she was pale and exhausted. Evidently, because she did not come,

Norton's friendship with the waitress grew more intimate. A few weeks later, he came to see Sylvia and confessed; her resulting anger ruined their day, and much of the coming year. In his July 18 letter, Norton signed himself "Truly and faithfully" and pointed out that *his* indiscretions occurred only because *she* had failed him by not coming to Brewster.

Sylvia was appalled, not only because of Norton's acts but also because of his attempts to justify those acts. She had thought she was his girlfriend. She had taken a miserable summer job in order to be near him, and the extent of their summer was going to be a few days together. She felt only "a deep hurt" at his treatment. She had idealized their relationship, but her pain was no less real for her naive trust in those idealizations.

What she saw as Norton's betrayal colored his every word and action. She was so angry about the double standard behavior—that he could simply confess his intimacy and expect to be forgiven—that she had sleepless nights. Sylvia expressed her anger only in her journal ("Being born a woman is my awful tragedy," she raged) and sometimes on the Mayo piano, if no one else was in the house. She had already invested years of thought, talk, and guilt in the subject of sexuality. Especially at Smith, she had listened well to other women: "Once a woman has intercourse she isn't satisfied," "You need time and security for full pleasure," and the dire "You'll be finished at Smith." She was remaining a virgin so that she could continue school, but more importantly because she wanted to be virginal for a husband. Now the very man she thought would be her husband had just made love with someone he cared very little about. In another year, Sylvia was to write in her journal, with predictable self-disgust, that she was still a virgin but that her love-making was "Everything but: what a pretty compromise between technical virginity and practical satisfaction."

During the 1950s, before birth control pills and in the days of illegal and dangerous abortions, American women knew all too well the destructive potential of sex. There was much frustration and anger about it—and so it was for Sylvia. But despite her disappointment with Norton, she persisted in the relationship. Dick had become her choice for a mate, regardless of the way he treated her. He seemed to be everything her family and friends admired—ambitious, talented, handsome, well educated, and from a good family. He was also studying to be a doctor. With characteristic stubbornness, Sylvia tried to live with the situation. The four days in September that the Plath and Norton families shared at Brewster, however, were agony, and Sylvia found herself spending more time with Perry than with Dick. Dick too was airing hurt feelings. Their anger finally culminated in what Norton called a "truth talk." Sitting back to back in the center of an open field, Sylvia and Dick asked tough questions and gave candid answers. They decided to continue their relationship, although Dick seemed to think that they were engaged, while Sylvia promised herself that, if she chose, she would date other men as well.

A few weeks later, Dick entered medical school at Harvard and Sylvia returned to Smith, ready to do even better than she had freshman year. At chapel on September 28, she was named one of twenty-four outstanding sophomores. Classes during her second year were more to her liking. She took English, creative writing, government, religion, art, and physical education. Except for B's in the latter, all her grades were A or $A-$.

Along with creative writing, Mr. Crary's Religion 14 was her favorite. Partly historical overview, partly philosophy, the course required a term paper about a belief system. Sylvia's was about Unitarianism. The most interesting assignments, however, were the precourse and postcourse "personal history" essays. In the precourse paper, Sylvia discussed what she called her unorthodox religious background—her mother's having left the Catholic faith, her own lack of interest in religion until she joined a "vital" Unitarian congregation the previous year. Then she had become convinced that "religion *was* life." She described her ideas as "anti-Christian," even pagan. She believed that people were born without purpose, that there was no "kind Father" and no such thing as an inborn conscience. Each person therefore was responsible for his or her destiny. People were not perfectible, and there was no afterlife.

Sylvia's postcourse essay was much the same, although she admitted that she was more sympathetic to Christianity than she had been before taking the course. She still defined herself as an "agnostic humanist'" who agreed with Nietzsche's criticism of

the "weak and passive" elements of religion. "Heaven, hell, original sin, and redemption, as commonly thought of, do not have
any part in my philosophy," Plath wrote. For Sylvia, religion
remained a curiosity, something of interest intellectually, but
not a matter of faith. Her friend Ellie Friedman attested to Sylvia's interest in Judaism, and described Sylvia's effervescent
questions—"300 at a time"—when she was interested in a topic.

What interested Sylvia more during this sophomore year was
Ortega y Gasset's *The Revolt of the Masses.* When he said that out
of struggle and hardship came a strong, vital nature, she wrote
in the margin, "My *own* philosophy." She also underlined many
places that said, in effect, that the mass crushes beneath it everything that is different—"excellent, individual, qualified and select." Part of Sylvia's hesitation about adopting a religious belief
beyond her Unitarianism was that she saw such belief as a lev-
eling process. She liked being what she saw as different.

She used these ideas in essays about both Thomas Mann and
Dostoevsky. Both men believed in a creative dialectic by which
a person makes his or her own purpose on earth, "striving always
for a dynamic becoming." For Mann, conflicts between his father's materialism and his mother's artistic nature led to what he
called "the artist's bad conscience." Plath felt that Mann's story
"Tonio Kröger" reflected this philosophy. Although adolescent
depression had led Mann to plan suicide when he was twenty,
his later work shows his secure sense of self. He continued,
however, to acknowledge what he called "the magnetic attraction" of death.

Margaret Mead's *Male and Female* was another important book
for Plath during this sophomore year. Much of chapters 12
through 18, Mead's analysis of gender differences in America, is
underlined; and Sylvia used that information as her Bible. Mead
championed the need for an integrated person, "high and low,
animal and spiritual, body and spirit." She insisted that people
recognize that sex drives have a place in human personality: "We
are creatures who are made not only to be individuals, but to
continue the human race." She lamented the American lack of
"skin sensuousness" and what she saw as a tendency to idealize
the Puritan code of restraint. Mead described the plight of the
well-educated American housewife, infernally busy but "not

working," questioning what she has done with her life. Heavily underlined, Plath's copy of *Male and Female* contains ideas that Plath would enthusiastically embrace: "the misfits are the gifted." "In educating women like men, have we done something disastrous to both men and women alike?" "Women will see the world in different ways than men."

In long journal entries during the fall of 1951, Sylvia drew on Mead's book as she tried to sort through her situation with Dick. She understood that she would always argue with him unless *she* changed:

> I can whittle my square edges to fit in a round hole. God, I hope I'm never going to massacre myself that way. . . . The most saddening thing is to admit that I am not in love. I can only love (if that means self-denial—or does it mean self fulfillment? Or both?)—by giving up my love of self and ambitions—why, why, why, can't I combine ambition for myself and another?

Characteristically, everything positive about her realizations seemed negative to Plath, and she continued to blame herself for the dilemma: "I am vain and proud. I will not submit to having my life fingered by my husband. . . . I must have a legitimate field of my own, apart from his, which he must respect."

For all the expert faculty at Smith College, Sylvia knew few women professors she could admire completely as role models. Many of her teachers were women who had given their lives to teaching and scholarship, most of them unmarried and, even if married, childless. Sylvia was looking for professors with families, women with what she regarded as rich, happy lives, full of accomplishment and pride in themselves. Even the successful Smith novelist Mary Ellen Chase was so modest, so deferential to the "great" writers about whom she taught, that she was embarrassed if students wrote essays on her fiction. Mentally and emotionally, Sylvia was trying out the roles of writer, wife, mother, professor.

Luckily, she had a chance to work out her ideas and emotions in Evelyn Page's creative writing course. Page was inspiring and shrewd, warm and practical (she limited her students to one story about suicide in each course); she understood adolescence, and she respected her students. For her course, Sylvia wrote three stories that later appeared in *Mademoiselle* and *Seventeen*, and other stories and poems as good. Before class met, Sylvia and Enid Epstein read and critiqued each other's writing. Always enthusiastic about her friends' work, Sylvia praised whatever Enid wrote—and then worried about her own writing. Enid in turn encouraged Sylvia, but Sylvia needed several cups of coffee and much praise before she was ready to submit her work.

Sylvia's creative writing and essays during her sophomore year were polished and sophisticated. When she took courses where she could work independently, her intellectual strengths became obvious. She was adept at selecting and correlating details and shaping material. Every professor who knew her work was impressed with her skill, her vivacity, and her hunger for learning. Robert Gorham Davis, a well-known American literature scholar who was then chair of the English Department, said about Sylvia's presence in class, particularly her smile:

> It was not just a smile for the photographer. It was certainly not the ambitious, ingratiating, falsely-open smile of someone eager to please and be accepted. . . . It was a radiant smile (I thought) of happiness at what was being offered, being shared. . . . I was conscious of Sylvia from the beginning, before I knew the quality of her work, because she was always attentive, always looking up at me as I spoke, always smiling. I can still see her very clearly.

Sylvia was once again submitting work to national magazines. *Seventeen* bought the story "The Perfect Set-Up" for $25 and "Initiation" for $200 (the prize in its annual fiction contest). *Seventeen* also bought five poems, "To a Dissembling Spring," "The Suitcases Are Packed Again," "Carnival Nocturne," "Twelfth Night," and "Cinderella." "Crossing the Equinox" appeared in the *Annual Anthology of College Poetry*. *The Christian Science Monitor* took "As a Baby-Sitter Sees It," her essay about the Swampscott summer, which ran in two issues and included her drawings of the Mayo children; the *Monitor* also printed the poems "White Phlox" and "Riverside Reveries." "Sunday at the Mintons' " took the $500 first prize in the 1952 *Mademoiselle* Fiction Contest.

Sylvia was also successful on campus. She belonged to several councils, boards, and committees (including PUSH, the sophomore honorary) and was asked to be on the board of *Smith Review*, the campus literary magazine. Her biggest honor was being chosen for Alpha Phi Kappa Psi, the arts honorary, at a time when most inductees were juniors. She was also named assistant correspondent on Press Board, writing news releases about Smith for area papers. Compelled by her conscience to share her time in ways other than for pay, she also volunteered to teach a children's art class at the nearby People's Institute, a service she continued during her junior year as well.

Volunteering helped to relieve the guilt that still dotted her letters home (Is she really "good enough" to be a Smith girl?) but campus recognition helped her to realize that her talents were exceptional. She was happier than she had been during her freshman year, in great part because she was rooming with Marcia Brown. Sylvia became a "celebrator," enjoying friends, listening, laughing. She left time for bull sessions with other Smith women, usually in the carved wooden booths at Rahar's (a local hang-out) and about what she called "monumental topics of interest: Sex and how can there be a god? Sex and why is there segregation? Sex and have you read D. H. Lawrence's poem 'Tortoise Shout'?" Marcia and Sylvia were close, unquestioning friends. They were not inseparable but they kept the same hours and liked many of the same things. They took walks together whenever they could. Because of the Cape Cod summer, Marcia had come to love the sea and its beaches almost as much as Sylvia did.

She also continued her correspondence with Ed Cohen, a literary and philosophical connection that she needed. His anger at their meeting the previous spring had worn away, and the two bantered about many things, including Sylvia's ideas about marriage, family, and career. Cohen—whom Sylvia described as "lovely, immoral, radical"—understood the Ivy League marriage patterns:

You might as well face it—we "radicals" believe that a wife should share her husband's life and experiences, but for most of the world a woman has a definite social role in marriage which will not permit the existance [sic] which I am inclined to feel you want before you start on the home and kiddies and dinner-everynight stuff. If I may get bitter for a moment, the nice clean boys of your acquaintance (you know, the ones who want the mother of their kids to be a virgin, etc.) would probably faint dead away at the thought of their wife living in the jungles of Mexico or on the left bank of Paris. Which means only this—that the type of individual who believes in what I somewhat contemptuously refer to as conventional morality also leads the type of life which is apt to be somewhat conventional. Literarywise, such a situation is likely to be rather sterile. . . . You can have your career, or you can raise a family. I should be extremely surprised, however, if you can do both within the framework of the social structure in which you now live.

With Marcia and Ed as confiding friends, Sylvia was more stable emotionally during her second year at Smith than she had been during her first, though she experienced some depression. Cohen returned that fall to visit with Sylvia in Boston—sightseeing, going to hear jazz, and spending time at the Plath home. He brought a Chicago friend along with him, so he and Sylvia were seldom alone. The chemistry that was so powerful on paper lessened in person, but Ed talked seriously to Sylvia about what he saw as her destructive relationship with "Allen" (her name for Dick in her letters to Cohen). He predicted that if they did marry, there would be unhappiness, if not violence.

Dick's attentiveness from Cambridge, however, was consistent. His regular letters were full of medical school worries, and detailed replicas of drawings from his anatomy textbook. He planned weekends for them at Harvard (for some of which Sylvia fell ill) and they dated on vacations. She spent much of her Christmas break with Dick and his family, though she also saw what she called "a daze of men." Once the pressure of his studies lessened, Norton began taking advantage of the literary resources of Cambridge: he heard Wallace Stevens read, as well as Merrill Moore, a physician who wrote sonnets. Trying to understand—and impress—Sylvia, he brought out notes from a literature course at Yale. For her birthday, Dick gave her T. S. Eliot's *Four Quartets*. Toward the end of the year, his letters, many of which had been decidedly impersonal, grew more sensual and more openly displayed his affection.

From Sylvia's journal, it is clear that she and Dick had become as physically intimate as they could be. Much of her correspondence with Ed Cohen discussed this involvement; she was both bothered and intrigued by the sexual play. She was also concerned over their many disagreements. When Sylvia visited Harvard for the first time, in October, she was hit with a number of upsetting experiences. She went with Dick on his tour of duty at Boston's Lying-In Hospital and spent the entire night watching dissections of cadavers, inspecting fetuses in jars arranged chronologically to show development, listening to a lecture on sickle-cell anemia, making visits to seriously ill patients, and, as a climax, seeing a live birth, complete with the mother's episiotomy. With her usual poise, Sylvia acted as if she were fascinated by everything. Her comments to friends at Smith revealed the truth, that she found having to match Norton's enthusiasm tiring, particularly about these experiences.

Many of the things Dick planned for them to do he chose because he knew more about them than Sylvia did. Sylvia, however, was sensitive to anything she considered an attempt to overshadow her or her interests. Her unhappiness over the medical school weekend in October lasted into Thanksgiving, when they had another "truth talk" and decided to conduct their relationship, in Sylvia's words, "more realistically." Their holiday dialogue did not, however, persuade Sylvia that her dating other people was wrong. Dick evidently agreed; when he was too ill to take her to the house dance at Smith, he sent a friend from the Harvard Business School to escort her. He had less control over other men that she was seeing—dates from Williams, Yale, and Princeton.

At a formal ball in Connecticut to which about thirty Smith girls were invited, Sylvia met a suave, articulate Russian-American student from Princeton. They danced a great deal, then went driving until 5:00 A.M. Sylvia didn't have to play dumb with this man; she needed all the intelligent conversation she could summon. After the next day's brunch, she and Marcia were driven back to Smith in a Cadillac. Sylvia felt even more like a princess when the cosmopolitan Princetonian asked her to a weekend in November.

But she refused. She had been ill and was behind in work and tests. She did see him several times that year, however. He appealed to her as a man of the world—wealthy, well-educated, "golden" in many ways. She described him to her mother as "a potential." He is "the only boy I have met . . . (after Dick) that I could really become greatly interested in. As far as my future life is concerned, doesn't it bear a whirl?"

Both her letters home and her fiction make clear how much thinking Sylvia was doing about possible husbands. Her prize-winning story "Sunday at the Mintons' " (the name not far removed from Dick's family name of *Norton*) explored some of the problems in Sylvia and Dick's relationship. Elizabeth Minton, the retired librarian housekeeper, was Sylvia; her controlling, scientifically-minded brother was Dick. She said as much in a letter to Aurelia, "Henry started out by being him [Dick] and Elizabeth me (and they grew old and related in the process)." In all respects Sylvia was sorting through, working through, the emotional dilemma: how to keep from being eclipsed by the older, stronger male whose mind was so different from hers. (Although Sylvia worried that Dick would recognize himself in the story, he thought it was modeled after Virginia Woolf's *To the Lighthouse*.)

Plath's worksheets for the story show that the pivotal differences between Henry and Elizabeth were her primary concern. The worksheets give an interesting glimpse into her working method. She made lists of adjectives, nouns, and a few verbs to describe her main characters. For Henry she chose *perseverance, firmness, stability, solid, sturdy, staunch, indefatigable* and the more negative *plodding, obstinate, dogmatic, peremptory, inexorable, indomitable, relentless, calculating,* and *designing;* for Elizabeth, *vacillate, fluctuate, irresolute, tremulous, capricious* (twice), *frothy, volatile, frail, pliant, erratic, fitful, fanciful, whimsical, spontaneous, impromptu,* and the somewhat more critical *eccentric, freakish, wanton,* and *giddy.* But what occurred in the story was a moderation of those qualities, as the tale went "soaring" past her plan, in her words, with Henry's character becoming less sinister and Elizabeth's becoming both stronger—even defiant at times—and more likeable.

The difference between the two characters is treated succinctly in careful dialogue:

"Last spring . . ."

"The week of April sixth," Henry prompted.

"Yes, of course. You know, I never thought," she said, "of what direction I was going in on the map . . . up, down or across."

Henry looked at his sister with something like dismay.

"You never have!" he breathed incredulously. "You mean you never figure whether you're going north or south or east or west?"

"No," flashed Elizabeth, "I never do. I never saw the point."

She thought of his study, then, the walls hung with the great maps, carefully diagramed, meticulously annotated. . . . She imagined herself wandering, small and diminutive, up the finely drawn contour lines and down again, wading through the shallow blue ovals of lakes. . . .

Henry was looking at her still with something akin to shock. She noted that his eyes were very cold and very blue. . . . Elizabeth could see him now, standing brightly in the morning on the flat surface of a map, watching expectantly for the sun to come up from the east. (He would know exactly where east was.) . . . Feet planted firmly he stood with pencil and paper making calculations, checking to see that the world revolved on schedule.

It took Plath many years to see that her kind of intellect—the penetrating and seemingly unsystematic insight of the poet—was as valuable as the more scientific ability of Otto Plath and Dick Norton. Ages of stereotype about the fallacies of "woman's intuition" set against man's "logic" didn't help her. In a late essay, she complained that the American educational system during the Fifties did a poor job of recognizing and nurturing individual talent. There was no place in the American culture, she wrote, for the artist.

As sophomore year ended, once again Sylvia was spending her summer on Cape Cod, this time at a $40-a-month waitressing job at the Belmont Hotel on West Harwichport. Once again she was near Dick Norton. But since neither of them had a car, the distance as measured in bike miles was forbidding. This time she was without Marcia. When she began working at the Belmont on June 10, she was the only female waiting on table.

Because she was a novice, Sylvia was assigned to the Side Hall dining room, which served staff instead of guests. This disappointing assignment meant no tips. Sylvia wrote Aurelia that she was "exhausted, scared, incompetent, unenergetic and generally low in spirits." As was her usual pattern, in a few weeks she was running a fever, miserable with another sinus infection. On a moment's impulse, one afternoon in early July, she decided to go home to Wellesley to recuperate.

Once home, she called and quit the job at the Belmont, partly because the satisfaction of having won the $500 fiction prize from *Mademoiselle* for "Sunday at the Mintons' " lulled her into thinking she did not need to work. Within days, however, as she came into what was now customary conflict with her mother over what was "useful" work for a vacationing college student, Sylvia regretted her choice. She then found an ad for a mother's helper and teenage companion with the Cantor family in Chatham. Sylvia began working there on July 21 and stayed for six weeks. For the first time, she enjoyed being a part of another household. She admired the Cantors, liked their children, and was interested in their belief in Christian Science. They liked Sylvia enormously too, and on her last day Marv Cantor presented her with a wonderful mock check, made out "To the gal with the winning smile, 1,000,000 thanks for the 1,000 things so lovingly and cheerfully done" and signed "Your devoted 'Family.' "

As the summer ended, Sylvia chose to return to Wellesley instead of going with the Nortons to Brewster for a week. She needed time to prepare for what she knew would be a grueling year, and she was avoiding Dick. Her relationship with him continued to be a source of frustration; she had dated a number of men in Chatham, and she was thinking more seriously of herself as a writer, not just a girlfriend. The summer had brought two important events in Sylvia's professional life: *Mademoiselle* published "Sunday at the Mintons' " in August and, about the same time, Sylvia met Val Gendron, a professional fiction writer. She spent several evenings at Val's, talking shop and being encouraged to take herself seriously. These two events, so close together, were watershed experiences for Sylvia. As she wrote to Aurelia,

> I took the car alone for a blissful two hours at the beach with a bag of cherries and peaches and the Magazine. I felt the happiest I ever have in my life. I read both stories and already feel that I have outgrown mine, as I saw a great many errors, artistically. . . . I read it . . . chortled happily to myself, ran out on to the sand flats and dog-trotted for a mile far out alone in the sun through the warm tidal water . . . talking to myself about how wonderful it was to be alive and brown and full of vitality and potentialities, and knowing all sorts of wonderful people. I never have felt so utterly blissful and free.

The summer of 1952, Sylvia Plath became a writer.

6

Junior Year

1952-53

"The Doomsday of the World"

Sylvia returned to a troubling situation in her junior year. Smith had raised tuition by $150, and she had not won another Elks' Club scholarship. She therefore had no choice but to move to Lawrence, one of the scholarship houses, where students did work in exchange for part of the cost of room and board. She knew very few women at Lawrence. Marcia Brown had moved off campus to live with her mother, and Sylvia also missed her other Haven friends. A few days after classes started she wrote to Warren, with whom she was more honest than she was with her mother: "God, those first few days were awful. . . . I got scareder and scareder thinking of how I didn't know anybody hardly in the house and hadn't even seen my room . . . —it was like being a freshman all over again, only worse."

Sylvia turned for help to Mary, her science-major roommate, but they had almost nothing in common. She had a substantial workload in the house. Part of her duty at Lawrence was cleaning and food preparation, peeling large quantities of potatoes and turnips, chopping onions, etc. She also had waitress duty for lunch, and phone and reception duty. Sylvia grew friendly with Jane Truslow, who had younger brothers at Exeter, where Warren was. Jane, however, dropped out of school during fall term and Sylvia was lonely once again. She also disliked the "fluttering idiot" who was the new housemother at Lawrence.

There were other losses. Many women had not returned after sophomore year: quite a few had married, others were working. Of the remaining class members, more than eighty were spending junior year abroad. Sylvia was envious of them and continued to long for foreign travel. Perhaps more important was an atmosphere of trouble: several women had either attempted suicide or had mysteriously left campus. Sylvia's junior year was marked with episodes of friends' having abortions (seeing "Dr. No") or making hasty marriages (the married women were subsequently asked to move out of campus housing while they completed the term; in at least one case, all scholarship aid was revoked).

Fall courses were also disappointing. Sylvia could no longer delay taking the required science course—she had put it off from sophomore year—and she hated every minute of it. Worries about that class hounded her, and she finally concocted a scheme whereby she was allowed to audit the second semester of the course because she had gotten an A for the first term. (She went to class but surreptitiously wrote poems while she was there.)

Even her English classes worried her. She took a Milton course and got only a B in it. The medieval literature unit, taught by the austere and imposing Howard Patch, was a nightmare. Huge quantities of memorization and exceptionally demanding requirements made the class a full-time load. In addition to the quantity of work, Patch's teaching strategy was to humble his students; of the ten English majors in the seminar, only Sylvia received an A. By the beginning of her junior year, Sylvia had declared that she would "honor" in English, a program which required that she write a thesis and pass comprehensive examinations in both English and American literature. She had no idea what to write a thesis about, and the reading list for the examinations was long and difficult.

It was a fall of lonely hours at Lawrence House; difficult classes; and a busy schedule writing for Press Board, attending the Electoral Board's "smoky midnight meetings," and the *Smith*

Review; being secretary of Honors Board; and teaching the children's art class. In the midst of all this came a phone call from Dick, with the news that he had tuberculosis and would be spending at least a year in a sanatorium in Saranac, New York, and that Sylvia should have a chest X-ray as soon as possible. Plath felt guilty about Dick's illness in the face of her increasing withdrawal from him so, beginning in mid-October, much of her remaining energy went into a lengthy and cheering correspondence with the ailing Norton. Because Dick had never been ill, and had little sympathy for illness—as she had seen during her own bouts with sinus infections—he was emotionally adrift during this time. He often wrote to Sylvia several times a day. She had become his beloved, his anchor. Considering that he was not usually demonstrative in his writing, Dick's love letters were not only surprising, they were in some ways manipulative; now Sylvia had the commitment she had always pushed him for.

Another change in their relationship also occurred. Because Dick had so much leisure, he began to read seriously. He wrote critical essays about what he read, including one on the work of "Miss Plath" and another on William Carlos Williams (from whom he had received a letter in answer to his own admiring one). Some of Norton's reading complemented hers: they both liked Salinger's *Catcher in the Rye* and Lawrence's *Women in Love*. But Dick also enjoyed contradicting Sylvia, as when he wrote a scathing parody of one of her favorite authors, Virginia Woolf.

Norton had always accepted the world of science as his province. Now he was moving into Sylvia's domain of literature and writing. He was writing his own poems, too, and Sylvia was hard put to say anything good about them. She wrote enviously in her journal about Norton's "lying up there, rested, fed, taken care of, free to explore books and thoughts at any whim."

Her envy broke out in the midst of her November 3, 1952, journal entry, typical of what she was writing and feeling that fall:

God, if ever I have come close to wanting to commit suicide, it is now, with the groggy sleepless blood dragging through my veins. . . . I fell into bed again this morning, begging for sleep, withdrawing into the dark, warm, fetid escape from action, from responsibility. . . . I thought of the myriad of physical duties I had to perform. . . . The list mounted obstacle after fiendish obstacle; they jarred, they leered, they fell apart in chaos, and the revulsion, the desire to end the pointless round of objects, of things, of actions, rose higher. . . .

Depressive as this was, her real anger was directed not so much toward Smith and her work there as toward Dick at Saranac, "lifted to the pinnacle of irresponsibility to anything but care of his body."

Sylvia's self-doubts grew stronger than ever. All she saw was her own "naked fear," her own inadequacy:

I am afraid. I am not solid, but hollow. I feel behind my eyes a numb, paralyzed cavern, a pit of hell, a mimicking nothingness. I never thought. I never wrote, I never suffered. I want to kill myself, to escape from responsibility, to draw back abjectly into the womb. I do not know who I am, where I am going. . . .

Several letters home echo this entry. On November 19, she signed herself "Your hollow girl" and cried to Aurelia,

Oh, Mother, I hate to bother you with this, but I could cry. Life is so black, anyway, with my two best friends, Dick and Marcia, so far removed I hardly see them. And this course: I actually am worried over my mental state! . . . God, what a mess my life is. And I know I am driving myself to distraction. Everything is empty, meaningless. This is not education. It is hell.

There was more. Relentlessly critical of herself, Sylvia wrote about her failures. This time, however, writing about them did not help her.

Her mother's characteristic response was to cheer her up. Mrs. Plath believed that Sylvia was a girl with many talents. She could always do well at whatever she tried, but she was subject to these fears and anxieties. Mrs. Plath's correspondence gives no indication that she tried to understand the root of Sylvia's fears. Her letters remained cheerful, encouraging, and somewhat uncomprehending.

Sylvia finally spent a night off campus with Marcia, who knew how to listen to her. Enid Epstein, too, was a loyal friend, and she and Sylvia took long walks. They saw each other at meetings of the *Smith Review* and Press Board, and Enid remembers sitting with Sylvia in Seelye Hall as they both counted the A's on their grade slips. Both women knew they would be junior Phi Beta Kappas, but the honor seemed crucial to Sylvia. Her deep-rooted insecurity would not disappear; it was the product of years of frantic searching for ways to excel. By this time, Sylvia believed that love was a consequence of her achievements and without those achievements she would not be loved. Without "success," Sylvia thought she would be unloved.

During her difficult junior year, the changes and challenges at Smith were less important than Sylvia's enervating emotional turbulence. Talented women as different as Jane Addams, Margaret Sanger, Charlotte Perkins Gilman, and Edith Wharton had each known this crippling indecisiveness as they tried to choose what kind of life they wanted. Plath's depression was partly of that nature. She knew she wasn't ready to be a great writer, yet that was her dream. Neither could she imagine living a life as curtailed and dependent as that of a physician's wife, or that of her own mother. Sylvia's ambition warred with her responsiveness to her culture. As a woman in the 1950s, she should marry and become a mother. How could she—unloved and guilty as she saw herself—dare think of a life other than that?

Everywhere she looked, Sylvia was disappointed. She was upset by Eisenhower's election as President and wrote angrily to Aurelia about the loss for Stevenson ("the Abe Lincoln of our age") and about her mother's stupidity in voting for Eisenhower: "I hope you're happy with McCarthy and Appropriations, Jenner and Rules and Civil Rights, Taft and Foreign Policy, and our noble war hero and his absurd plan to fly to Korea like a white dove with a laurel leaf in his mouth. . . . I felt that it was the funeral day of all my hopes and ideas."

More customarily, however, whatever happened anywhere in the world Sylvia saw as being entirely *her* fault. In the bleakest days of fall term, she made a terse, admonitory list. One column was headed "Escape" and the other, "Wisdom." Under Escape came the items "Mary? [Mary was her roommate.] Science? Job? Girls in house? Patch? Responsibility?" and under Wisdom, three phrases, all sensible but hardly helpful in a crisis: "More time," "More rest," "Less physical danger." The item that might have been helpful to Sylvia would have been *reevaluation*—of both her life goals and of her daily schedule. Such reevaluation, however, would have taken the help of a trained therapist, able to talk with this talented girl who had for so long confused what she accomplished with who she was.

By the fall of 1952, Sylvia had been working hard almost nonstop since the summer of 1949, and her body showed the strain: breaks of three to five months in her menstrual cycle were common. Her seemingly inexplicable angers spoiled friendships, although the hallmark of her personality was cheery calm. Shortly before Christmas, Sylvia wrote her mother that she had gone to the infirmary after an appointment with the college psychiatrist because of her terrible insomnia. And friends from Lawrence House remember that when Sylvia phoned her mother—from the only pay phone in the house, located just outside the housemother's suite and therefore public—arguments between them were clearly audible.

The symptoms of Sylvia's growing anxiety during the fall of 1952 were evident. Ed Cohen, 1000 miles away in Chicago, responded immediately to a letter she wrote in December, urging her to get counseling regardless of cost. Cohen wrote that he was concerned over her state of mind, "the agitation, the dissatisfaction, the unrest, the annoyance, the lack of co-ordination, the nervous tensions that mark the time that a person approaches the ultimate breaking point. Syl, honey, I think you've moved much too close over these past few months." Ed knew her well by this time; he also knew that much of her concern for her family was concern for money. Despite this, his advice was "Shoot the cost!"

One must wonder why, if Ed Cohen could assess Sylvia's health so accurately, no one else saw what was happening to her. Marcia Brown would have seen the changes, but living off campus meant that she saw Sylvia rarely. Dick might have noticed but he was hundreds of miles away and totally absorbed in his own health problems. Each of her teachers knew Sylvia only during this term. Even her mother, to whom she was writing about suicide, seemed to disregard the literal meanings of her daughter's words. Perhaps Aurelia simply could not believe them; perhaps she did not know what to do about them. And it must also be recognized that Sylvia was usually an expert at assuming a confident manner.

The December holiday only added to her depression. Instead of catching up on studies (exams at Smith fell in late January), Sylvia was expected to spend the days before Christmas with Dick, who was home for the holiday, and then on December 26 she returned with him by train to Saranac for a week's stay. Arrangements had been made for her to stay with the Lynns, a young physician who had himself had TB as a medical student, and his vivacious family. Although she did not admit it, Sylvia was disturbed by the Saranac plan. It assumed that she and Dick were inseparable and that she had nothing to do but spend her vacation with him. It also located her in the midst of a traditional family with, as she saw it, Dr. Lynn representing Dick, cured and returned to a dominant role in society, and his wife the helpmeet Sylvia was expected to become.

By this time, Sylvia knew that she did not love Norton, but there are indications that they talked seriously about getting married soon after they arrived at Saranac. The next day— angry with herself for not being honest with him—she went downhill skiing, with Dick, who did not himself ski, as her teacher. Her re-creation of the scene in *The Bell Jar* seems accurate. After a fleeting sense of freedom, she crashed. Her leg was severely broken.

> Break break break on the cold white slopes oh knee. Arriving Framingham Tues. night 7:41. Bringing fabulous fractured fibula. No pain just tricky to manipulate while Charlestoning. Anything to prolong vacation.

Sylvia's telegram to Aurelia belied the real pain and torment of the injury: how would she get around the Smith campus in midwinter with no car and no bus service? For the next eight weeks, the busy girl dragged a heavy cast over an icy, snowy campus. For Sylvia, who always raced from job to job, class to class, her situation was impossible. The broken leg was the final blow to her already troubled psyche. As her January 8, 1953, letter to Aurelia shows, she was beside herself and losses of temper were not uncommon: "I'm sorry I made such a fuss by being a baby and crying but forgetting that carton broke the last straw of my nervous control: I felt so badly and scared by so many things that I could hardly manage to be gay and cheerful."

No one would expect a student with Sylvia's workload facing the sheer physical labor of getting to and from class to be "gay and cheerful." Again, the discrepancy between the behavior that was normal and the behavior Sylvia felt she had to maintain was obvious, and confusing.

Letters from Norton were no help, either. He seldom even mentioned her leg. His attention remained entirely upon his own health. Later in the winter, he wrote disapprovingly that his mother had told him that Sylvia was taking sleeping pills because her leg hurt at night. Not only was Dick doing nothing to help Sylvia's state of mind, he was also giving her a running account of his budding romance with one of the other patients.

As 1953 moved toward spring and Sylvia's cast finally came off (she wrote a friend that she was going to build a bonfire of the pieces of the cast), her spirit received other setbacks. The Lynns' charming son had been accidentally killed. Dick was not improving and would not go back to Harvard in the fall as he had planned. He was, in fact, scheduled for surgery in May. Meanwhile, Sylvia's relationship with the Norton family was disintegrating. Dick's mother thought that Sylvia was selfish because she refused to work as a waitress in Saranac during the summer. Mrs. Norton also complained that because Aurelia Plath always taught in summer school, Sylvia should also be working. Sylvia replied that she had made $1000 during the year from her writing. She did not need a low-paying, exhausting job, especially not in Saranac.

Her relationship with Dick could only have been weakened by her romances with other men during the school year. Over Thanksgiving break, she had met Myron (Mike) Lotz at the Nortons' home. She found him handsome, talented, intellectual, and athletic, and invited him to the Lawrence December dance.

93

Number one in his class at Yale (Perry Norton was second), Mike during the summer pitched for a Detroit Tigers farm team. From Warren, Ohio, the son of an Austrian steel worker, he was a scholarship student at Yale, but he also had money from playing ball and was about to buy a car so that he could drive to Smith. He had been accepted at Yale Medical School.

Aside from Lotz's height, build, and dark good looks, Sylvia admired Mike for his ambition: "power, strength. Mentally and physically he is a giant. . . . He wants very hard what I want very hard." Mike asked Sylvia to go to the Yale Junior Prom. From then on, they saw each other every few weekends. With him she had her first plane ride; they went to see the Northampton mental hospital; they shared long afternoons in the country, and became both physically and intellectually close. In her journal, Sylvia wrote that Mike was the only man she would consider marrying, though she then asked herself, "Do I want to crawl into the gigantic paternal embrace of a mental colossus? A little, maybe, I'm not sure." She did stress that "with him there would be a great, evolving intellectual dignity to life."

In late spring, however, the relationship with Lotz cooled suddenly. Over spring break, Sylvia had visited Dick at Saranac. She had also spent a weekend in New York with a casual boyfriend from the previous summer. While Sylvia was gone, Mike dated someone else. Angry over what she called his "betrayal," she was honest enough to admit her behavior was as bad. But the truth was that Sylvia reacted furiously and vindictively whenever a boyfriend showed signs of losing interest in her. She usually called that behavior betrayal, while at the same time she nearly always pretended to be so absorbed in other aspects of her life—or other men—that she hardly noticed the absence of the beau. The cultural emphasis on a woman's belonging with (and to) a man combined with Sylvia's personal insecurity to make her relationships with men the most important—and the least rational—part of her life.

Toward the end of the term, coming back from a poetry reading by W. H. Auden, Sylvia met Gordon Lameyer, an Amherst English major whose home was also in Wellesley. Ready to go to Officers' Candidate School for his Navy service, the tall blond Lameyer asked Sylvia out and they dated much of the summer of 1953. Whatever her situation with Norton and Lotz, Sylvia ended spring term angry, describing her dates as "unlovers," men who were not worthy of her affection. Although she felt that she had not found the right man yet, she knew what she wanted. It was, she wrote, "to live hard and good with a hard, good man."

Meanwhile, she continued to publish and to win honors on campus. (She had been chosen editor of *Smith Review* and had a prize assignment on Press Board.) She sold three poems to *Harper's* for $100; won two Smith poetry prizes for $120; won third prize in *Seventeen's* fiction contest with "Initiation"; sold a poem called "Mad Girl's Love Song" to *Mademoiselle*, and was doing well in that magazine's College Board contest (the completion of exercises in design, writing, and critiques of previous issues took most of the year).

Much of the fiction and poetry Sylvia wrote during this year was done on assignment for Robert Gorham Davis's creative writing class. One interesting piece was a long dialogue between the characters Alison (probably Sylvia) and Marcia (Marcia Brown). Written in January of 1953, the dialogue drew heavily on Sylvia's anguish during the fall. Alison, described as a "free spirit," criticizes Marcia for her "rotten layers of middleclass morality." Marcia, in turn, asks Alison if all the responsibility for making up her own rules, her own world, isn't frightening. Alison then describes her fall depression: "I wasn't anybody at all. And I began to get afraid that all at once maybe my eyes would break open like soap bubbles and everybody would see there wasn't anything there, just a vile mess. And I was afraid that maybe the rot inside me would break out in sores and warts, screaming: 'traitor, sinner, imposter.' "

Part of her unrest during her junior year resulted from the fact that she was trying to break away from the most basic of her family's ideals: working hard, behaving impeccably, always aiming for self-betterment, living thriftily. While she quietly tested the boundaries in some areas of her life, she flaunted her extravagance in other areas. Clothes continued to attract her (she sometimes stayed on at Smith after vacations began, shopping alone for bargains in the Green Street shops), and during the 1952–53 year, she spent $310 on her wardrobe, much more than she had spent the first two years together. Such spending was never guilt-free, however, as this passage from her journal shows:

> Today I bought a raincoat . . . with a frivolous pink lining that goes good to my eyes because I have never ever had anything pink-colored, and it was much too expensive—I bought it with a month's news office pay, and soon I will not have any money to do anything more with because I am buying clothes because I love them and they are exactly right, if I pay enough. And I feel dry and a bit sick whenever I say "I'll take it" and the smiling woman goes away with my money because she doesn't know I really don't have any money at all.

Part of Sylvia's clothes-buying at this time was in preparation for a major event: the big news during spring term was that she had been chosen for the *Mademoiselle* College Board. Working on the staff of the glossy fashion magazine, "the magazine for smart young women," she would live in New York from June 1 through 26, along with nineteen other outstanding women from campuses across the country.

Reaction at Smith to this honor was all Sylvia could have asked. Robert Gorham Davis and his wife Hope invited her to dinner; Smith's novelist Mary Ellen Chase invited her to a celebratory coffee. The news even overshadowed her interview with W. H. Auden, who spent several days on the Smith campus that spring. As a favored student of Elizabeth Drew's, Sylvia took her poems to the great poet and came back—all too quickly—with his word. She was to work hard on verbs. She also took the time to go to Amherst to hear Dylan Thomas, one of her favorite poets, read.

Arriving in New York on May 31, Plath made her way to the Barbizon Hotel at Lexington Avenue and 63rd Street, where all the guest editors were to stay. The plush lounge and library contrasted with the cell-like rooms, where green walls matched the green and pink coverlets and drapes. The young guest editors were impressed with even these modest surroundings, however, and with the Barbizon's indoor swimming pool. They felt like real New Yorkers in their hats, heels, and gloves. Eating breakfast at the hotel or a nearby drug store, they set off for the magazine offices in groups, arriving around 9:00. They spent much of their time at special events—luncheons, fashion shows, art galleries, performances, including a Balanchine ballet, visits to the United Nations and the *Herald-Tribune*, movie previews and television shows, and a formal dance on the St. Regis Starlight Roof.

Mademoiselle also tried to arrange individual activities according to personal interests. Sylvia asked to meet the writers she admired: J. D. Salinger, Shirley Jackson, E. B. White, Irwin Shaw. None of her choices was available but she was assigned an interview with Elizabeth Bowen and treasured the meeting and the thank-you letter Bowen wrote her afterward. Other of the guest editors met Imogene Coca, William Inge, Hubert de Givenchy, and Richard Rodgers.

In the words of one of the guest editors, Sylvia was regarded as "one of the leaders of the group, one of the smartest and funniest." She usually was outspoken and a little argumentative, a hard worker who was proud of her talents. In the words of another guest editor, Sylvia was "filled with a healthy love of mankind and great artistic vitality." She kept her smile even during the torrid afternoon in Central Park when all the guest editors were photographed in their human star formation, each wearing wool kilts and long-sleeved blouses.

A few days after they arrived, assignments were made, and Sylvia was thrilled to be chosen guest managing editor, the second-most-important position on the staff. She worked directly with Cyrilly Abels, *Mademoiselle*'s managing editor. Fiction editor might have been the ideal assignment for Sylvia, in that it would have meant less involvement with layout and business details, but Abels herself was interested in fiction and poetry (she later became a successful literary agent), and she wanted someone in her office who had strong literary abilities. A few days after the assignments had been made, Abels asked Sylvia to move her desk into Abels's office. Initially, Sylvia was excited; the days wore on, however, through the oppressive city heat, and Sylvia often worked till 6:00 and had a late supper in the cafeteria.

The work the twenty guest editors did was unequal. Some of

the women reported to editors who had very little planned for them; actually, by mid-June, the September issue of the magazine was nearly finished. Sylvia's role was busier, however. As Anne Shawber, another of the editors, said, Sylvia had "*the* toughest job on the magazine. Sylvia was an artist. She was sensitive . . . lacking confidence in the world outside the mind."

The job Sylvia was asked to do was difficult, but it was especially difficult for her. The atmosphere at *Mademoiselle* was sometimes critical and threatening. Barbed comments from staff members were common. In addition Cyrilly Abels was known at that time as a tough editor who insisted on nothing less than perfection, as she defined it. For her, Sylvia wrote and rewrote her feature on five rising young poets (Richard Wilbur, Anthony Hecht, George Steiner, Alastair Reid, and William Burford). She had begun writing the story, "Poets on Campus," during May, corresponding with the poets. She thought the feature was done before she arrived in New York, but for the next three days Abels taught her what *Mademoiselle* style meant. Sylvia was no novice; she had written hundreds of press releases and features as a Press Board correspondent, in addition to her published essays, fiction, and poetry. But Abels's criticism shook her confidence about her writing abilities. She signed herself "Syrilly" in her letters home, but she also wrote to Aurelia that she had trouble remembering who Sylvia was.

Working so closely with Abels also meant that Sylvia got to know very few of the other staffers. She was therefore completely dependent on Abels's opinion of her. Although Abels included Sylvia in lunches with young writers such as Vance Bourjailly and introduced her to people who came into the office (Paul Engel and Santha Rama Rau, for instance), she was also critical of Sylvia's proper, demure intellectualism. "Where is your own thinking, Sylvia?" Because Sylvia did not know at this time, and was bright enough to sense that she did not have the answers Cyrilly wanted, Abels's blunt interrogation devastated her. As she wrote candidly to Warren,

Somehow I can't talk about all that has happened this week at length, I am too weary, too dazed. . . . I can't think logically about who I am or where I am going. I have been very ecstatic, horribly depressed, shocked, elated, enlightened, and enervated—all of which goes to make up living very hard and newly. . . . It is unbelievable to think of all this at once—my mind will split open.

In addition, worries about money peppered her letters, and she said she was planning to find some men to date "so I can go out without paying for it myself." Her fellow guest editors frequently found Sylvia in tears.

Sylvia's letters home did not tell the whole story, however. She may have been tired at 6:00 P.M., but she loved talking and giggling and eating with the other guest editors till early morning. She was usually ready for long walks and scouting expeditions to bars—where they might find the self-styled Western disc jockey she wrote about in *The Bell Jar*—and one night's wait in the hallway of Dylan Thomas's hotel, hoping to catch sight of him as he returned to his room.

The four weeks in New York City were frantic, but one of the most memorable events was the luncheon at the huge advertising agency, BBD&O, at which Sylvia and many of the other guest editors contracted ptomaine poisoning. After a long night of relentless vomiting, she was shaken with fear, but also aware of the irony of having eaten beautiful gourmet food only to be poisoned by it.

Weak from several days of ptomaine agony, Sylvia experienced more pain on the day of Ethel and Julius Rosenberg's execution, June 19. Typical of her earlier behavior patterns, she focused on politics when her personal depression intensified. In the midst of her disappointment at the way her work with Abels was developing, she reacted strongly to the enormous public debate over the Rosenbergs' electrocution. Her old friend Phil McCurdy was marching in Washington, D.C., to protest their deaths, yet when she tried to talk to her friends at the Barbizon about what she saw as the horror of their executions, she got very little response.

The situation peaked on the morning of the execution, when Sylvia criticized the women eating breakfast for their lack of concern, their being able to eat "at a time like this." According to Janet Wagner, the peacemaker of the group, Sylvia left her coffee in disgust and stormed out to go to the office. Janet went along, at least partly because she did not want Sylvia to be alone. As they walked to the *Mademoiselle* offices at 575 Madison Avenue, Sylvia kept asking Janet what time it was. At 9:00 A.M., the time Sylvia thought the execution was set for, she turned to her friend and said, "Now it's happening." Then she turned the insides of her arms to Janet. Each arm was covered with red pinprick bumps and, as Janet watched, they elongated into each other and formed a series of welts running up and down Sylvia's arms.

It was a dramatic reaction, but Sylvia had long thought of herself as having psychic powers. She often found that she was in painful empathy with troubled friends, and she remembered episodes from her childhood when she seemed to know well in advance of events what was going to happen. On this particular day, Sylvia let herself be assured by Janet's telling her that the welts were only hives, and that she was having them because it was hot and she had not eaten breakfast. Neither of them ever spoke of the episode again to each other.

Fixed up soon afterward for a date with "a wealthy, unscrupulous Peruvian delegate to the U.N. at a Forest Hills tennis club dance," Sylvia found herself paired with a violent woman-hater, a man who tried to rape her amid a torrent of verbal abuse. Traumatized, she found the male escort from *Mademoiselle* who was there as a chaperone, and he drove her and Janet Wagner back to the Barbizon. Although the women laughed about their respective dates all the way back, Sylvia was also angry: not even blind dates were safe in this mad city.

By the last night of her editorship, Sylvia was as bewildered as she was angry. She threw many of her clothes—old and new —out the window. Although she had spent more money on clothes for New York than she had thought possible, she now rejected the world of women's fashion. It was as though she was announcing that the Sylvia Plath who was a guest editor for *Mademoiselle* would become someone different in the future.

Throwing away clothes was hardly characteristic behavior for Sylvia. It was certainly a cry for help. But the other guest editors were themselves so exhausted from the month in New York that few of them noticed what she had done. Even her friend Janet, to whom she turned to borrow an outfit to wear home, didn't stop to think why Sylvia was asking her for clothes. As Janet recalled, "I didn't pay her much attention, but I remember telling her she could have anything on the bed. . . . She went over to the bed and chose that green dirndl skirt and the white peasant blouse with the eyelet ruffles on the sleeves. She insisted on giving me her bathrobe with the little blue flowers on it." It *was* characteristic that Sylvia would never take a gift without paying for it.

She arrived home to bad news. Her mother told her that she had not been accepted into the Harvard summer school fiction course taught by Frank O'Connor. Added to Abels's criticisms of her and her writing, this rejection was shattering. Sylvia felt that she was a complete failure. All the prizes she had won scarcely a month before were forgotten as she continued her steady slide into depression. She would be living at home the rest of the summer, instead of moving to Cambridge; sharing her room with her mother; dependent on the family car and the family schedule for any time away from Elmwood Road.

Dating Gordon Lameyer the two weeks before he left for OCS helped. They spent long days together, driving to New Hampshire and to the Cape. More often they went to Gordon's mother's apartment and listened to his record collection—Beethoven, Brahms, Sibelius. Sylvia was fascinated as well by recordings of Dylan Thomas, Edith Sitwell, Robert Frost, e. e. cummings, and James Joyce reading from their own work, and she and Gordon read aloud to each other from *Finnegans Wake*, Gordon having begun his study of Joyce several years earlier.

After Gordon left on July 13, Sylvia's depression grew worse. She did little but sleep. She did not call friends or go to Cambridge to see Marcia; she seldom sunned. Even the mail delivery did not rouse her, although letters from Dick at Saranac came frequently. "How's the shorthand going?" he would ask. Dick and her mother had decided that, since she hadn't made the fiction class, she should study shorthand at home with Aurelia. Norton had learned it several years before and thought no girl should be without it. Dick's other theme in his summer letters was his excited discovery of James Joyce, the writer Sylvia had tentatively decided to work on for her Honors thesis. And she

101

heard from both Ed Cohen and Phil McCurdy, either of whom might have been able to understand her depression. Circumstances, however, made both unavailable to her. Cohen had married in June and was honeymooning in Mexico for two months with no forwarding address. McCurdy, too, was unreachable as he traveled the United States, hitch-hiking on his grand tour.

Concerned about Sylvia's lethargy, Aurelia arranged that she take a nurse's aide job at the Newton-Wellesley Hospital. She worked mornings, feeding patients who were too ill to feed themselves. But she did not stay long at the hospital; she was herself too ill. Her lethargy had changed to insomnia and she had found that—tired and distraught as she was—she could no longer read Joyce. The linguistic difficulty of *Finnegans Wake* was far beyond her comprehension at this time. Worse, she could no longer write; her handwriting was nearly unrecognizable. Desperate, Sylvia called Marcia to meet her for dinner in Boston. When she told her friend that she had not slept for many nights, Marcia responded calmly and soothingly, thinking that Sylvia was once again exaggerating.

As days passed, time became Sylvia's worst enemy. Each morning brought her closer to her senior year, the year in which she would write her thesis, for which she had no definite topic, and take the extensive comprehensive examinations, for which she felt completely unprepared. Each day also brought her closer to the planned late-summer vacation with Dick, who was coming to Wellesley at the end of August and then returning to Saranac, with Sylvia accompanying him. It would be a repetition of Christmas vacation.

Entries from Sylvia's July journal chart the self-inflicted pain she experienced. Guilt and shame once again blinded her: whatever was wrong with her was *her* fault. She called herself "an Over-grown, Over-protected, Scared, Spoiled Baby," unable to meet real life. In a harsh scolding tone, she addressed herself in second person: "You are so obsessed by your coming necessity to be independent, to face the great huge man-eating world, that you are paralyzed . . . shocked, thrown into a nausea, a stasis." Later she cajoled herself, "I must make choices clearly, honestly, without getting sick so I can't eat." There was no reason, she continued, that she could not be "cheerful and constructive." For a young woman to live the "good" life, the suitable life, especially in the wealthy suburb of Wellesley, she must have the right attitude and wear the proper face, even amid deep depression. Near the end of this July 14 entry, she raged, "Stop thinking selfishly of razors and self-wounds and going out and ending it all. Your room is not your prison. You are."

Mrs. Plath described the horror of the summer in *Letters Home*, recounting the morning in July when she saw gashes on Sylvia's legs. Sylvia admitted that she had tried to kill herself, " 'I just wanted to see if I had the guts!' " Then she took Aurelia's hand in her own burning hot ones and cried, " 'Oh, Mother, the world is too rotten! I want to die! Let's die together!' "

That morning Aurelia took Sylvia to the bright and sympathetic woman who was the Plath family doctor. She of course referred them to a psychiatrist, a young man who talked with Sylvia and then recommended shock treatments. There was no second opinion. Sylvia received out-patient shock treatments— bipolar, electroconvulsive shock, given with no preparation and no follow-up counseling—at the direction of a doctor she disliked intensely. No sooner were the treatments begun than August came and the supervising doctor went on vacation, referring Sylvia to a colleague of his.

Her experience with shock treatments horrified her. "By the roots of my hair some god got hold of me. / I sizzled in his blue volts" is a description in a late poem. Sylvia felt intense pain. She was frightened beyond the words left to her at this point in her depression. Her mother told her the treatment would make her well, but it was doing nothing of the kind, and her resentment at Aurelia's advice would be a source of later anger.

In reality Aurelia and the Schobers were equally horrified, bearing their anxiety over Sylvia (and their fear of financial ruin from the expense of the therapy) in almost complete secrecy. Characteristically for the time, no one outside the family knew that Sylvia was in therapy or having shock treatments. Nor did Sylvia let on. She dated Gordon on two weekends when he was home from OCS, and as late as August 18, she wrote to Mike Lotz at his summer baseball camp that she was having a "placid" summer. The word was chosen with her usual wry irony. On August 24, she received a letter from Gordon asking whether he could come over in a few days when he was home on liberty.

But that same day, several days after a shock treatment, Sylvia broke open a cabinet that held sleeping pills and took the nearly full bottle, along with a container of water, to the crawl space under the first-floor bedroom, the entrance to which was usually blocked by a pile of firewood. She was wearing Janet Wagner's green dirndl skirt and white peasant blouse. She left a note for her mother propped plainly on the dining room table: "Have gone for a long walk. Will be home tomorrow." Then she crawled inside the hideaway and took such a quantity of sleeping pills that she lost consciousness for more than two days.

Otto Plath in 1930, when he was Professor of Entomology at Boston University. Years later, Plath wrote in her poem "Daddy" about the image of her father as he appears in this photo.

Aurelia Schober Plath, teaching in 1930 at Brookline High School, Brookline, Massachusetts

The Plath family in 1933:
Aurelia, Sylvia, and Otto

3

4

The Schober home in Winthrop, Massachusetts, on the bay side of the Atlantic. Sylvia spent long happy days with her grandparents here until she was ten.

Sylvia playing in the ocean near her grandparents' home

The Plath home on Johnson Avenue, also in Winthrop. Otto's study was on the front porch of the home. Sylvia lived here until she was ten.

6

5

Sylvia in one of her usual photogenic poses

7

Sylvia and her younger
brother, Warren, with
Mowgli, their cat

8

Otto Plath's grave (to the right of Azalea Path) in the Winthrop Cemetery. Sylvia wrote
about her visit to her father's grave in "Electra on Azalea Path."

9

26 Elmwood Road, Wellesley, where Sylvia grew up

Sylvia in junior high school

The Norton boys *(left to right):* Perry, Charles, and Dick

13

Above right: Mrs. Freeman, whose children Ruth and David were Sylvia's playmates in Winthrop. The Freeman house was a second home to Sylvia.

14

Wilbury Crockett, Sylvia's beloved English teacher at Bradford High School

15

Sylvia wearing the regulation physical education uniform in high school

Sylvia sunbathing on the Cape 16

17

Sylvia's high school graduation photo, 1950. As editor of the school paper and an outstanding student, Sylvia still worked diligently to maintain an image of popularity. Throughout her life she was influenced by the 1950s standards of what girls should be.

18

Olive Higgins Prouty, the well-known author who became Sylvia's friend and benefactor while she was at Smith. Sylvia corresponded with Mrs. Prouty throughout her life, and looked upon her as a second mother, one who shared a life of writing.

Ed Cohen, the Chicago college student who corresponded with Sylvia during her college years

19

At Smith College: members of the Press Board. Sylvia is second from left, back row.

21

22

Marcia Brown, Sylvia's sophomore-year roommate and close friend

Above right: Adlai Stevenson gave the graduation speech at Smith when Sylvia graduated in 1955 and was her "Lincoln."

23

Mademoiselle, summer, 1953: Sylvia as poet

24

Sylvia interviewing Elizabeth Bowen during the *Mademoiselle* summer

25

The twenty-member College Board at *Mademoiselle* in their Central Park formation

Sylvia at Yale on a weekend *(front row, third from left, in hat)*

Sylvia with Bob Riedeman at the University of New Hampshire, 1950

Sylvia with Dick Norton, Yale Junior Prom, 1951

Sylvia with Perry Norton, Yale, 1953

Sylvia with Myron (Mike) Lotz, Yale, 1953

Sylvia babysitting on Cape Cod, 1951

31

Sylvia shared first place in the Mount Holyoke poetry contest. Sylvia, *far left;* Marianne Moore, one of the contest judges, *third from left*

32

33

Ruth Beuscher, Sylvia's psychiatrist and friend. She corresponded with Sylvia throughout much of Sylvia's life.

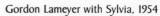
Gordon Lameyer with Sylvia, 1954

34

Sylvia's graduation photo, Smith, 1955

35

Newnham College, Cambridge, England, where Sylvia took a second B.A. as a Fulbright student

Right: Dorothea Krook, Sylvia's favorite professor at Cambridge. Like Ruth Beuscher, Dorothea Krook became a role model for Sylvia.

Whitstead dormitory in Cambridge, where Sylvia lived

Sylvia and Ted Hughes after their marriage, living in Boston and writing

9 Willow Street, on Beacon Hill in Boston, "home" for Ted and Sylvia in 1958–59

Robert Lowell, in whose writing workshop Sylvia wrote during the spring of 1959. Sylvia was not as enthusiastic about Lowell's methods of teaching as many of the other workshop students were.

42

Anne Sexton, Sylvia's good friend from the Lowell workshop. Sexton's reminiscences of Sylvia are among the most
touching in print.

W. S. Merwin, with whom Ted and Sylvia became friendly
during their London years. It was in the borrowed Merwin
study that Sylvia and Ted wrote for part of every day during
1960.

"Three Generations of Faber Poets," June 1960 *(left to right):* Louis MacNeice, Ted Hughes, T. S. Eliot, W. H. Auden, and Stephen Spender

Sylvia and Ted with Frieda, 1961

46

4

Court Green, Sylvia and Ted's Devon country home in 1961
and 1962: back view, *above;* lane view, *right.*

Bottom right: Clarissa Roche, a friend during the Smith
teaching year, 1957–58, and after, with whom Sylvia corresponded frequently

Elizabeth Compton, Sylvia's Devon friend

48

4

Ruth Fainlight, poet and wife of Alan Sillitoe. Sylvia was planning to spend time at Court Green with Ruth in the spring of 1963.

Sylvia with Nicholas, July 1962, in Devon

Sylvia with Frieda and Nicholas, July 1962, in Devon

REGISTRATION DISTRICT St. Pancras

1965. DEATH in the Sub-district of South West St. Pancras in the Metropolitan Borough of St. Pancras.

Columns:— 1	2	3	4	5	6	7	8	9
No.	When and Where died	Name and surname	Sex	Age	Occupation	Cause of death	Signature, description and residence of Informant	When registered	Signature of registrar
12	Eleventh February 1963 Dead on arrival University College Hospital St Pancras	Sylvia Plath HUGHES	Female	30 years	23 Fitzroy Road St Pancras an authoress wife of Edward James Hughes an author	carbon monoxide poisoning (domestic gas) while suffering from depression did kill herself	Certificate received from the W M Tavern Deputy Coroner for London Inquest held 15th February 1963	Sixteenth February 1963	Alice L Hemmen... Registrar

CERTIFIED to be a true copy of an entry in the certified copy of a Register of Deaths in the District above mentioned.
Given at the GENERAL REGISTER OFFICE, LONDON, under the Seal of the said Office, the 18th day of June 1985

(330044

A504M D4 8349843 50m 2/85 Mcr(306278)

53

Sylvia Plath's death certificate

Yeats' house (123 Fitzroy Road in London's Primrose Hill area), the flat where Sylvia and the children lived from December 1962 to the time of her suicide, February 11, 1963

54

Sylvia's gravestone in Yorkshire, located in the Heptonstall churchyard near Hepden Bridge, where the Hughes family lives. The inscription reads, "In memory/Sylvia Plath Hughes/1932–1963/Even amidst fierce flames/The golden lotus can be planted."

5

7

Smith, a Culmination

1954-55

"I Shall Be Good as New"

On August 24, 1953, Aurelia reported Sylvia missing. Then followed what she called "the nightmare of nightmares": police investigations; reporters; a volunteer group of nearly a hundred Scouts and Wellesley citizens, complete with bloodhounds, searching Lake Waban and Morse's Pond; national news coverage. The story of Sylvia's disappearance was carried in most papers, complete with a photograph and the caption, "Beautiful Smith Girl Missing at Wellesley."

Two days into the nightmare, Warren heard a moan coming from below the house. He dashed from the lunch table and soon was shouting "Call the ambulance!" On Wednesday, August 26, at 12:40 P.M. the "beautiful Smith girl"—semiconscious, bruises and cuts under her injured right eye badly festering—was taken by ambulance to the Newton-Wellesley Hospital at Framingham, where the nurse on duty described her as "more dead than alive."

Disfigured, temporarily sightless in one eye, and still thoroughly depressed, Sylvia had been saved. Although her mother had blamed the debacle on her daughter's "writing block," Sylvia's writing block was itself more a symptom of her problem than a cause.

When her mother reached the hospital and was allowed to see Sylvia, her daughter's first words were a moaned "Oh, no!" And when Aurelia assured her that she was much loved, that the family rejoiced in her having been found, Sylvia replied faintly, "It was my last act of love." She went on to say, sadly, "If I could only be a freshman again. I so wanted to be a Smith woman."

Bewildered by these responses, Aurelia tried to do what was best for Sylvia. She tried to find good psychiatric care, asking her minister to bring a psychiatrist he recommended as a consultant. She quickly wrote to Olive Higgins Prouty, Sylvia's benefactor at Smith, who was then vacationing in Maine. Although Mrs. Plath had told reporters that Sylvia's suicide attempt resulted from her inability to write, she told Mrs. Prouty that it probably was caused by Sylvia's realizing, belatedly, how much she cared for Perry Norton, Dick's younger brother, who had recently become engaged. Aurelia also gave another explanation: that Sylvia's suicide attempt had occurred because her daughter knew that she was very sick and did not want to be a financial burden. Aurelia had saved a $600 emergency fund, but she was worried about costs of Sylvia's treatment.

Mrs. Prouty replied promptly. She had wired Aurelia when she first saw the news stories about Sylvia. In the coming months, she would assume both the cost and the control of Sylvia's treatment; and in the years to come, she would remain a constant source of both funds and encouragement.

Aurelia's first plan was to have Sylvia live for awhile in Provincetown on Cape Cod with a friend who was a trained nurse. Mrs. Prouty, who had herself successfully recovered from a breakdown twenty-five years earlier, cautioned that Sylvia would eventually need "the constructive help and advice of some wise doctor" in order to recover. Mrs. Prouty understood the complexity of the situation better than most of Sylvia's friends. A few days after she had been found, for example, Sylvia heard from both Gordon Lameyer and Dick Norton, each of whom planned to come visit her on the weekend. They assumed that she was at home and that convalescence would be simple.

Expectations were that Sylvia would fully recover quickly. Psychiatrists found "no trace of psychosis" and no schizophrenia; several of her doctors predicted that she would recover "completely." But her attitude was discouraging. It became clear that Sylvia did not want to recover and go home. In fact, she was soon taken from Framingham Hospital to the locked psychiatric wing of Massachusetts General Hospital in Boston, where insulin shock treatments were begun.

In mid-October, Sylvia was moved to McLean Hospital in Belmont, traveling in Mrs. Prouty's car. The quality private institution boasted an excellent physician-patient ratio, beautiful grounds, and conscientious care. Most important for Sylvia, her treatment was taken over by Ruth Beuscher, an attractive young psychiatrist who Plath thought resembled Myrna Loy. Beuscher became both counselor and role model for Sylvia.

On arriving at McLean, Sylvia could neither read nor write. The one person she asked to see, Wilbury Crockett, her high school English teacher, then began visiting her at least once a week, bringing with him an anagram game. At first, Sylvia could hardly recognize any letters. He would begin with *a* and *n*; some days Sylvia could add a *d* to make the word *and*. Some days she could not. Crockett's patient work, even to helping Sylvia move her hand to pick out letters, was a crucial part of the therapy that led to her recovery.

The key to Sylvia's recovery lay at least partly in being accepted for herself, and by herself. As Evelyn Page, one of her favorite Smith teachers, wrote to her after her breakdown, "I want you to know that I am proud of you with the kind of pride that makes no demands upon you." Page assured Sylvia that everyone who writes hits "rock bottom" at times, and that she would share her own history with Sylvia when Sylvia returned to Smith.

Dr. Beuscher continued the insulin therapy at McLean, and that treatment led to a significant weight gain. Sylvia was miserable about her appearance. As she wrote in a later story, "Tongues of Stone," "she was caught in the nightmare of the body, without a mind, without anything, only the soulless flesh that got fatter with the insulin and yellower with the fading tan." She was sensitive about the unsightly scab under her eye, which later became a dark scar. She stopped using makeup. She did not bathe or wash her hair.

Ruth Beuscher had her work cut out for her. She had to overcome Sylvia's hatred of psychiatrists and her fear of electroconvulsive shock treatment. So frightened had Sylvia been by the earlier treatment during the summer that even the suggestion of it terrified her; she withdrew quickly into her most hostile posture. Beuscher was working to gain Sylvia's trust, so that eventually the girl would allow electroshock, but she would not order it—or any other treatment—without Sylvia's agreement. To that end, she set up an honor system: she and Sylvia would always communicate honestly.

As one step toward granting Sylvia her wishes about her own care, Beuscher restricted visitors. For several weeks during the autumn, Sylvia saw only Crockett and Prouty. By the end of that time, Sylvia had improved: she was typing manuscripts for Prouty, doing "exquisite" weaving, and asking for books on contract bridge—or so Prouty wrote to Aurelia Plath. To her own psychiatrist, however, Prouty wrote that Sylvia was still "feeling terribly inadequate, and inefficient, and inferior." She was planning to remove Sylvia from McLean and place her in a hospital further away from Wellesley.

Beuscher's rapport with Sylvia finally allowed her to begin the electroconvulsive shock treatments which, combined with the insulin shock, led to Sylvia's recovery. During late November and December, Sylvia took one hurdle after another: she drank coffee with friends (a Vassar songwriter, a fellow Smith student), took ceramics classes, tobogganed, played badminton and bridge, typed and designed the hospital newspaper, saw movies, and celebrated Christmas at McLean with caroling, mass, and a holiday dance. She wrote to Enid Epstein and Marcia Brown, who were both recently engaged, that she was happy for them and that she was looking forward to being a bridesmaid in Marcia's June wedding. She told them she was excited about coming back to Smith, although she would take things "more slowly but surely." By late December, Sylvia had been given ground privileges at McLean, and by the first of February, she was back at Smith for spring term, taking three classes and doing her usual *A* work.

Beuscher and her treatment had worked a miracle. Following her suicide attempt, Sylvia had been completely hopeless. As she described her feelings, "There was no more sanctuary in the world. . . . Her grandparents would soon die, and her mother would die, and there would finally be left no familiar name to invoke against the dark." Always dependent on people taking care of her—family, friends, teachers—Sylvia raged whenever those caretakers turned away from her. She was not yet ready to take care of herself. As she wrote to Ed Cohen toward the end of the year, although she was stronger she remained incredibly lonely: "I need more than anything right now what is, of course, most impossible, someone to love me, to be with me at night when I wake up in shuddering horror and fear of the cement tunnels leading down to the shock room, to comfort me with an assurance that no psychiatrist can quite manage to convey. . . ."

Part of Sylvia's therapy was to learn to trust herself. Beuscher tried to teach Sylvia to see that her relationship with her parents —her dead father as well as her mother—was crucial. She had to understand that she did not need to "do" anything to be worthy of love: love was a natural part of a loving family. And if Sylvia had difficulty relating to her family, then Beuscher was willing to stand in for family during the transition away from the angry dependence that now dominated her relationship with her mother.

Mentally and emotionally, Sylvia recovered in 1953 by leaving the hospital for home and then leaving home. She left 26 Elmwood Road to return to Lawrence House and Smith, and she tried to stay away from Wellesley after that whenever possible. Visits home were replaced by letters.

And the perfectionism that Sylvia had grown accustomed to was also subdued. Beuscher's therapy tried to show her that her desperate and nearly insatiable demands for recognition through success were bound to meet with failure. Her unrealistic expectations about what she could accomplish led to her tendency to collapse when she felt unsupported, and to her quick anger when she felt that someone she had counted on had let her down. Sylvia still could not rest so long as she was trying to create "the self that should be," the ideal Sylvia; but she had at least learned to watch for that obsessive pattern.

While Beuscher was trying to teach Sylvia to rely on herself, and to expect only reasonable successes, Sylvia had decided on her own program for recovery. She felt that it was time for her sexual emancipation. Hungry for experience and, always, hungry for caring and affection, she took lovers. Spring semester of 1954, when she returned to Smith, and her senior year there were marked by weekends away from campus that her family could never have approved. Sylvia came to see herself as a 1950s version of Brett Ashley—free-thinking, free-loving—but she actually was far from free of her earlier guilt and anger over sex and the double-standard social codes of the time.

During 1954, Aurelia heard from Otto's sister that the women in the Plath family had histories of depression. Otto's mother had been hospitalized at least once; his other sister and a niece also struggled with the problem. But Mrs. Plath never told Sylvia this—nor, so far as is known, did she ever tell her daughter's psychiatrist. Her tactic with Sylvia was not to discuss her breakdown or anything relating to it.

She found Sylvia very moody, alternately affectionate and remote. There was a noticeable tone of command in Sylvia's 1954 letters home: her daughter insisted that Aurelia cook a steak dinner for a roommate's birthday, that Sylvia be allowed to have the car for a trip to the Cape, that she be allowed to invite a boyfriend for a weekend. From Smith, Sylvia asked repeatedly for cookies. Needing assurance that she was central in her mother's life, Sylvia might have been forced into more realistic behavior if Aurelia had ever refused her. But the pattern had been set years before: her mother would never refuse to supply Sylvia's physical needs, especially when she had been ill.

Sylvia returned to Smith in February of 1954 as a witty, sophisticated advisor to younger women—women new to Lawrence House, women who admired her writing skills and were, perhaps, intrigued with the notoriety of her attempted suicide. The truth of Plath's return was that her earlier friendships were bound to change. As one woman who had been a close friend during Sylvia's sophomore year remembered, it was as if Sylvia were a different person. Instead of the eager, vivacious, talkative Sylvia, she was now a person with an enveloping past: *attempted suicide. Who did any of us know who had ever done that? Missing a semester was bad enough, but missing a semester because of a suicide attempt!* Enid Epstein remembered that, for all their earlier closeness, she could never bring herself to ask Sylvia how she had gotten the scar on her cheek.

Nancy Hunter, a transfer student who had been given Sylvia's room in Lawrence House, recalled the aura of mystery and envy that Plath's absence evoked during fall term. She also wrote about her surprise when Sylvia returned, to find her so beautiful:

> Her photographs are misleading; Sylvia was a remarkably attractive young woman. She was impressively tall, almost statuesque, and she carried the height with an air of easy assurance. Her yellow hair, which had been lightened several shades from its natural light brown, was shoulder length and had been carefully trained to dip with a precise and provocative flourish over her left eyebrow. Her eyes were very dark, deeply set under heavy lids that give them a brooding quality in many of her photographs. Her cheekbones were high and pronounced, their prominence exaggerated by the faint, irregular brown scar that was the only physical reminder of the suicide attempt. The face was angular and its features strong, a fact that may explain the dark shadows that seem to haunt it in photographs.

Beautiful, fun-loving, and crazily humorous, Sylvia was an appealing new friend to Nan Hunter, Sue Weller, and Ellie Friedman. Most Smith women who knew her remembered Sylvia as a great talker, a genuine story teller. Ellie Friedman recalled long afternoons talking in her room about writing, acting, and the usual Smith topics—grades, clothes, careers, sex, and gossip. Sylvia was able to entertain with hilarious stories about teachers and dates or serious discussions about depression, her attempted suicide, and recovery—which she called "rebirth."

Sylvia spoke to her new friends about the sheer pain connected with her illness. She said that "everything hurt," that she was "on fire under her skin." She vowed that if she ever were insane again, she would kill herself because "the pain is just too great. I cannot live through it again." She spoke, too, about the supposed connection between writing and madness, and made clear that so far as she was concerned, there *was* no such connection. Her writing, she said, came from her sanest self. As she repeated, "When you are insane, you are busy being insane—all the time. . . . When I was crazy, that was *all* I was."

What Sylvia feared most was the loss of self. When mad, she explained, no person possesses a self. With her customary thoroughness, Sylvia read widely in the psychology and sociology of identity. Whatever was known about the problem in the 1950s, Sylvia researched. One of the results she seldom talked about, however, probably because it was frightening, was the effect shock treatments had had on her long-term memory. When she did talk about it, she said it was like being in a dream; she never knew whether she was awake or asleep and dreaming. It was as if she had lost events, people, years from her life.

Although Sylvia was the witty and irreverent star of some campus conversations, she was not popular on campus. One friend described her as a dramatic loner. Off on picnics with a date, she would not be huddled in conversation. Rather she would be posing—blanket or towel wrapped around her—at the center of some admiring group. People were more likely to be in awe of Sylvia Plath than close to her.

Sylvia's campus identity during 1954 was that of the academic star, the writer who won all contests, the girl who had worked too hard and suffered a breakdown from fatigue. George Gibian, the young, dynamic professor of Russian and English who taught the course in Tolstoi and Dostoevsky which Sylvia took that spring and who eventually directed her honors thesis, wrote that she was, simply, the "exceptionally gifted student" that the English Department was so proud of. Gibian recounted Robert Gorham Davis's having told him that Sylvia was the only talented writer in his course who was not in some way neurotic. She instead impressed her teachers as being "completely wholesome, healthy, and creative. . . . Her manner gave the impression that she was just back from skiing in Vermont or from the beach in Bermuda."

Gibian knew her name even before she took his class, because he had been one of the judges for the Smith poetry prizes. Smith students annually competed for prizes under pseudonyms. Sylvia had submitted two groups of poems, using two different names—and she was awarded both prizes. When the names were decoded and the committee found that Sylvia had won twice, there was talk of giving one prize to another student. Gibian held out for Sylvia's receiving both, which was what finally happened.

His description of Sylvia was typical of comments made by most of her teachers: "I came to know her handwriting—very clear, rounded, legible. Her exam was excellent (to the point, brief, right on target)—and then later I got to know her in person. Her work was absolutely brilliant. She just seemed to UNDERSTAND things, to get the idea, and to be able to push it further." Although he did not know her well personally (she babysat for his young children on occasion), she wrote an essay about Dostoevsky for him and explained some of her personal circumstances in that paper: "I did not believe that psychic regeneration was possible. Then, unbelievably, a slow regenerating joy began to grow out of my gradual determination to live creatively." She compared herself to Andreyev's Lazarus, and to Kilroy in Tennessee Williams' play *Camino Real*, as a character who found nothing in life.

Besides Gibian's Russian literature course, Sylvia was studying nineteenth-century American literature with Newton Arvin, a teacher and scholar she much admired, and intellectual history with Mrs. Koffka. She received A's in all three classes and wrote to Aurelia that she had, indeed, recovered.

Although she would not graduate with her class, Sylvia kept busy spring term. She was chosen president of the arts honorary, and she was elected to Phi Beta Kappa. She invited Evelyn Page, Elizabeth Drew, and Hope and Robert Gorham Davis to the Phi Beta Kappa dinner. Later she wrote caustically about the pink rose she was given as part of the induction ceremony, "symbol of god knows what: virgin intelligence with a faint blush of knowledge, mayhap!" She met weekly with Dr. Booth, Smith's psychiatrist, and once in a while with her therapist and friend Ruth Beuscher.

Determined to continue at Smith as though her breakdown was only an aberration, Sylvia filled her days with activity—or so she wrote to her mother. Because Aurelia thought that Sylvia's depressions occurred when she "did too much," Sylvia cruelly emphasized how busy she was in all her letters home. It seems evident that Dr. Beuscher wanted Sylvia to break her close ties with her family, as a way of finding self-confidence and strength. Sylvia accordingly wrote home less often than she had before her breakdown, and she used her breaks to travel instead of returning to Wellesley. During this spring break, she spent a week in New York, visiting her Lookout Farm artist friend, Ilo, and having lunch and dinner with Cyrilly Abels. In April, she wrote her first poem in nearly a year. The creative center of Sylvia's life had taken the longest to recover, and she was ecstatic about "Doom of Exiles"—both because it was an effective poem, soon published in *Harper's*, and because she knew she had recovered.

She continued to have a busy social life. She wrote regularly to Gordon Lameyer, who was on a five-month naval cruise and would not return to Boston until summer. She also wrote to Ed Cohen and Phil McCurdy. She saw Mike Lotz several times, once making an obvious play for a proposal from him. The spring of 1954 saw the beginning of the romance of Sylvia's last year at Smith: on April 19, she met Richard Sassoon. A Yale rebel, who defied authority by cutting classes and making sly remarks about faculty, Sassoon was a history major who devoured Hegel, Kierkegaard, Nietzsche, Rimbaud, Baudelaire, and Sartre and other contemporary writers, as well as nihilistic philosophy. Continental in dress and manners, Sassoon was related to the English poet Siegfried Sassoon. He and his roommate, Mel Woody, whom Sylvia dated simultaneously for a time, regarded themselves as existentialists.

Sylvia was fascinated by the intellectualism of the Yale campus, with Henri Peyre and Ernst Cassirer teaching there. She also enjoyed the expensive weekends with Sassoon in New York. One entry from her scrapbook, dated May 8–9, 1954, read: "Weekend in NYC—ecstatic rapport with intuitive and solicitous Sassoon—play in village—nuit d'amour, wine, poetry— gray dawn—enormous two-hour feast at Steuben's." Each weekend away was filled with theater, films, food both exotic and plentiful (another scrapbook list read, "Oysters, snails, herring and sour cream, onion soup, steak, lamb chops, avocados, strawberries all washed down with good French wine"). And love. Sylvia was dedicating herself to the experience of sexual love. Sassoon took the place once held by Sylvia's best friends—Marcia Brown, Nancy Hunter, Perry Norton, and Ed Cohen. He was another searching, rebellious spirit. Part of his charm for Sylvia was that he cut classes and scoffed at his teachers with a wit that she envied. But while Sassoon pretended to be disdainful of Yale and its traditions, he belonged to the very elite Renaissance Club, and many of the letters he wrote to Sylvia were actually part of his assignment for a creative writing class that she did not know he was taking. He also did not tell her that he planned to publish their correspondence, at least his side of it.

Sylvia the rebel and outsider, as she now saw herself, responded totally to Sassoon. But it is revealing that she described their weekends away, which continued for several years, as "living as man and wife." Sex may have been easier for her to accept, but she continued to think of such intimacy as the prelude to marriage.

Marriage was much on her mind that year. Besides housemates, friends from Wellesley and from Smith were married during the summer of 1954, most notably Marcia Brown. Sylvia was a bridesmaid for Marcia's wedding and, again the next summer, for the wedding of her childhood friend, Ruth Freeman. That year she also received wedding invitations from several of her fellow guest editors at *Mademoiselle*, Janet Wagner among them. All Sylvia's friends were marrying.

She tried to repress her worries. During the summer of 1954, Sylvia bleached her hair a brazen blonde and roomed with Nancy Hunter and two other Smith women in a sublet apartment just one block away from Harvard Square. She was on scholarship to Harvard for that "platinum summer," as she called it, taking an intensive German course. The rest of the time she sunned, played tennis, met men, and learned to be a gourmet cook. She served her excellent meals, with dramatic flair, to Gordon Lameyer, finally home from his tour of duty; to a Harvard economics instructor; to a physics professor from M.I.T.; and to men from other campuses in town for the summer. Nancy Hunter remarked that Sylvia's flamboyant menus made heavy demands on the women's joint grocery fund.

Sassoon was abroad for the summer, so Sylvia became involved in a sexual relationship with the physics professor. She simultaneously maintained her serious affair with Gordon Lameyer, discussing long-range plans—even marriage—on occasion. The relationship with the physics professor had an unexpected repercussion when Sylvia suffered a vaginal tear and lost a substantial amount of blood before the tear was stitched in a hospital emergency room. Sylvia's story, when she retold it to Gordon and others, was that she had been attacked and that the bleeding was *not* the result of her being deflowered but of the professor's manually raping her without provocation.

As Lameyer remembers it, Sylvia was deeply concerned about sexuality—she feared pregnancy, she feared losing her reputation, but she also feared seeming inexperienced. As their letters indicate, Sylvia and Lameyer were now quite in love. Knowing what Sylvia had been through the previous year, and knowing also that she was still meeting Dr. Beuscher for therapy, Gordon did not want to force his attentions on her before she was ready.

One weekend in late August, however, about two weeks after the incident with the physics professor, Sylvia abruptly indicated that she wanted to change their relationship, pretending, however, that she was still a virgin. As a result of this one evening, she became convinced several weeks later that she was pregnant, although her menstrual periods had never been normal. In early September, although she had not confirmed this suspicion with a doctor, Sylvia called Gordon with the news that she was probably going to have a child. What grieved her most, she said then, was how much she felt she had let down those who believed in her and who had helped her return to Smith for her senior year.

Lameyer was very deeply in love with Sylvia. He wrote her a letter, reassuring her of his intentions to marry her. Soon, however, her period began and Sylvia found that her driving ambition was not to marry, but to continue her stellar record at Smith. So that she need not work during her senior year, Smith had awarded her "the biggest scholarship yet," for $1250. (The previous term, since Sylvia was not eligible for aid, Aurelia had cashed in an insurance policy to pay her expenses.) She concentrated on finishing her honors thesis on Dostoevsky's use of the double in his fiction; she won high praise from Alfred Kazin for her creative writing; and then she took an independent study course in poetry with Alfred Young Fisher, for whom she wrote at least fifty-five new poems. She submitted nearly everything she wrote for publication.

Much of her time during the fall of this belated senior year went to applying for fellowships and for admission to graduate schools at Radcliffe and Columbia. She had recommendation letters from Alfred Kazin, Mary Ellen Chase, Newton Arvin, and Elizabeth Drew. Interviews for the prestigious fellowships were crucial. Rather than offend or alarm a committee of conservative professors, Sylvia decided to let her hair return to its natural brown color.

Through this senior year, Sylvia continued the discreet weekends in New York with Sassoon, seeing plays and good films, eating at good restaurants. She could also count on Gordon's coming to Smith every weekend she would allow him to do so, because his ship was being overhauled in a Boston drydock and he was living at home in Wellesley. She often put him off with the excuse that she was working on her thesis, but she needed to know that she was still his best girl. Sylvia seldom ended relationships; she drew on everyone around her for support and admiration. As Nancy Hunter, Ellie Friedman, and Sue Weller could attest, Sylvia was demanding in her friendships, asking that her friends be understanding, supportive, and trustworthy. As Nancy Hunter realized after a year of being close friends with Sylvia, "I could not promise to keep her going like some intricate, erratic timepiece, and I could not face the guilt that would result if I failed to try. So I drew back instinctively. . . ."

Sylvia's relationship with Sassoon also had a dark side. A sadistic tone ran through his letters, a recurring emphasis on the notion that pleasure is enhanced by pain. His ideal, he wrote, was to "play daddy" to a naughty girl and Sylvia was, he said, the only woman he ever wished "to please and to punish." Sylvia did not share any reservations about Sassoon with her friends, although she did humorously describe his comparatively small physique, as when she told Nancy and Ellie that when he embraced her, she felt like Mother Earth with a small bug crawling on her. Sylvia's wit was consistent, though she used it carefully. She did not go after people publicly. She did, however, complain regularly to the Lawrence House president about women she disliked whenever they broke quiet hours. Sylvia could be difficult.

Her writing during senior year indicated a full recovery from her breakdown. Some of the best of her fiction included "The Smoky Blue Piano," a story about her Cambridge apartment; "Superman and Paula Brown's New Snowsuit," an oblique treatment of a child's loss of her father; and the deftly written "In the Mountains," a story about the Norton-Plath relationship, which she described as "Hemingway-like." She deserved her *A* in Alfred Kazin's creative writing course. He had also taught her that "great works of literature come out of passion."

The fifty-five poems she wrote for Professor Fisher would have profited from that lesson. Her use of controlled stanza forms such as sexain, rondeau, and villanelle undermined the effects she might have achieved, although these poems later won many prizes. Her senior-year collection was titled "Circus in Three Rings" and her current pseudonym was "Marcia Moore." The collection was dedicated to "My Favorite Maestro, Alfred Young Fisher." It included poems which had already appeared in *Harper's* (three poems), *The Atlantic Monthly*, *The Nation*, and *Mademoiselle* (three poems). For an undergraduate, Plath was being published in amazing places. The only other young woman poet in the country who was achieving more notice in 1955 was Adrienne Rich, already a winner of the Yale Younger Poets contest. Sylvia's envy of Rich is clear in a letter to Gordon: "I keep reading about this damn adrienne cecile rich, only two years older than I, who is a yale younger poet and regularly in all the top mags. . . . Occasionally, I retch quietly in the wastebasket."

Competitive and always aware of markets and marketability, Plath was not content to write for herself. She had become "the" area poet, giving readings on other campuses and winning (in a tie) the Mt. Holyoke Glascock Prize, a marvelous two-day event with competitive readings before an audience. Sylvia had good conversations with judges Marianne Moore and John Ciardi, with whom she drank bourbon. She also came to know the other college poets who were competing. A month later, she was asked to staff a New York state writing festival for high school students, at which Mickey Spillane was also an instructor.

As graduation neared, Sylvia won several major awards at Smith—for her honors thesis, her poetry, and for being the outstanding English student. She was one of only four students to graduate *summa cum laude* at the June 6, 1955, commencement. She had also been paid over $200 by magazines for stories and poems. Her most important award during her senior year, however, was her Fulbright fellowship to Newnham College at Cambridge University in England. The fellowship paid all her expenses including travel and a generous book allowance.

Winning the Fulbright solved several personal problems for Sylvia. She had a glamorous opportunity before her—at least one year of study in England, possibly two. She did not have to marry anyone ("but English men are wonderful," she wrote to Aurelia). And she could graduate from Smith and spend the summer at home without the feelings of failure or guilt that usually plagued her when she was "doing nothing."

Although Sylvia wrote that she was totally cured, she was still insecure, still trapped in her family's value system, which, even if she learned to question it, she could not reject entirely. After all, it had been her dream just two years earlier, as she had written in her application for the *Mademoiselle* guest editorship, that she would someday have "a tall brilliant husband," and that together

> We will work hard, have vital, intelligent friends, go to plays, concerts, and exhibits, and subscribe to the *Atlantic*, the *New Yorker*, the *Saturday Review of Literature*, *Time*, the Sunday *Times*, and the *Monitor*—and I will be able to buy all the poetry books and tweed suits I want!

Cambridge may have sounded exciting, but she was still single, and nearly twenty-three. By itself, the fellowship was not the fulfillment of Sylvia's earlier dreams.

8
England

1955-56

"In the Sun's Conflagrations"

If only I get accepted at Cambridge! My whole life would explode in a rainbow. Imagine the wealth of material the experience of Europe would give me for stories and poems—the local color, the people, the fresh backgrounds. I really think that if I keep working, I shall be a good minor writer some day. . . .

This letter from Sylvia to her mother, written during the spring before she went to England, captured two of her dominant personality traits: her tendency to place great weight on something scheduled to happen in the future (and then to be disappointed when it failed to meet her expectations) and a corresponding harshness in her assessment of her own abilities. Why would Sylvia be content to become "a good *minor* writer"? She had immense talent, an excellent education, the encouragement of many professional writers who had either taught her or befriended her or both, and an impressive number of publications, prizes, and awards. Within an outer shell of polished self-confidence lived the timid child-woman who listened all too well when inner voices reminded her that she was "just" a middle-class girl with unrealistic dreams.

Nevertheless, when she sailed for England in mid-September of 1955, she was exuberant. She planned to become at least a professional writer, if not a Ph.D. in literature as well. Her horizons seemed limitless. She was always cheered by having "new worlds" ahead.

She heaved a sigh of relief when the cab pulled up beside her at the small Cambridge train station. Her luggage had grown heavier as she lived and traveled in London for ten days, and she had no idea where Newnham College or Whitstead dormitory at 4 Barton Road was. Much to her dismay, Sylvia found that Whitstead sat at the back of the Newnham playing grounds, far from the classroom buildings, and that Newnham itself was not central to Cambridge. She had had her bike shipped over and would often ride ten miles a day from Whitstead to classes to friends' rooms and back. Wearing her short black undergraduate gown, Sylvia pedaled robustly through her schedule, until her colds and sinus trouble began. Then her daily treks loomed insurmountable.

But she loved Cambridge. She raved about its formal gardens, King's Chapel, and the Bridge of Sighs. Surrounded by the archaic walled colleges and lovely stone buildings, Sylvia felt tranquil and happy when she arrived. An academic world was her world; people here would understand and approve her aims, and would nourish her in attaining them. She bought furnishings for her third floor single room—a black pottery tea set, a large earthenware fruit plate, sofa pillows, and some prints— and she got to know Irene Morris, her tutor, and her housemother and housemates (largely Commonwealth women, but among them several other Americans). She wrote home frequently, letters that provided both a bridge and a safety net for her.

By early October Sylvia had settled in. Whitstead was a rambling frame house, large enough for a dozen students, surrounded by a wide tree-dotted yard. It was somewhat dilapidated, but Sylvia described her room glowingly:

> The roof slants in an atticish way, and I have a gas fireplace
> which demands a shilling each time I want to warm up the
> room (wonderful for drying my washed hair by, which I did
> last night) and a gas ring on the hearth where I can warm up
> water for tea or coffee. . . . I love the window-sofa—just big
> enough for two to sit on, or for one (me) to curl up in and read
> with a fine view of treetops.

The woman who had earlier questioned her tutor about whether
or not to bring Bermuda shorts to Cambridge seemed secure and
happy there.

Some of Sylvia's happiness that fall in Cambridge must also
have stemmed from her relief at having made it through the
summer at home. Partly because of her mother's health, life at
26 Elmwood Road had been tense. During the spring, Mrs.
Plath had been forced to have a subtotal gastrectomy to avoid
further problems with her ulcer. (Aurelia had not missed Sylvia's graduation, however, although to get there she had to be
taken from the hospital to Northampton, lying on a mattress in
a friend's station wagon.) Much of the summer Aurelia spent
convalescing on the Cape with the Schobers, leaving Sylvia—at
her request—alone in Wellesley, where she was getting ready
for England. Sylvia saw Sassoon occasionally—usually in New
York but for one weekend at her home—and she dated Peter
Davison, a young poet and editor at Harcourt Brace whom she
had met through Alfred Kazin. And before she left for England,
she spent several days with Lameyer.

By the summer of 1955, Sylvia's relationship with her mother
was fragile. In a letter written after he had spent the weekend in
Wellesley, Sassoon urged Sylvia to be kind to Aurelia, pointing
out that Sylvia would not be home for two years. Peter Davison's account of the relationship was critical of Sylvia, who he
said privately criticized her mother but in person deferred to
her. After Davison and Sylvia became lovers late in the summer,
she took him home to meet her family. Davison thought that
Sylvia's treatment of her mother epitomized what he considered
her worst trait, "her impersonal appetite for experience." (Describing their romance, Sylvia said that her "intensity" had bothered Davison, and he does write, in a memoir, "Her quest for
knowledge was voracious. I felt as if I were being cross-exam-

ined, drained, eaten.") It seems that much of the tension between Sylvia and her mother was visible to her dates, and may
have occurred in part because of them. Aurelia could never accept Sylvia's sexual involvements.

The poems Plath wrote during 1955 reflect the tensions in her
life. "Aerialist" is about a tight-rope walker, an acrobat doing an
amazing balancing act. Horrible things happen to the woman:
trucks crush her, weights fall on her, bowling balls threaten to
smash her. Staying alive is her feat. As in "Circus in Three
Rings," in which the woman is a lion tamer, in this poem the
men in the protagonist's life are either evil or unreliable. Some
of Plath's poems are about an absent lover—"Cinderella," "On
Looking into the Eyes of a Demon Lover," "Denouement," and
"Two Lovers and a Beachcomber by the Real Sea." Still other
of her 1955 poems convey a fear of death and loss. "Temper of
Time" speaks of the character Kilroy from *Camino Real*, walking
the earth while "all the gold apples/Go bad to the core" and
skeletons surround him.

Sylvia's poems suggest a number of unresolved problems. She
may have been ecstatically looking forward to living in England
for two years (she would spend her vacations traveling throughout Europe), but she was no clearer about where she fit into the
world than she had been before her breakdown. Whenever she
was dissatisfied with a situation, she tried to leave it, to find
some more exciting new world. Sylvia's search for the new,
then, including her stay in England, was less healthy than it
might have appeared.

According to both her journal and many of her 1955 poems,
the only genuine alleviation of Sylvia's "doomsday" gloom came
from the pleasure she took in her developing sexuality. She spent
much of her time enroute to England, crossing on the S.S.
United States, flirting with men and then making love. She did
more of the same during her ten days in London. Lovemaking
blotted out her anxieties about going to Cambridge—once again
in that all-too-familiar role of the pressured scholarship student
—and about leaving home for such a long time.

Her aims in England were twofold: Sylvia was going to get
the best possible education, by reading widely and not overspe-
cializing; and she was going to find a husband. She wrote her

mother late in 1955 that she would not return to the United States until she had married. Hearing that Dick Norton was engaged only confirmed her decision. Before she had left for England, she had broken up with Peter Davison and had been chilled by Sassoon's casual responses to her now that he had graduated and planned to live in France. Her romantic relationship with Lameyer was over, although they were going to travel together in Europe during the 1956 spring break. (Like many women at that time, Sylvia's pattern was to keep as friends men she had been romantically involved with. This practice reflected her understanding of the patriarchal world she was moving in. As British writer Hilary Bailey Moorcock, who had been a classmate of Plath's at Newnham, observed: "There would be no point in cultivating the society of women for practical reasons. Obviously, no woman would marry you. Equally, no woman, with only a few exceptions, could advance you in the world. Women had no power to help you in any important way; nor could they defend you from male power.")

Men at Cambridge outnumbered women ten to one in 1955, and Sylvia was a dramatic, attractive American. She was bound to be noticed. She was slightly older than most of the Newnham students—they being undergraduates, she, at twenty-three, the equivalent of a graduate student. She impressed other students as being even older and also seemed to be a worldly and highly competitive person. (In Cambridge, one of the arts was to appear noncompetitive, although everyone was fiercely so.)

Plath's bright lipstick, her height, her usually solemn expression, her aura of defiance, and her unshakable poise made her someone to talk about. She sometimes wrote articles for *Varsity*, the weekly Cambridge paper, and she modeled for a two-page feature on fashions. Christopher Levenson, the Cambridge poet who edited *Delta*, an influential magazine, recalled the awe that Plath tended to inspire:

She was almost a golden girl, gifted and poised, energetic, serious and intent. . . . My main impression remains one of the combination of intensity and sophistication. For me at least she came across as a strong, confident, experienced young woman: I remember her on one occasion describing driving through, or very close to, a tornado. I remember the vividness and intensity of her gestures and eyes, the way certain words, like the word "strong" itself, were elongated to our English ears, almost physically savoured in the telling. I think she must have been aware of the sense of power, and of a larger, less controllable world, that she projected.

Sylvia was capable of holding her own with her Whitstead housemates. She dressed as she pleased, particularly for breakfast. She also had the habit of cutting her fried eggs into careful shapes as she ate them. One morning Margaret Robarts, a South African student, asked Sylvia impatiently, "*Must* you cut up your eggs like that?" Sylvia quickly answered: "Yes, I'm afraid I really must. What do you do with your eggs? Swallow them whole?" Jane Baltzell, a Marshall scholar from the United States who also lived in Whitstead, found that being friends with Plath was sometimes difficult. Jane borrowed some books from Sylvia and made penciled notes in them, intending to erase the marks before she returned them. She forgot to erase the notes, however, and when Sylvia saw her annotations, she was furious. A similar episode occurred once when the women were traveling together and Jane inadvertently locked Sylvia out of the room they were sharing. Once Sylvia was angry, becoming friends again was a slow and testing process.

But to casual acquaintances, Sylvia seemed to be the heart of good fellowship. She was an animated story teller, a vibrant talker. She insisted on learning to eat in the British manner, knife in right hand and fork in left. No one at Whitstead cared whether or not Sylvia ate in this fashion, but she kept her housemates posted on her progress in this and in most of her activities. Everyone heard about her experiences with the theater group, her bike rides, and her dates. (On a date with a friend from America, Plath rode a runaway horse named Sam through the Cambridge streets, barely escaping injury. The ride became one of the recurring images in her late poems, always a symbol of her daring.) Sylvia was intense, nervous, and skittish at times, crossing her legs and swinging the one crossed over, threading her fingers together endlessly. For the women who lived near her in Whitstead, the fact that she often typed before 6:00 A.M. was a cross to bear.

Sylvia's classes at Newnham fascinated her. Kathleen Burton,

her director of studies and supervisor, helped her plan the two
years of work. There would be no examinations until June of
the second year, but prior to that time she would write weekly
papers for each supervision (one hour a week with Burton and
another with Dorothea Krook, a young and attractive woman
who resembled Ruth Beuscher and became Sylvia's favorite
teacher at Cambridge). She attended eleven hours of lecture a
week, all in the mornings and given by David Daiches, Basil
Willey, and F. R. Leavis. She read independently in three areas,
which she chose from the six offered: tragedy of all periods;
literary criticism and British literature; and the English moralists
(Aristotle to D. H. Lawrence), the last chosen because it included philosophy. It was an ambitious program, perhaps
frighteningly so. The areas that Sylvia had studied at Smith—
the modern novel and poetry—were not among those offered at
Cambridge.

Sylvia enjoyed her time with Dr. Krook, a bright woman who
taught Henry James and the moralists—chiefly Plato. Sylvia
admired the fact that Krook was a success academically and yet
was also personable and feminine. She was not pretentious.
Wendy Campbell, a friend of both Krook's and Sylvia's, wrote
about the latter's supervision sessions that even though Sylvia
was extremely bright, she

> did not feel the need to define herself in intellectual combat.
> . . . There was nothing of the preacher, the enthusiast or the
> persuader about Sylvia. Her point of reference was always
> firmly fixed within herself. She seemed to use her mind as a
> set of antennae with which she assessed her own experience
> and felt it over. She wanted "to know" for her own subjective
> purposes.

For Krook, Sylvia's chief strength as a student was not her
brilliance—although she wrote solid, intelligent essays—but
rather her responsiveness. "I felt the things I said, we said, her
authors said, mattered to her in an intimate way, answering to
intense personal needs, reaching to depths of her spirit to which
I had no direct access." Krook observed that Sylvia loved literature, loved to study it and talk about it, and loved the humane-

ness of discussion with her tutor. Meeting with Krook at her house at 111 Grantchester Meadows was the high point of Sylvia's week, and she accumulated a long row of alphas (*A*'s) for her essays.

Because her lecture schedule seemed light in comparison to her days at Smith, and because studying was only one of the reasons Sylvia was in Cambridge, she tried out for the Cambridge Amateur Dramatics Club (ADC). She was one of only nine women chosen to be a part of that elite group. She played minor roles during fall term, the comic part of a mad poetess and that of a screaming whore in *Bartholomew Fair*. She also joined a political group, the Labour Club. Men were plentiful and Sylvia dated a good deal. For the first time in her life, she had money to spend without guilt. She was living on what the Fulbright committee thought students in her position should spend.

And Sylvia was always in love—and always with some giant of a man. This was the perception of her friends, anyway. In fact, according to her journals, Sylvia avoided serious relationships at Cambridge by telling men there about "this boy in France." Sassoon was the subject of much conversation, the object of much correspondence. They did spend the Christmas holiday together, traveling in Europe and staying at the Sorbonne in Paris, reviving their former intimacy. Sassoon, however, also loved women in Switzerland and France. After their holiday together, he asked Sylvia not to write to him until he had sorted through his future plans.

She did write to Sassoon, but she did not mail the letters, and some of them appear as entries in her journals for 1956. Being forbidden to write while separated from him was a restriction she could hardly bear. Once again, she had idealized a situation so that it bore little resemblance to reality: Sassoon clearly was not ready for marriage but Sylvia was looking for permanence. She not only wanted to love Sassoon; her repeated references to wanting to bear his child would have frightened the hardiest playboy.

Returning in January from her romantic vacation, Sylvia was faced with the depths of the English winter. She learned what room heaters were for. As she wrote to Aurelia, "I wear about five sweaters and wool pants and knee socks and *still* I can't keep my teeth from chattering. I was simply not made for this kind of weather." Soon after winter term began, to add discomfort of a different type, Sylvia got a splinter in her eye. She went to the infirmary in great pain, afraid of being blinded. She also had the flu, more colds, and depression. Her grand plan—to conquer Cambridge academically and socially—seemed as impossible as her dream of conquering New York had been during the summer of 1953.

By mid-February of 1956, Sylvia was in the same kind of inert, angry depression that had preceded her earlier breakdown. The language of her 1956 journal entries echoes that of her writing in 1953. According to that journal, her behavior was a mixture of rash impulses. She wore only black clothing, with red gloves and a hairband; she was aggressive, sexual, shrill; she scolded herself for doing little studying. She admitted that she was unbearably lonely ("I long for Mother, even for Gordon"), fighting what she called "the old beginning-of-the-week panic," wanting to cry "to Richard, to all my friends at home, to come and rescue me. From my insecurity, which I must fight through myself." Physically, too, she was far from being at her best: "I am tired and have been very discouraged by having sinus for so long."

Her letters to Ellie Friedman, as well as those to her mother, did not suggest depression, however. Comedy was Sylvia's pattern on paper, and every love affair, every adventure, became the stuff of good stories. Socially Sylvia was sometimes less than polite to the students who surrounded her. Ildiko Hayes invited Sylvia to tea to meet Hilary Bailey, but Sylvia was remote and taciturn. (Bailey remembers, "We crouched by a gas fire, gnashing crumpets.") It was as if Sylvia's attention was on students who could do her some good, male students for the most part, or those who were already established. She did go to the poetry readings held in Chris Levenson's rooms, partly because Levenson was editor of *Delta*. There, Plath criticized fellow poets freely. According to Philip Gardner, a Cambridge student and poet, at one meeting Sylvia read a poem that she had already published in the United States as though it were new work, and she just smiled when listeners criticized it. Gardner felt that Sylvia's practice showed her need to be successful on the British literary scene and belied her apparent self-confidence. The work that Sylvia submitted to the local poetry magazines—*Granta, Delta, London Magazine*—was, for the most part, rejected. Levenson described the poems Sylvia sent to his magazine as being "too tricksey, too self-consciously clever."

On February 20, 1956, Sylvia was back to her old habit of analyzing everything in her journal. She listed as her problems: "men (Richard gone, no one here to love)" and "writing (too nervous about rejections, too desperate and scared about bad poems)" and "girls (house bristles with suspicion and frigidity)" and "academic life (have deserted French and feel temporarily very wicked and shirking, must atone: also, feel stupid in discussion; what the hell is tragedy? I am)." Another journal entry, all too reminiscent of those 1953 prebreakdown entries, began,

> Dear Doctor: I am feeling very sick. I have a heart in my stomach which throbs and mocks. Suddenly the simple rituals of the day balk like a stubborn horse. It gets impossible to look people in the eye: corruption may break out again? Who knows. Small talk becomes desperate.
>
> Hostility grows, too. That dangerous, deadly venom which comes from a sick heart. Sick mind, too. The image of identity we must daily fight to impress on the neutral, or hostile, world collapses inward: we feel crushed.

Burdened with her self-imposed responsibility, Plath turned every event into a symbol. When a group of young boys threw snowballs at her, she concluded that they had chosen to attack her because they could see the rottenness within her.

On February 25, recognizing the old symptoms for herself, she went to see Dr. Davy, a psychiatrist, a fatherly man who impressed her. Her guilt, in that day's journal entry, turned to anger against Sassoon. He was responsible for her being this age —23—and single. But the chief problem was that Sylvia had not yet found that "blazing love" she had believed would surround her: "My God, I'd love to cook and make a house, and surge force into a man's dreams, and write, if he could talk and walk and work and passionately want to do his career. I can't bear to think of this potential for loving and giving going brown and sere in me. Yet the choice is so important, it frightens me a little. A lot. . . ."

As if in answer to her journal entry, that very afternoon she bought a copy of the first issue of the new literary magazine, *St. Botolph's Review*. Bert Wyatt-Brown, an American acquaintance of hers, was selling copies down by the Anchor at the Queen's Street bridge. Several hours later she returned and asked where she would meet Ted Hughes. His poems particularly impressed her.

Sylvia turned up that night at the *St. Botolph's* celebratory party in Falcon Yard, and she met Hughes. Yelling exuberantly at each other, stamping their feet and drinking brandy as they talked about poetry, Ted and Sylvia exchanged kisses in a re-mote room. As she described it in her journal,

> then he kissed me bang smash on the mouth and ripped my hairband, off my red hairband scarf which has weathered the sun and much love, and whose like I shall never find again, and my favorite silver earrings: ha, I shall keep, he barked. And when he kissed my neck I bit him long and hard on the cheek, and when we came out of the room, blood was running down his face.

The incident quickly made the rounds of the Cambridge gossips.

For several weeks, however, the only place the romance ex-isted was in Plath's journal. Hughes worked in London as a reader for the film production company of J. Arthur Rank. Syl-via wished that he would come to Cambridge. She lamented that he did not, worried that he had a girlfriend. Finally Ted and Luke Myers, an American poet friend, did come to Whitstead. They came, however, to the back of the house, calling the name Shirley. Sylvia never knew they were there. When the students who lived on that side of the sprawling house told her of the incident, Sylvia was furious. He had no respect for her, that was clear. She wanted nothing to do with him.

But of course she did. Spring was spinning through the chill British air, and Sylvia was apprehensive about her travels in Europe. She had heard from Sassoon; he would not be able to see her. She had plans to meet Gordon Lameyer for a trip through Germany, but she knew her spring break was going to be less than idyllic. The night before she was to leave for vacation, however, she saw Ted. They spent the night at his second-floor flat on Rugby Street in London, reciting poetry, making love, finding their alter ego in each other—rebellious and isolated, strong and erotic and gifted. The "twentieth-century Brownings," as friends later called them, loved the power each seemed to command, the promise each had in writing, the sensual responses each was capable of.

Tired but euphoric, Sylvia rose early and left. It was March 24, 1956. She traveled to Paris only to find that, indeed, Sassoon was gone. She tried to enjoy her isolation, the superb French food and drink. She was tempted to pick up men to be companionable with but not to love. As she later wrote to Aurelia,

In the last two months I have fallen terribly in love, which can only lead to great hurt. I met the strongest man in the world, ex-Cambridge, brilliant poet whose work I loved before I met him, a large, hulking, healthy Adam . . . with a voice like the thunder of God—a singer, story-teller, lion and world-wanderer, a vagabond who will never stop.

She had difficulty not thinking of Hughes, especially when she received his March 31 love letter, telling her that her memory went through him like brandy. He would come to her in Cambridge if she did not come to London. Her impulse was to return immediately, but Gordon was planning to meet her so she stuck it out. Besides, there might be some chance that Sassoon would return. She had some happy times, and the loneliness finally brought tranquility.

Several days later she began her travels with Lameyer. On April 12, she could resist no longer. As she later wrote her old friend Marcia Brown, "I flew back from Rome to London on a black Friday the 13th of April, and we haven't been apart a day since."

Born August 17, 1930, in West Yorkshire, Ted Hughes was the youngest of three children. He had served as a radio operator in the RAF and was a 1954 anthropology graduate of Pembroke College, Cambridge. Hughes was somewhat outside the academic tradition: his father was a tobacconist. His family home, The Beacon, in Heptonstall village, was both comfortable and secluded. Six feet tall, a hunter and fisherman, Hughes was primarily a writer. He had begun writing poetry at fifteen, and knew Chaucer, Shakespeare, Donne, Blake, Yeats, Hopkins, Lawrence, and Dylan Thomas better than Sylvia did. She and Ted shared these writers. They also shared a deep understanding of the power of language (especially Ted, with his boyhood in the Yorkshire dialect), as well as that of mythology and folklore. They prowled the British Museum, listened to Beethoven, and read Nietzsche and—in Ted's case—Schopenhauer. Ted kept himself steady through a balance of mind and body, the natural and the sophisticated.

At Cambridge, Ted had rejected the preciousness of some of the students and the English faculty and had managed to remain himself. He did not try to become a literary figure, and he avoided most of the campus writers. He instead chose his friends from other Cambridge outsiders, people who were Irish, Welsh, and American. According to a friend, Ted was bound to his companions through a love of "talk, song, and outrageousness." Ted's Cambridge was not the one Sylvia was trying to conquer. In fact, the appearance of *St. Botolph's Review* was meant to state a new order of business for the poets of England—a more vital and rigorous effort than that which Levenson, Spender, and Leavis represented. Prior to the party for the publication, Ted's friends complained of Sylvia's association with the *Granta* crowd, although they did not know her personally. David Ross, the editor, Daniel Weissbort, Luke Myers, and others told each other that Sylvia's writing was superficial. They belittled the appearance of her poems in American middle-brow journals. Male jealousy was part of the criticism. But there was also the feeling that she was "on the make" and that her pursuit of Ted (as the courtship was interpreted) was yet another manipulative attempt to promote her career by attaching herself to someone as promising as Hughes seemed to be. While that opinion did not dissipate at once, Ted's response to her as well as a better acquaintance with Sylvia herself led to that crowd's eventual welcoming of her as a poet and friend.

For her part, Sylvia thought that she had found exactly the

sort of man she had long sought for a husband. Her letters home that spring were rapturous. In April, her beloved grandmother died of cancer, but even that great loss did not dampen her happiness. And then her mother was coming to England in June and would get to meet the "huge derrick-striding Ted," who, according to Sylvia, knew everything, had done everything, was willing to try everything, and wrote expert poems besides.

Her litany of praise continued. To Warren she called Hughes

the only man in the world who is my match. . . . His voice is richer and rarer than Dylan Thomas, booming through walls and doors. He stalks into the room and yanks a book out of my case: Chaucer, Shakespeare, Thomas, and begins to read. He reads his own poems which are better than Thomas and Hopkins many times, better than all I know: fierce, disciplined, with a straight honest saying. He tells me endless stories, in the Irish spinning way, dropping his voice to a hush and acting some out, and I am enchanted: such a yarn-spinner. He is 25 and from Yorkshire and has done everything in the world: rose-grafting, plowing, reading for movie studios, hunting, fishing. . . . He is a violent Adam.

She had some worries, however. She had written to Olive Higgins Prouty, whom she consistently saw as a more worldly and experienced woman than her mother, that Ted's behavior was sometimes unruly, and that she suspected that he loved to drink and make conquests of women. Much as Sylvia admired what she called Ted's "ruthless force," she knew that she named it accurately: "He is a breaker of things and people," she wrote. When Mrs. Prouty replied in early June, she warned Sylvia not to marry Ted—at least not so soon. "You don't really believe, do you, that the characteristics which you describe as 'bashing people around,' unkindness and I think you said cruelty, can be *permanently* changed in a man of 26?"

That spring Sylvia and Ted saw each other nearly every day. They ate together, and read books—plays and poems—together, often aloud. Ted would recite a line of poetry or drama and—to Sylvia—shout "Finish!" They drank with Ted's friends and partied with their poetry friends, but most of their time they spent alone together.

Sylvia was her most dynamic. She brought Ted all the love and affection, all the talent and curiosity, all the childlike winsomeness and contrasting sophistication she possessed. She loved him and poured all her energy into the relationship. But she was also idealizing. She was not only romanticizing Ted; she was idealizing her own powers to change that already wonderful man into someone more impressive. As she boasted to Aurelia, loving Ted had changed her for the better: "I have become a woman to make you proud. . . . Although this is the one man in the world for me, although I am using every fiber of my being to love him, even so, I am true to the essence of myself, and I know who that self is."

On June 16 (James Joyce's Bloomsday) in 1956, Edward James Hughes and Sylvia Plath were married in the Church of St. George the Martyr, Queen Square, a five-minute walk from Ted's London flat. Aurelia Plath was present, a curate was witness, but otherwise the marriage was secret, even from Ted's family and friends. Despite rain and Sylvia's anxiety about the haste of the wedding (they had spent the morning shopping for shoes and trousers for Ted), she thought the ceremony was beautiful. She wore Aurelia's new pink knit dress with a matching hair ribbon and carried a pink rose from Ted, and she cried when he placed the gold ring on her finger.

Because Sylvia was afraid she would lose her Fulbright if people knew she was married, the ceremony remained secret. After a summer honeymoon in Spain, they planned to live separately—Ted was going to teach in Spain, and Sylvia would return to Newnham. Because of the marriage, Aurelia's long-planned visit to England changed dramatically. She and Sylvia spent a few days in Cambridge together, while Ted returned to Yorkshire to tell his family he was going to Spain, but not that he was traveling with Sylvia or that she had become his wife. Then Aurelia and the Hugheses went to London and then to Paris, where she saw Ted and Sylvia off for Madrid and then Benidorm, a remote fishing village on the coast. Aurelia traveled alone in Europe from June 29 till August 5, when Ted and Sylvia returned from Spain to see her off from London.

Sylvia loved almost everything about Spain—the sun, the colors, the air, the people, the food. Early in July, she wrote Aurelia that she had never been so happy: she was proud of Ted; she was reveling in the sea, the hills, her perfect health. She wrote that she and her husband were "fantastically matched; both of us need the same amount of sleep and food and time for writing; both are inner-directed, almost anti-social." Some bad experiences in Spain, however, where Sylvia felt that she was being asked to keep house in primitive conditions, upset her, and she wrote very little. Even after she and Ted had moved into a pleasant stucco house with a yard, grape arbor, and fig tree, she resented having to do the marketing and cooking as well as the housework. In a late July journal entry she recorded the anger that she did not otherwise express.

> The hurt going in, clean as a razor, and the dark blood welling. . . . Sitting in nightgown and sweater in the dining room staring into the full moon, talking to the full moon, with wrongness growing and filling the house like a man-eating plant. The need to go out. It is very quiet. Perhaps he is asleep. Or dead. How to know how long there is before death. . . .

For someone so recently married, the words of this entry—in which she and Ted are described as "two silent strangers"—are ominous. The progression in Sylvia's thoughts to Ted's death might have suggested her childhood days, when she wished her father dead so that she would not have to play quietly—only to have him in fact die. Whatever the association, in July of 1956, Sylvia was in angry turmoil, sorting through feelings of love marred by disappointment that she had not known since she was a child. And she felt alone in her quandary—far from her therapist, far from her family, far from her country. Being married to the most wonderful man in the world was not the consistent bliss she had envisioned. Her July journal entry closed, sadly, "The world has grown crooked and sour as a lemon overnight."

9
Marriage
1956 - 57

"I Am Learning Peacefulness"

Sylvia's humor was not improved when she and Ted returned from Spain completely broke. Partly because their funds were depleted, in September, after Aurelia had gone back home and Warren had come and gone with the Hugheses to Paris, she and Ted went to visit Ted's family. Sylvia had thought Cambridge was cold, but in Yorkshire she would experience England at its chilliest. And at its most historic: Heptonstall, where the Hughes family lived, was one of the last villages to have fallen to the Angles. A part of Elmet, the last Celtic kingdom, the whole Calder valley had for centuries been considered a desolate wilderness, a hide-out for criminals. Steep roads led to the area; narrow path-like streets wound at odd, fortifiable turns through the village; and ferocious winds off the Pennine moors waited just beyond the village walls.

Traveling by train and bus, Ted and Sylvia finally arrived, dragging their cumbersome luggage as best they could. The breathtaking expanse of moor, dotted with somnolent sheep, extended to the clouds. It was Brontë country (the Haworth parish where the Brontës lived and wrote was only a few miles away)—wild, beautiful, trackless, and colored at times with a fragile, almost fantastic, light.

At first, Sylvia loved it. A walker, she enjoyed the seemingly chartless distance, the loping fields, sometimes hidden in woods, then etched by deep blue rivers and accented with rock formations. Heptonstall was the land of the unexpected. For Sylvia, it was as good as the sea.

She wrote to Aurelia about the kindness of Ted's parents and their welcome at the news of the marriage, about her sharing Ted's room and writing in it during the days while he worked downstairs. Mostly she wrote about the long walks, picnics at old ruins, and a day's trip to the Brontë house with Ted and his Uncle Walt, who became a favorite of Sylvia's. As she described Wuthering Heights:

> Imagine yourself on top of the world, with all the purplish hills curving away, and gray sheep grazing with horns curling and black demonic faces and yellow eyes . . . black walls of stone, clear streams from which we drank; and, at last, a lonely, deserted black-stone house, broken down, clinging to the windy side of a hill.

During the last week of their visit, Sylvia and Ted were joined by Ellie Friedman, Sylvia's friend from Smith who had planned to travel with Sylvia during the summer. They took Ellie, at midnight, to see the neighborhood witch, a wise old woman who did little but gossip about the villagers. They talked about astrology, went on long hiking trips (to and from the Brontë house, barely finding their way home) and to local pubs. While much of the Yorkshire life was exotic and interesting, Ellie was as attracted by Ted's commentary on it. At all times, Ted was in charge; this was his home territory. Born nearby in Mytholmroyd, he had lived near the imposing Scout Rock, which might have been the site of Celtic ceremonies. At times, Ted played the part of the primitive Celt telling the story of a dream he had had his second year at Cambridge. Then an English major, he was writing countless critical essays, not very happily. One night in a dream, a fox (Ted's totem) appeared—erect, man-sized, and with human hands. It walked to Ted's essay and put a charred hand on it, saying sternly, "Stop this. You are killing us." The next day, Ted said, he changed his major to archaeology and anthropology.

Sylvia was fascinated by the stories Ted's mother told about ghostly appearances and mysterious deaths on the moors. While in England, Sylvia had discovered the British interest in what she called "scientific mysticism, probability in foreknowledge in cards, hypnotism, levitation, Blake." This treatment of the occult was a comfort to Sylvia, who had long thought of herself as clairvoyant. Since she had come to England, she was having what she called mystic experiences regularly. She described an Advent service at King's College Chapel in Cambridge in that way, and connected it with the way she felt when literature struck her hard—"as if an angel had hauled me by the hair in a shiver of gooseflesh"—as it did when her mother had read her a Matthew Arnold poem, or when she read the ending of James Joyce's story "The Dead," or when Dr. Krook read from D. H. Lawrence's "The Man Who Died." Sylvia insisted that "The Man Who Died" was *her* story, that many of the events were similar to happenings in her own life, and that the temple of Isis had long been one of her key images: "All seemed shudderingly relevant. . . . I have lived much of this." With Ted, Sylvia could share these experiences, as she could not with some of her intellectual friends. For instance, she and Ted enjoyed astrology, and when Ted gave her tarot cards for her birthday in 1956, Sylvia wrote her mother that the two of them would become a "better team than Mr. and Mrs. Yeats."

The Yorkshire visit gave Sylvia a sense of Ted's home territory in the rural and sometimes brutal country that was so different from London and Cambridge, and showed him to be a part of a highly traditional culture. His good-humored father drove to his tobacco shop in Hebden Bridge every day. His mother cooked and kept house, visiting with friends and trying to forget her debilitating arthritis. Neither was a workaholic. Both were capable of spending long hours in conversation. Because the atmosphere of The Beacon was different from that of the Plaths' efficient Wellesley household, Sylvia did not always appreciate it.

In October, Sylvia and Ted left Yorkshire to return to Cambridge. Ted stayed briefly, but since the Newnham College authorities did not know that Sylvia was married, he returned to Yorkshire to live when she moved back to Whitstead. Their separation lasted not quite four weeks. Ted's letters to Sylvia during that time show a tender, passionate love, full of concern for her health and her ability to work. Sylvia, meanwhile, was undergoing what she called "a hectic suffocating wild depression." The first week she was at Whitstead, she said she could not read at all.

After Ted had been in Yorkshire several weeks, he came to London to read a program of Yeats's poems for the BBC. He was paid $150, money he badly needed. He and Sylvia spent two days and nights together and by the end of that time, realized that they could not live apart again. It was not much of an exaggeration when Sylvia wrote to her mother, "Both of us have been literally sick to death being apart, wasting all our time and force trying to cope with the huge, fierce sense of absence. . . . It is impossible for us to be whole or healthy apart."

Near tears, Sylvia went to Dorothea Krook with the situation. When she told Dr. Krook she was married, her mentor urged her to talk with her tutor, Irene Morris. Morris went to the authorities on Sylvia's behalf, and both Newnham College and the Fulbright committee agreed that she could complete her year. She would stay in university housing until December, and then move to 55 Eltisley Avenue, several blocks beyond Whitstead in the Grantchester Meadows area, where Ted began living in November.

Happy as she was to be living with Ted, Sylvia was disappointed in the apartment. She and Ted shared a bathroom with the couple upstairs. More upsetting were the layers of dirt and grime. Even though the landlord allowed them to paint, Sylvia never felt that the place was clean ("How I long to get away from the dirt here. Everything is so old and dirty; soot of centuries worked into every pore"). Their £4-a-week apartment was a far cry from the houses with immaculate modern kitchens in the women's magazines that Sylvia had grown up reading. She rode her bicycle to market, cooked with erratic heat, and—acting as Ted's agent and business manager—tried to keep at least twenty of his poems and stories out to magazines at all times. By the second term, Ted had found a job teaching adolescent boys in a day school. For relatively low pay, he taught nearly every subject, including physical education. Now his days, too, were long. When he had time at home, he used it to write. (Sylvia wrote to a friend that, over spring holiday, she and Ted got up early and worked from 7:00 A.M. to 12:00 on their own writing, "very hard.")

The first year of his marriage was a culmination for Ted. Although as a teenager he had written poetry and had read English when he was first at Cambridge, he felt that he had written his first successful poetry only a year or so before his marriage. In 1955 he had come across a copy of the Penguin collection of modern American poets and became fascinated with the work of Robert Lowell, W. S. Merwin, Richard Wilbur and, somewhat anachronistically, John Crowe Ransom. (Hughes was one of the few Ransom admirers to see the strikingly personal voice in that poet's work.) With these writers as models, Hughes had written the poems Sylvia admired in *St. Botolph's Review.* He was working toward the forceful, sometimes violent, wrenchings of speech that would mark his early mature work. Meanwhile, he was having considerable success; he had published poems in *Poetry, The Nation,* and *The Atlantic Monthly* as well as in the British journals *Granta, Gemini, Nimbus,* and *London Magazine.* Sylvia had promised him that she would be a great agent, and would place at least fifteen poems a year for him—and she did.

At this time, Sylvia felt that Ted's writing was more important than her own. She shopped, cooked, kept house, typed Ted's manuscripts, and studied for her exams. She could do little more. As she wrote to Aurelia, "It is heaven to have someone like Ted who is so kind and honest and brilliant—always stimulating me to study, think, draw and write. He is better than any teacher, even fills somehow that huge, sad hole I felt in having no father."

But as her marriage satisfied one of her lifelong dreams, it took away time from her other roles. Sylvia dragged through the winter, working hard, worrying about money, and behaving erratically at times. Sue Weller, a Smith friend who was also studying abroad, remembered visiting Ted and Sylvia that winter, only to find Sylvia "wandering around the house with tears streaming down her face." She was upset because a paper she had turned in was not up to her standards. Although her marriage necessarily took time away from her scholarship, Sylvia could not adjust to that situation. In Weller's words, Sylvia "was very, very driven."

This strain to be excellent at everything she did was not apparent to everyone. One friend thought Sylvia *could* do it all:

> She had a sort of natural excellence at whatever she turned her hand to. If she wrote an essay it was effortlessly good, if she kept house it was done easily and well, and she even cooked superbly, with enthusiasm and discrimination, and she enjoyed it almost as much as she enjoyed eating. But her very remarkable efficiency was also very natural to her and was never accompanied by any sense of strain.

Sylvia's journal entries show all too well, however, the difference between that surface impression and the truth. There she was writing about her frustration with no time to do anything right, feeling her mind "shut off like an untidy corpse under the floorboards during the last half year of exam cramming, slovenly Eltisley living, tight budgeting . . . a space of paralysis."

Despite the pressures that Sylvia was feeling, her marriage was a source of great satisfaction and happiness to her. She and Ted loved each other. They worked hard, wrote seriously, and explored London, especially the British Museum with its rare treasures of art and archeology. Together they read mythology and anthropology, including Robert Graves's *The White Goddess*, a book that became a source of poetic symbols for both of them. They saw Luke Myers, Dan and Helga Huws, and other friends from Ted's Cambridge years, but they were happiest at home, sharing their lives with each other.

Sylvia remained as keenly interested in politics as ever, angry now over both the Suez crisis and the Russian invasion of Hungary. Her outspokenness about politics marred friendships with some of her British acquaintances. When she wasn't worrying about international affairs, Sylvia worried about money. Writers both, she and Ted did not want to take permanent jobs, but the lure of college teaching was appealing. So Sylvia wrote application letters for both of them to any school that had available positions. Following a suggestion from Mary Ellen Chase, who was spending time in England after her retirement from Smith, Sylvia applied to her alma mater. In April of 1957, Robert Gorham Davis, Chair of the English Department, invited Sylvia to teach three sections of freshman English at Smith, at a salary of $4000 for the year. Sylvia accepted, thinking that Ted could perhaps get a job at Amherst or the University of Massachusetts nearby. (Fearful of the predatory Smith students, Sylvia said she thought it best that Ted not teach at Smith, even had he been asked.)

With the Smith job secured, Sylvia made plans for returning to the United States. After a winter of financial worry, she and Ted would have money to enjoy. And Aurelia planned a garden reception for them on June 29, where Ted could be displayed like a jewel in Sylvia's crown. To follow the party, Aurelia had rented a cottage for them at Eastham, on Cape Cod, as a belated wedding present. For seven weeks, Sylvia and Ted could live in the sun and the sea, write, and be alone. After the year of inconvenient housekeeping and hard studying, Sylvia saw those seven weeks as an oasis.

As it happened, Ted would be coming to America with some fanfare. His poetry manuscript, *The Hawk in the Rain*, had won the first book prize of the prestigious Poetry Center at the 92nd Street Y in New York, which meant that Harper's would publish the collection. The judges for that international competition —who chose Ted's book from 286 entries—were W. H. Auden, Marianne Moore, and Stephen Spender. (Later, Faber & Faber would agree to bring the book out in England, and Ted would receive a letter of praise from T. S. Eliot.)

But before the move back, Sylvia had an important spring ahead of her. First as part of her tripos, Cambridge's honor examinations, she finished and turned in a collection of poems, many of which came from her Smith manuscript of two years earlier, "Circus in Three Rings." Then she took the examinations in her chosen areas for her official degree, a second bachelor's. Receiving a second, she was disappointed that the result was not a first. Dr. Krook commented that, despite Sylvia's excellent work, she had learned that Sylvia was a poet rather than a scholar. She was committed to becoming a better writer and approached her studies from the perspective of what she could learn that would relate to her own writing. Had she chosen, she could have stayed on for a Ph.D. in literature, but Sylvia wanted to write now. She had not written much that she liked during the year, although she had published in *The Atlantic Monthly*, *Poetry* (six poems, for which she won the Bess Hokin prize), and *The Christian Science Monitor* (an essay about life in Spain and four drawings to accompany it).

After several weeks of packing their belongings, crates of books and china, Sylvia and Ted sailed for America. After another week, they were celebrating at Aurelia's garden reception. A huge success, the party brought together Sylvia's neighbors and the Crocketts, the Cantors, the Freemans, Ellie Friedman, Marcia Brown and her husband, Gordon Lameyer's mother, Peter Davison, and other Smith friends. Radiant, Sylvia hugged the people she had not seen for two years, happily described her accomplishments, and introduced Ted, who felt somewhat lost in the hubbub of congratulations. He was a little overwhelmed by Sylvia's steady exuberance. She, conversely, was euphoric over the striking effect Ted—her colossus—had on people.

Sylvia began her summer on the Cape writing stories about her own experiences, even though they were disguised. One story was called "Trouble-Making Mother," a narrative about a mother who dominates her teenage daughter, even to flirting with her dates. Within a week, Sylvia had finished the story and sent it off, pleased. She wrote in her journal that it was a gripping story with a dramatic crisis, and growth in the protagonist. But it was to be the only fiction she finished that summer, though she intended to write another about a sister-in-law and one "like Kafka, simply told, symbolic, yet very realistic. How one is always and irrevocably alone."

Mining the emotional centers of her life, Sylvia also planned to write a novel about her love for Ted and their first meeting in Falcon Yard—"*love, a falcon*, striking once and for all." In her journal, she traced much of her sense of fiction to Virginia Woolf, and she also admonished herself not to tell too much of the daily life of "Judith Greenwood," her *Falcon Yard* protagonist. Several years later, Plath used the name Esther Greenwood for the main character in *The Bell Jar*. "Greenwood" was her grandmother's maiden name, but it also had the connotation of growth and youth. As she reminded herself in her journal, the character of Judith, or Esther, was to be symbolic: "Make her a statement of the generation."

Ted meanwhile was writing fables for children, and having some success placing them in children's magazines. He also was having considerable success with his poetry. Sylvia wrote to her mother that Ted would have fifteen poems coming out in August and September of 1957. In contrast, she got back her rejected manuscript of poems from the Yale Younger Poets competition.

Sylvia desperately wanted to write during those weeks on Cape Cod, but she was dissatisfied with what she was doing: "not touching on my deep self." The days went on, adding to her litany of guilt. Either she spent too long in the sun and lost her energy, or she wrote badly and was even more disappointed in herself. Aurelia and Warren came for several visits, and she hid the real state of her work from them. Panic was setting in; the summer was going fast.

To make matters worse, Sylvia's menstrual period was two weeks late. From late July to August 8, she was sure she was pregnant—and the plans she had made for the two of them, to be able to write and live without responsibilities until they had been successful, were ruined. As she wrote in retrospect,

> I have never in my life, except that deadly summer of 1953 and fall, gone through such a black lethal two weeks. I couldn't write a word about it, although I did in my head. The horror, day by day more sure, of being pregnant. Remembering my growing casualness about contraception, as if it couldn't happen to me then: clang, clang, one door after another banged shut with the overhanging terror which, I know now, would end me, probably Ted, and our writing and our possible impregnable togetherness.

Pregnant, Sylvia would not be able to teach the year at Smith.

She described as well "crying sessions in the doctor's office, the blood test Sunday, in avalanches of rain and thunder, riding the streaming roads, up to our knees on our bikes in the dips filling inch by inch with rainwater, drenched to the skin." Already the pattern of Sylvia's taking responsibility for their lives is obvious, another kind of burden that would unbalance and slant the ledger for the rest of the marriage. Her hysteria, her guilt, suggests that she thought Ted had no part in the problem —whereas his own view of the matter was quite different. He thought he was being as helpful and responsible as she expected. Once Sylvia had been tested for pregnancy, her period started. What was harder to erase was the deep anger she felt at the end of the summer—toward the loss of her writing opportunities, toward Ted for not assuming what she saw as his share of the household burden, but most of all toward herself for allowing these all-too-human things to happen.

10
Marriage in America

1957-59

"I Boarded Your Arc"

Ted and Sylvia were lucky to find a three-room apartment at 337 Elm Street in Northampton, less than a mile from the Smith campus. Owned by a local police officer and his young wife, the third floor of the house had been remodeled into an apartment with its own back stairway and private entrance. The $85-a-month flat had a large bedroom and living room, and a smaller dining-room–study with no windows. The owners left the Hugheses to their quiet life, though the wives occasionally discussed recipes.

During the first semester, Ted wrote at the apartment most of the time. He was experimenting with radio drama and writing for children. His part-time teaching job at the University of Massachusetts, a few miles away in Amherst, would not begin until spring term. In late September, his collection *The Hawk in the Rain* came out, to good reviews and some invitations to read. *Sewanee Review* and *The New Yorker* accepted Ted's new poems, and *Jack and Jill* his children's stories.

For Sylvia, returning to Smith meant an even busier schedule than she remembered from her student days. Coming back was hardly a triumph; no one much noticed her and once she had been given the syllabus for the freshman course, she was on her own. Mary Ellen Chase had retired. Her former professors seemed less friendly than they had been when she was a student. Depressed by her interpretation of her reception, she wrote in her journal on October 1,

> I am middling good. And I can live being middling good. I do not have advanced degrees, I do not have books published. I do not have teaching experience. . . . I must face this image of myself . . . and not freeze myself into a quivering jelly because I am not Mr. Fisher or Miss Dunn or any of the others.

To Warren, she called herself "the returned and inadequate heroine of the Smith campus."

Sylvia's students, however, thought otherwise. To them, she was dramatic, beautiful, glamorous, with long hair and different dangling earrings each day. She read poetry aloud wonderfully, and her performance in front of a class was enhanced because of her reputation as a Smith woman, a star who had studied at Cambridge and married a British poet. She and Ted were invited by students to houses for dinner. They were the Smith poets, along with Anthony Hecht, Marie Borroff, and Paul Roche, a British poet and translator who was teaching at Smith for a second year.

Sylvia's colleagues, too, thought she was enjoying her teaching. The younger faculty—Marlies Kallmann, Wendell Johnson, Joan Bramwell, among others—saw her as a favored alumna and were relatively cool about making advances to her. Sylvia was also married and therefore less free to be friends with other faculty women who were still single—or so they thought. One day in the middle of fall term, Sylvia asked Marlies whether she might sit in on a class that Kallmann was teaching; she felt that she was having trouble getting students to participate. That was the only indication anyone had that Sylvia was worried about her teaching, and she told Marlies afterward that she had learned a great deal and that she felt much better.

Like most freshman English courses of the 1950s, the program at Smith combined literature with writing. Dostoevsky's *Crime and Punishment* was a standard novel, as was James Joyce's *A Portrait of the Artist As a Young Man*. The bewildered freshmen struggled hard with William James's *The Varieties of Religious Experience*. Short stories by Henry James, Hawthorne, Joyce, Faulkner, and D. H. Lawrence; an anthology of poetry, much of it modern; and plays from Seneca to Ibsen were some of the texts Sylvia had her students read. Each class met three times a week, either Monday-Tuesday-Wednesday or Thursday-Friday-Saturday. Sylvia's classes met at the end of the week so she had Monday, Tuesday, and Wednesday free. Each writing assignment, however, meant that she would have seventy themes to read, and every third week a new stack of papers appeared on her dining room table.

She was bothered less by the work of teaching than by its performance aspect. She quickly came to realize that it was not enough to love literature and to be interested in students; the expert teacher controlled the classroom and the students' responses every minute. Teaching was difficult for Sylvia, who called herself "a being who gets tired, has shyness to fight, has more trouble than most facing people easily." Temperamentally, she was not a teacher. Every interaction with students was draining, and when she had to discipline one of the women, she anguished over the case for days. As an October journal entry recounted, "could not sleep, although tired, and lay feeling my nerves shaved to a pin and the groaning inner voice: oh, you can't teach, can't do anything. Can't write, can't think. . . ."

Outside the classroom, other events also affected Sylvia, most notably the suicide of a freshman found in the woods near Paradise Pond on November 7. The woman had hanged herself, supposedly because of either a pregnancy or an abortion. Later that fall, according to the Smith newspaper, *The Sophian*, there were other attempted suicides. When Sylvia was writing *The Bell Jar*, she used the paper's account of the 1957 suicide as her model for the death in the novel.

Meanwhile, the Smith English Department disappointed Sylvia. During faculty meetings, she discovered that some people she had previously admired were less than perfect. The inevitable squabbles over petty matters, which mark most academic departmental discussions, were unexpectedly revealing. Sylvia came to see the teaching profession as less noble than she had thought and quickly decided that she did not want to continue teaching.

In the autumn, Ted broke his foot getting up suddenly from a chair. Sylvia was reasonably healthy until mid-December when she was struck by the flu, which had reached epidemic proportions on campus. Later, she developed pneumonia and was in bed for more than two weeks. Her illness cost her the holiday break, time she had planned to use to prepare for second semester courses, and it left her depressed because she was now not only weak and ill but behind in preparation. Her list of things to feel guilty about grew longer. She worried about "owing" people socially, and planned countless dinner parties for the Roches, the Hechts, and others. Most of them never materialized. She worried about preparing for her own courses and that of Newton Arvin—a class in Hawthorne, James, and Melville—which she was to grade papers for. (She thought the extra grading would pay $300, but the fee was only $100, which disappointed her.) She worried about household duties and cooking, about Ted, and about her own writing. She had no time to do anything creative. She resented the fact that Ted did have that time.

Recovering from pneumonia at her mother's home in Welles-ley, where she and Ted had been headed when she was taken sick, Sylvia realized that she could not teach a second year at Smith. She was exhausted; she was in worse physical and mental shape than she had been as a student. She was not happy—she was not happy teaching and, as she told friends, if she could not write, nothing else seemed meaningful. She wrote to Warren about her decision to give up the Smith job, hoping he would break the news to Aurelia. Sylvia knew her mother would think she was foolish to quit the post, but, as she explained, she and Ted hoped to rent a small apartment on Beacon Hill in Boston and write, "me part time and Ted full time" for the year. Then, on the basis of that year's manuscripts, they would try for grants. Sylvia knew now how important writing was to her. She was becoming so jealous of Ted's writing time that she complained about having to vacuum the rug under his desk because he threw down scraps of paper as he wrote. She still affirmed that Ted was "This one I have chosen and am forever wedded to," but she found it easy to forget the Saturday afternoons they spent napping and making love, their walks gathering pine boughs and watching animals, their shared writing exercises and reading, and their excitement when the mail arrived.

Back at Smith after her illness, Sylvia continued to slide behind. She grew increasingly angry about teaching, about the quantity of time it took. By February, she had insomnia: "I've been through the worst, the hells of explaining snippets of ambiguous, ambivalent William James on 3 days and nights of no-sleep. . . . Tonight I shall manage dinner for 5 and coffee for an extra 2 with ease." Her journal entries are less angry than they are guilty, however, even when she describes herself doing the clearing up alone, "elbow-deep in last night's dishes." She implies that if she were somehow better, she would be able to manage everything. She berates herself: "married gold ring, heels, silk stockings, hair up: how I confront myself and disbelieve. I am again behind, cramming: only till next weekend, then the next." Sylvia seemed to believe she was a fraud, that Sylvia Plath Hughes the teacher was really Sylvia Plath the student. Worse, the world would soon discover that fact.

At times she cajoled herself into believing that such unremitting work was good for her (there are many echoes of the Plath family philosophy here). As she wrote after a dinner party for Ellie Friedman and her husband,

> Work redeems. Work saves. Baked a lemon meringue pie, cooled lemon custard and crust on cold bathroom windowsill. . . . Set table, candles, glasses sparkling crystal. . . . Making orders. Shaping a meal, people, I grew back to joy.

But more often, she described her life as "a grim grind." She wrote, "I deserve a year, two years, to live my own self into being."

Depressing as the Massachusetts winter had been, spring brought vacation time and a miraculous flowering: Sylvia wrote eight good poems. During break, she scarcely stopped to do anything else. She felt revitalized. She could sleep, her "back quirk" was better. During spring term, however, she and Ted disagreed more often and, tired from the year and anxious for the term to end, Sylvia lost what little tact she had. They disagreed about money, about their future plans (should they move to Boston in June or wait until September? should they return to England?) and about their professional lives. Sylvia had felt only disapproval from the older faculty when she decided to give up her teaching post at Smith, and it was hard for her to withstand the pressure. She sensed that her colleagues thought that she had let down the very people who had gotten her the position, Miss Chase and Mr. Davis. It was also hard to relinquish the security of another year's good pay.

While Sylvia was a fledgling teacher, Ted was a published and sought-after poet. He gave a reading at Harvard in the spring, followed by a houseparty in Boston, given by Jack and Moira Sweeney; and he read the part of Creon in the Smith College presentation of Paul Roche's translation of *Oedipus*. Sylvia and he disagreed over whether she should come to hear the staged reading. She did; he seemed displeased. Then on the day she taught her last classes of the year, she had arranged for Ted to meet her both before the last class and after it, to celebrate. He failed to meet her as arranged and later, according to her account, she found him coming up the road from Paradise Pond with a student. Furious, she accused him of being like all men—faithless. She deserved different treatment, better treatment, she wrote. She had given him all her trust and love, not to mention money. Perhaps the last item was the most difficult for her. As she wrote angrily in her journal, "I have served a purpose, spent money, Mother's money, which hurts most, to buy him clothes, to buy him a half year, eight months of writing." Ted's protestations of innocence only added to her fury. Then, after a fight complete with physical injury to each, everything was all right once more, wrote Sylvia. But as her journal entries record, Sylvia was developing a good deal of resentment toward Ted.

Summer was slow, relaxed, and—for Ted—productive. Everything he wrote was good. Summer vacation began with five wonderful days in New York. Ted and Sylvia had dinners with Ted's publishers and went to parties and visited Oscar

Williams, Marianne Moore, Babette Deutsch, and other literary acquaintances. They celebrated their second wedding anniversary in Wellesley, and then Sylvia read for a Harvard Library recording of her poetry. (She had earlier done a recording for the Library of Congress.) And then home to 337 Elm Street in Northampton, where the most appealing feature of their location was Child's Park, the small natural area that adjoined the house. She wrote to her sister-in-law, Olwyn, that she and Ted were thriving, and that they were working out a plan to somehow clear the next five years for writing. Political as always, Sylvia asked Olwyn to tell her more about De Gaulle, who had just founded the Fifth Republic in France.

Her tranquil tone in her letters, however, is contradicted by her anguished journal entries. Filled with the anxiety that attacked her whenever she had time to write (was she "good enough" to be a writer? should she be doing something to make money instead of trying to write?), she sank into her doldrums. Ted's analysis was that Sylvia had gone to school for twenty years and that without that external structure she was apprehensive. Ted seldom had such worries. He judged his work by whether or not it satisfied him; publication was secondary. For Sylvia, however, being unsure of her role as writer, publication was all-important. She marked her progress in the field by the places her work appeared. When *The New Yorker* accepted two of her new long poems in June (her first acceptance by that magazine), she was jubilant. Not only would the payment ($377) take care of several months' rent, but appearing in *The New Yorker* was one of her lifelong goals. She dreamed about the way her poems would look on the pages, and planned a strategy for placing fiction there as well.

In the next few weeks, *The Nation* and *Sewanee Review* accepted Sylvia's work, but she was already moving in a downward spiral. Her journal charts the decline: "I felt sicker and sicker. I couldn't happily be anything but a writer and I couldn't be a writer. I couldn't even set down one sentence: I was paralyzed with fear, with deadly hysteria." "Paralysis still with me." "My mind is barren. . . ."

She spent her free summer time avoiding chances to write. She rescued a dying bird and allowed its struggle for life to occupy a week of their time, night and day. Finally Ted gassed the bird—and Sylvia wrote of its being "composed, perfect and beautiful in death"—and they buried it with ceremony. Sylvia visited her old friend Ruth Freeman Geissler and envied her her three young children. She wrote a few poems she thought good enough to be included in a collection she was putting together ("Owl," "Lorelei," "Whiteness I Remember") and thought about prose, which now seemed incredibly difficult to her. Her lethargy wore on, accompanied by intermittent high fevers, into the fall. Even after she and Ted moved to Suite 61, 9 Willow Street, in the Beacon Hill area of Boston, Sylvia could not shake her depression.

Moving to Boston was a part of Sylvia's plan to surround Ted with the best of the American literary world. He had been bored in Northampton, impatient with what he saw as the parochial concerns of the Smith College faculty. Surely Boston—where, in Adrienne Rich's words, "the world of literary celebrity and success was deeply meshed with that other world of Boston, old money and Harvard"—would be more interesting to them both. Sylvia knew some of Boston's literati; Jack and Moira Sweeney had entertained after Ted's Harvard reading, their apartment full of Picassos and Matisses, overlooking Boston Common. The back of Beacon Hill—Boston's Left Bank or Greenwich Village —was the ideal place for two young, ambitious writers. And the tiny two-room apartment had two bay windows, one for each of them to write in. Sylvia loved the light, the quiet, and the sixth-floor view of the river.

But writing was the reason Sylvia and Ted had moved to Boston, and once again, Sylvia was blocked. She tried writing on the hoard of pink memo paper she had purposely taken from Smith to write her novel on. She set aside regular times for writing and other times for reading and studying languages. She pushed herself, cajoled herself, argued with herself—and worried about money. The plan for the year had become that Ted would take a full-time job, but he saw no reason to look for work. He was confident that they could live on their incomes from writing. He had applied for a Saxton grant, but that funding was administered by his publisher, Harper & Row, and he was therefore ineligible. He also applied for a Guggenheim fellowship but that funding—if he were fortunate enough to win the award—would not begin until the next summer. It was Sylvia, not Ted, who claimed to feel the pressure of financial responsibility, and toward the end of September she applied for a part-time job. As she wrote in her journal, she panicked. She wanted to write, but she also felt compelled to have a "real" job, to live in a world where people worked at things they might not care about doing. Even though Ted had just received a check for $150 along with an $850 prize for his poem "The Thought Fox," Sylvia felt more comfortable having a regular job. She took work transcribing the dreams of patients, and acting as receptionist and general office clerk, in the psychiatric clinic of Massachusetts General Hospital.

Her job there put her in contact again with Myron Lotz. After his year at Oxford, Lotz had finished medical school at Yale and was now interning at Mass. General. Sylvia, of course, was delighted to see him and invited him and his fiancée for dinner. She served a traditional Boston seafood meal, which Mike raved about. He and Sylvia reminisced warmly; Ted seemed uneasy. When Mike teased his date about being so conventional, wanting to cook and keep house, Ted roused himself from a long silence to ask, "And what is so bad about that?"

After Mike and his date left, Sylvia and Ted repeated their argument from June. Each was capable of a powerful jealousy. Early in the summer, Sylvia had written, "I have a violence in me that is hot as death-blood. I can kill myself or—I know it now—even kill another." Ted insisted that they spend the night at a hotel, implying that Sylvia had somehow defiled the apartment, and their argument raged to such violence that the hotel-room furnishings were damaged, according to an account Sylvia gave to a friend years later.

Although Sylvia recognized her sexual jealousies, she may not have realized her literary ones. As her journals show all too clearly, she became sick—either depressed or physically ill or both—whenever she and Ted were both writing full time. As in their early months in Boston, working outside the apartment seemed to be her solution, but Sylvia soon quit what she referred to as her "amusing" job at Mass. General. Being in those surroundings surely took her back to the fall of 1953, when she was a ward patient there. But the position had at least helped to rid her of what she had for several years called her "panic bird," a state which froze her and kept her from any kind of profitable writing or living. At Mass. General, most of the patients had worse panics, and knowing their histories was in some ways a help to Sylvia, who wrote, "I feel my whole sense and understanding of people being deepened and enriched."

Back in the apartment to write, however, Sylvia became depressed again. She knew she needed help. In early December, she secretly began seeing Ruth Beuscher, her therapist from McLean. As she wrote on December 12, "If I am going to pay money for her time & brain as if I were going to a supervision in life & emotions & what to do with both, I am going to work like hell, question, probe sludge & crap & allow myself to get the most out of it." She was again working on the problem of her relationship with her parents, and after weeks of work with Beuscher Sylvia found that she could accept the situation she was left in when her father died. Beuscher helped her see that she could simultaneously love and pity her mother on the one hand, and also resent her for the attitudes about sexuality and work that Sylvia had come to mistrust. She was finally able to mourn her father's death, and to trace her suspicion of men— and her conviction that they would eventually leave her—to the early abandonment of her father's death.

She also realized how guilty she felt about disappointing her mother and all her benefactors and the other "mother figures" in her life: Mary Ellen Chase, Olive Higgins Prouty, Mildred Norton, Mrs. Lameyer, and other of her mother's friends. She concluded resentfully, "I get very sad about not doing what everybody and all my white-haired old mothers want in their old age." Her various mothers also represented the society that she felt expected her, and Ted, to work for financial gain, "The Writer and Poet is excusable only if he is Successful. Makes Money."

Within a week after she began therapy with Beuscher, Sylvia wrote "Johnny Panic and the Bible of Dreams," one of her best stories. In this fantasy about a hospital typist who becomes a dream connoisseur, she wrote in natural-sounding, humorous prose. The year before, when she had been reading a great deal of Woolf and Lawrence, she had asked in her journal, "What is my voice?" She then had answered, "Woolfish, alas, but tough. Please, tough." The Johnny Panic story is told in a slangy, tough woman's voice. It was a breakthrough in fiction to a recognizable artistic voice that Sylvia had not yet made in her poetry, and she wrote five more stories during the spring of 1959, each one a success.

After Christmas, which Ted and Sylvia celebrated with Mrs. Plath at their apartment, Sylvia got a tiger kitten with green eyes, which she named Sappho. She was spending more time with female friends—afternoons with Shirley Norton, Perry's wife, playing with the Norton baby and braiding rag rugs; having lunch with Norma Farber; entertaining Marcia Brown and her husband, Elizabeth Hardwick and Robert Lowell, the Philip Booths, Adrienne Rich and her husband, and others. Sylvia asked Rich, whose children were small, whether she thought a woman could both write and bring up children—to which Rich answered, "Yes, but it's hellishly difficult." Rich's sense of Sylvia at that time was that she was Ted's wife first, and a poet only after that. Charles Doyle, a young Australian poet who visited the Hugheses at the suggestion of Lowell, remembered Sylvia's cooking a chicken dinner, clearing and washing dishes, and then sitting in the living room where Doyle and Hughes were discussing their poems. As Doyle recalls, "Nothing was said about her poetry. I didn't know she was a poet."

In early spring, Sylvia wrote in her journal that men interested her less and less. What she found fascinating was "women and women-talk." At the same time, her marriage was evolving into a more traditional coupling, and less a partnership between two writers. Sylvia began thinking of Ted as the breadwinner, while he in turn berated her—sometimes publicly—for failing to sew on buttons or mend his clothes. It was an unsettling winter and spring, and any dissension between them was especially painful coming as it did while Sylvia was, in her therapy, reliving her father's abandonment of her through his death.

She often experienced immense grief, crying her way through sessions with Beuscher (her poem "The Ravaged Face" was written after one of these). She was indecisive at times, unable to make up her mind about getting her hair cut, about studying toward a Ph.D. in psychology, about whether to entertain. Then on March 9, 1959, she visited her father's grave on Azalea Path in the Winthrop Cemetery. Calling it "a depressing sight," she described its location "on a flat grassy area looking across a sallow barren stretch to rows of wooden tenements." The stone, marked *Otto E. Plath: 1885–1940*, was beside a path, likely to be walked over. Plath continued, "Felt cheated. My temptation to dig him up. To prove he existed and really was dead. How far gone would he be? No trees, no peace, his headstone jammed up against the body on the other side. Left shortly. It is good to have the place in mind." The terse description shows the power of her unexpressed grief. The visit—her first in nearly twenty years since her father's death—was crucial to resolving that relationship.

Later in the spring, Sylvia took another part-time job, this time as secretary to the head of the Sanskrit Department at Harvard. She relearned speedwriting and took comfort in the regularity of her hours and duties. She also was reading widely: Freud, Faulkner, Tolstoi, Ainu tales, the Bible (especially the Book of Job), lives of saints. She was fascinated by accounts of St. Thérèse, who was sanctifed after receiving visits from the Virgin. Sylvia's notes include a long description of Thérèse's many influenzalike illnesses with high fevers, her hatred of the cold, her fears before the visitations—tribulations which had echoes in Plath's own life. They also include a description of the earlier St. Teresa, who founded the Discalced (barefooted) Carmelite order in sixteenth-century Spain, and the nuns' early rising, fasting, meditation, and consistent gaiety (and Teresa's own pragmatic wit and stability).

During her years in America, Plath moved in her extensive reading between the established great works of literature and philosophy to the very new. She devoured existential playwrights such as Ionesco and Beckett, and during the summer of 1959 read two novels that she liked a great deal—Philip Roth's *Goodbye, Columbus* and J. D. Salinger's *Seymour: An Introduction*. She loved their terse humor and rapid pace, and laughed aloud at both books. Most important of all, she began to appear at

Robert Lowell's Boston University poetry workshop, where many young Boston writers gathered on Tuesday afternoons for several hours.

In 1959, Robert Lowell was regarded as America's most prominent younger poet. His taut, involuted early writing was influential, and he had begun his own process of breaking out of the tightly-structured lyrics in a new book, *Life Studies*, which would be published later that year. (Ted had previously given Sylvia a copy of Lowell's *Lord Weary's Castle*.) Kathleen Spivack had come to Boston from Ohio so that she might study with Lowell, and such poets as Stephen Sandy, Don Junkins, Henry Braun, Steve Berg, Anne Sexton, and George Starbuck were already in the class. Sylvia had an additional reason to be interested in Lowell's work: he was the victim of frequent breakdowns.

She found his teaching style more disconcerting than helpful, however. He taught by shifting part of his authority to the workshop members, but at the same time he was encouraging their participation, he continuously probed, "What does this mean?" To Lowell, there were "major" and "minor" categories of poets and poems, and the workshop students often remained silent rather than offer a judgment Lowell might disagree with.

Because Sylvia was more accustomed to the teacher as an authority figure, she was never entirely comfortable in Lowell's class. Sometimes she appeared, in Junkins' words, "mousy, almost totally silent." Other times, as Kathleen Spivack remembered her, she was curt and businesslike. " 'Reminds me of Empson,' she might drawl as a student's poem was handed around the table. Or she might cite a more obscure poet, out of another century." Sylvia was less the warm-hearted fellow student than she was the erudite somewhat older writer, and her relationships with younger students in the workshop were never close.

But there was a student in Lowell's workshop to whom Plath was drawn—talkative, vivacious Anne Sexton. A comparative novice to poetry (and to writing classes), Sexton did not have to unlearn all the rules that Plath was laboring under in 1959. Sexton was a fashionable and attractive suburban wife whose breakdown following the births of her daughters was the subject of some of her poems. She attracted Sylvia both because of her outspoken comments in class and because of their similar life experiences. Sylvia identified with what Sexton wrote; she also admired her innovative techniques. "You, Dr. Martin," a poem written to an analyst, was one of Sexton's workshop poems that Sylvia admired greatly. During workshop sessions, Sexton had also read "A Story for Rose," a poem about a woman as story teller, and her long sequence poem, "The Double Image." Plath's long years of conservative poetic training tumbled down. It took some months before she could discover a poetic direction for her work as satisfying as Sexton's was for her. Sexton's poetry and friendship were resources Sylvia could find nowhere else—not even at home, because the imagery and subjects of Ted's poems were remote from Plath. Sexton was already aware of her special province as a woman poet, and in that respect she influenced Sylvia as no male poet could.

After class, Plath, Sexton, and George Starbuck drove in Sexton's old Ford to the Ritz bar for martinis. Sexton parked her car in the Ritz's loading zone, shouting, when challenged, that it was all right for her to park there because the three of them were going to get loaded. Sylvia enjoyed every minute of it. Once in the red plush lounge, they huddled around the small table, eating dish after dish of free potato chips, talking poetry. Sometimes the two women discussed suicide. Then they all went to a cheap supper at the Waldorf Cafeteria.

Of all the many writers in the Boston area, Sexton most interested Sylvia. She took Ted to a meeting of the New England Poetry Club, which met monthly at the elegant Beacon Hill mansion of Mrs. Fiske Warren, so that he could hear Sexton and Maxine Kumin read their poems. Kumin (who, with Sexton, privately referred to Ted as Ted Huge) thought, "There was something very cleancut and lovely about Sylvia with her schoolgirlish good looks and long hair and very open and level way with people." And Sexton, too, although she did not at the time like most of Plath's poems, did like her—her shyly defiant manner, her sense of being someone, her intensity. Without a great deal of conversation, Sexton and Plath were good friends. They shared attitudes, knowledge, and experiences. They were women in a man's field, but they were confident in their aesthetic direction. They had both tested the line between death and life and had come back wiser. In the spring of 1959, Sylvia was in therapy with Beuscher, and Sexton was using analysis to help her face the deaths of both parents within a few months of each other.

In May, Sylvia's book of poems, which she now titled *The Bull of Bendylaw*, was chosen the alternate to the winner of the Yale Younger Poets contest. (Plath's book was eventually published in 1960.) She was disappointed not to win, especially when Dudley Fitts, who was judging the competition, wrote that she had missed "by a whisper." When she discovered that the winner was fellow poetry student George Starbuck, whose work she thought imitative and immature, she was furious. She raged to Fitts in her journal that he was wrong about what he called her "lack of technical finish," that the flaw in her poems was the opposite—too much finish. Sylvia found writing in formal patterns easy. What was hard was discovering the true life of the poem inside its technical scaffolding. Angry as she was, she knew her current poems did not do her ability or her vision justice, and she promised herself to work harder. Meanwhile, Sexton's first poem collection, *To Bedlam and Part Way Back*, had been accepted by Houghton Mifflin. Sylvia took pride in her friend's success, but she wanted it for herself as well.

As the year in Boston closed, Sylvia was productive. She wrote three of her best stories, "Sweetie Pie and the Gutter Men," "Above the Oxbow," and "This Earth Our Hospital," the latter drawn from her Mass. General stint, written with humor and compassion. She also finished a children's story, *The Bed Book*. *The New Yorker* took two more poems. She and Ted had decided to return to England to live, but before they returned, they planned to spend the fall at Yaddo, the upstate New York artists' and writers' colony, and during the summer they were taking a cross-country trip, driving Aurelia's car. Their leaving in June helped to bring to a close Sylvia's therapy with Ruth Beuscher. As she wrote at the time, "A happier sense of life, not hectic, but very slow and sure, than I have ever had. The sea, calm, with sun bland on it. Containing and receiving all the reefy narrow straits in its great reservoir of peace." No longer blocked by the Panic Bird, Sylvia was on her way to creating one of the most striking voices in contemporary literature.

11

The Colossus and Other Poems

1960

"A Dawn of Cornflowers"

Sylvia and Ted's cross-country trip in the summer of 1959 was a complete success. Months of hard work and financial worries fell away. They both loved the outdoors, the gorgeous scenery, the freedom of being on the road. Before they had left Boston, a gynecological examination had showed that Sylvia did not ovulate regularly, and she was depressed because her doctor had told her that becoming pregnant might be difficult. On the trip, however, Sylvia did become pregnant, and her suspicion that she was added to the happiness of the travel.

Returning to Aurelia's home in Wellesley, they stored many of their books and, on September 9, left for Yaddo. Sylvia told her mother that she thought she was pregnant, but she felt good so she did not see a doctor to confirm her condition.

Yaddo, in Saratoga Springs, New York, was beautiful, maintaining all the elegance it had had as a private estate—rose gardens, marble statuary, goldfish ponds, small lakes, woodland walks, and a greenhouse that fascinated Sylvia, who was reading Theodore Roethke's poems about the Michigan greenhouse he had worked in as a boy. The buildings were scrupulously cared for, decorated with valuable paintings and art objects.

Perhaps as important to Sylvia as Yaddo's physical beauty was the fact that she was well cared for. Meals were tasty, and served in a central dining room so that—for the first time in over three years—she did not have to shop, cook, or clean. Breakfast was served between 8:00 and 9:00 in the dining room; box lunches were available for the noon meal; and the guests met again for dinner. After that meal, guests went to each other's rooms to socialize or returned to their work. Being at Yaddo gave Sylvia the professional standing that she sometimes lacked as Ted's wife. As she wrote her mother, "I have never in my life felt so peaceful and as if I can read and think and write for about seven hours a day. . . . I am so happy we can work apart, for that is what we've really needed." Their bedroom was on the first floor of West House and Sylvia's studio was on the third. Ted's study was out in the woods, heated with a wood stove and surrounded with pines.

Sonia Raiziss, editor of *Chelsea* magazine and a poet and translator, thought that Sylvia and Ted's relationship was complex. Sylvia usually walked a bit behind Ted, she observed, "content to be there and almost secretively pleased with the status and circumstance of their attention—like a double billing." According to Raiziss, Sylvia's manner was one of "wry trustfulness" and she exuded a sense of satisfaction. Pauline Hanson, acting director of Yaddo at the time, remembered that both Sylvia and Ted were innately gracious, but that Sylvia said very little. Her chief pleasures were those things that pleased Ted (a dessert of crepes, maple syrup, sour cream and red caviar, for example). Modest and unassuming, she was happy to be at Yaddo and appreciative of its beauties.

Above all, at Yaddo Sylvia and Ted were the *young* writers. In contrast to the slacks and businesslike skirts of older women, Sylvia wore Bermuda shorts and short skirts. She and Ted rowed on the lake, took long walks, and after dinner visited Raiziss, Malcolm Cowley, the novelist Charles Bell, and composers Gordon Binkerd and Chou Wen-Chung. Late in their stay, May Swenson joined the group and described meeting

Sylvia, who was in bed in West House. In Swenson's words, it was late afternoon,

> already almost dark under the pine boughs outside their windows. A standing lamp was lit beside the bed in which Sylvia sat against pillows. A long-limbed, good-looking girl with blond hair worn to her shoulders, she looked languid and morose. There were books on the bed, and a cleared lunch tray being used as a desk held papers and a pen.

Usually Sylvia gave an impression of energy, sometimes directed, sometimes frustrated. Yet these were the months when Ted hypnotized her so that she could sleep, months when he made lists of possible subjects for her to write poems about—months of anxiety as real as any she had known before, even in the midst of her contentment about being pregnant. During her eleven weeks at Yaddo, Sylvia's moods fluctuated from recurring depression to calm tranquility.

The difference between Sylvia's polished outward manner and her inward anxiety shows again in the discrepancies between her letters home and her private journals. To Aurelia she described the marvelous food and scenery, and her poetry reading in September. But in her journals she wrote at length about her nightmares ("Full of them. Keep them to myself or I'll drive the world morbid"); her depression ("The old fall disease"); her anxiety ("Would getting a degree help me? Where is my willpower?"). Simultaneously, she was noting exciting things she had read—Roethke's poems, Jean Stafford's and Eudora Welty's stories, and, most important, those stories read aloud so she could "feel on my tongue what I admire."

Despite Sylvia's emotional uncertainties, she grew as a poet. After all her years of study, and her workshop experience with Lowell and Sexton, Sylvia possessed a great deal of knowledge about writing. She knew what she liked and she knew what would be useful to her own work. From that perspective, she admired Eudora Welty's remarkable ability to write in the voices of different characters, and Shirley Jackson's *The Bird's Nest*, a novel about psychosis in a young woman character, gave her important ideas that helped her in thinking about *The Bell Jar*.

Yaddo came at the perfect moment in Sylvia's development as a writer. She turned twenty-seven there, an occasion which Polly Hanson celebrated with *vin rosé* for everyone and a cake with candles. Sylvia could see that her writing was coming to fruition, after those years of work and study, and she was beginning to be as pleased with her poems as she was with the stories she had written the previous spring in Boston. Her journal is filled with admonitions to herself that she write in a more natural voice, that she open her experience like a wound and "then invent on the drop of a feather, a whole multicolored bird." She warned herself not to write by formula, but to use her writing as a voyage of discovery, to find by writing what was important about her experiences.

These were also months of trying Ted's exercises: deep-breathing, concentration on objects. Hypnosis was another way of reaching remote layers of consciousness; it was practiced by both Ted and Sylvia. Late in her Yaddo stay, Sylvia wrote in her journal that she had written two poems that pleased her, "Different. Weirder. I see a picture, a weather, in these poems." And in a later entry she admonished herself "to be honest with what I know and have known. To be true to my own weirdnesses."

One of the changes in Plath's work at Yaddo was the use of more colloquial, even slangy, language as a way to get rid of the sound of what she called "drawing room" speech. She wanted a voice that was witty, wry, American, brazen, arrogant and, at times, comic—like those of Welty, Roth, and Salinger. One of her frustrations at Yaddo was that she had already completed several versions of a poem collection, and her new poems were not going to fit into it. At Ted's suggestion, she began a new book (for which she did not have a publisher), calling it *The Colossus* after a poem she wrote at Yaddo, which she considered little and humorous.

The poem "The Colossus" is apparently about Sylvia's father, pictured as the ruin of a huge statue, over which the daughter crawls as she tries to repair it. The poem draws on imagery she had often used to refer to boyfriends, Mike Lotz and Ted among them. It describes Ouija board sessions in which her father was called "colossus" or "Prince Otto," as well as Sylvia's impression of the Elgin marbles and the many Egyptian colossi in the British Museum. Her tone of wry chagrin is clear from the start: "I shall never get you put together entirely / Pieced, glued, and properly jointed."

As the poet mends the statue, she regards it as an oracle, the source of wisdom she desperately needs but cannot quite understand:

> Thirty years now I have labored
> To dredge the silt from your throat.
> I am none the wiser.

The language is reminiscent of Sexton's; the comic yet matter-of-fact voice, the touches of absurdity, give the poem a more humorous tone than its subject would suggest. "The Colossus" is an important departure for Plath.

The book titled *The Colossus and Other Poems* contains many finished and expert poems. "Full Fathom Five," "Moonrise," and "Lorelei" are related poems in which Plath's language is both deft and surprising. They show her admiration for Wallace Stevens and her effort to apply his principle that the poet should mesmerize through language. In the new poems, word by patient word, Plath lets the poem go where it will; "Blue Moles" is a good example of her exploration. "The Disquieting Muses" and "Point Shirley" are tapestries of memory about mothers and grandmothers; "Medallion" is a stream-of-consciousness description of a dead snake; and "Mushrooms" is the first of her three-line-stanza poems that move rapidly, connected more often by images than by narrative.

Ted Hughes and others—Plath's college roommates among them—have given us the familiar image of Sylvia writing poems, sitting with the heavy, red-covered thesaurus that was her father's open on her lap, consulting it frequently. But as early as 1956, even before she had met Hughes, Sylvia had begun trying to write poems that spoke more colloquially. She had come to think of the poet as song-maker, not as scholar with her head buried in books. Plath did not break the thesaurus habit overnight but in 1959 she was working much more orally, listening to the language of the poem to see whether it was the language of speech. She was choosing her "book poems," those that would appear in her current collection, as much for the ease and naturalness of their language as for their subject matter.

Subject matter was an important consideration, but Sylvia at this point seemed unclear about what appropriate subjects for poems were. Because she relied so heavily on lists that Ted made up for her of subjects that he would consider possible writing topics, she was screened off from her own primary interests. Many of the poems she had written since her marriage were as much exercises as the poems she had written for college classes. In fact, many of the poems that Sylvia left out of *The Colossus* collection were among her best. They were also her most personal. For example, from her Yorkshire poems she chose to omit "The Snowman on the Moor," a narrative about a husband-wife argument; "Two Views of Withens," the Brontë country described first by a man and then a woman; and "November Graveyard," a poem about the Heptonstall cemetery where the Hughes family was buried. From her Boston poems, the more personal "Child's Park Stones" and "Electra on Azalea Path" were omitted. The latter poem particularly is important for its striking imagery and terse language, as well as because it tells directly some of Plath's early history—a possible suicide attempt after her father's death, her guilt over that death, and her attempt to remain a child so that she could escape any consequences. Rich with fragments of imagery that would later open into poems less hurried, "Electra on Azalea Path" is a marvel of mood. How Sylvia could have thought it unfinished is a mystery, especially when she included a much milder pastiche, "The Beekeeper's Daughter," which uses some of the same imagery to tell much the same story, but more obliquely.

Had Plath included some of the good poems she chose to omit, the reader of *The Colossus* as it was published in 1960 would have been better prepared for the culminating achievement of the seven-part "Poem for a Birthday." By far the most interesting and powerful poem Sylvia had written, it began as an exercise modeled after Sexton and Theodore Roethke (at Yaddo, Plath had been reading Roethke's sequences, "Words for the Wind" and "Meditations for an Old Woman"). Her own "Poem for a Birthday" combined history, clusters of strong and unexpected images, and haunting phrasing to create an exploration of the whole poetic self. Written in a childlike language reminiscent of Roethke, the poem included many of her dreams as she had recorded them in her journal, as well as images from Jung and Freud, and from Paul Radin's African folktales. Like Sexton's "The Double Image," her long poem about mothers and daughters, which Plath had discussed when Sexton read it in Lowell's workshop, Sylvia's "Poem for a Birthday" traces the poet's search for a mother's love. It also tells of her quest for the protection of a father and fuses the husband figure with that of the father. It recounts, usually in a surreal manner, details of Plath's childhood, her breakdown, her electroconvulsive shock treatments, her self-doubt, her marriage, and the problems of being female in midcentury America.

The Colossus and Other Poems was a varied and comparatively innovative collection, the fruit of four years of serious writing. Except for her Yaddo poems, nearly all the work had been published in good magazines. That the book carried as its title one of the Yaddo poems, and that it concluded with the major sequence "Poem for a Birthday," one of the last things Sylvia wrote at Yaddo, demonstrated that her fall experience at the writers' colony was crucial to her development as a poet.

It was a satisfied Sylvia who leaned against the rail of the *Queen Elizabeth* in December of 1959, pregnant with either Nicholas or Frieda Rebecca, the names she and Ted had chosen for their baby, luxuriating in a sense of accomplishment. She looked forward to living in England, although she hoped to have household help so she would not become, in her words, one of those English "drudges." She also, as she had told Polly Hanson, hoped to avoid the moors. Thoroughly American, Plath felt that agreeing to live in England was a kind of sacrifice on her part.

Sylvia and Ted spent the rest of December in Yorkshire. Olwyn was home from Paris for the holiday and she and a cousin, Vicky Farrar, spent hours playing cards with Ted and Sylvia. The weather was windy and rainy, especially unpleasant at the Heptonstall altitude, but they managed to get out for walks every day. They rested. Ted wrote and Sylvia typed his manuscripts and the final draft of her poem collection. She sometimes wondered whether their decision to move back to England had been wise, even though she knew that Ted would be happier there, and even though living in England as writers would be economically possible.

On January 2, 1960, they arrived in London for what they hoped would be only a few days of apartment hunting. They lived in a bed-and-breakfast place for $5 a day and began the search that Sylvia called "gruelling." Later they moved to an extra bedroom in the Bloomsbury flat belonging to Helga and Dan Huws, Ted's friends from *St. Botolph's Review*. There they had a central location in a picturesque part of London, and they also could cook. The search for a London flat was part of a depressing winter for Sylvia. As Ted recalled, "The December London gave her a bad shock—the cars seemed smaller and blacker and dingier than ever, sizzling through black wet streets. The clothes on the people seemed even grubbier than she remembered. . . ."

In some ways, apartment hunting showed Sylvia at her best. Both Dan and Helga Huws remember her energy, her readiness to start out early each day, her strategies for scouring the city, and her moments of happiness in the midst of the ordeal. Even when she was tired, Sylvia was good company, excited about Philip Larkin's poems in *The Less Deceived*, enthusiastic about teaching Helga to make Aurelia Schober's fish chowder. Sylvia would wrap herself in one of Helga's large aprons and chop and stir busily. After dinner, she usually wrote letters and talked with friends of Ted and the Huwses who stopped by.

Sylvia's living standards were still American. She wanted a flat that was modern, and she sometimes failed to appreciate the charm of traditional London housing. But she was grateful for the help Ted's friends gave them. Through the efforts of the American poet W. S. Merwin and his British wife Dido—a couple the Hugheses had met in Boston—Sylvia and Ted did find an unfurnished three-room flat at 3 Chalcot Square in the Primrose Hill area near Chalk Farm subway station. Sylvia was elated. The Merwins and Huwses helped them furnish the apartment, and the rent ($18 a week, gas and electricity extra) was reasonable. Even though the neighborhood was working class, filled with children and noise all day long, Sylvia described the location as a quiet square, overlooking a small green with benches and fence where mothers and children passed the day. The fact that she was only five minutes from beautiful Regent's Park, and near her doctors, a laundromat, and shops also impressed her.

Helga Huws remembers how hard Sylvia worked at cleaning the flat, even to scrubbing floorboards on her knees and sanding them. She was a relentless worker. Helga recalls, "Never—even when she was highly pregnant—did I see her sit down, hands in lap, just resting." Sylvia, by striking contrast, was surprised at her deep weariness and worried about the actual move. Her pregnancy had tired her beyond her expectations, and she was having trouble meeting the demands she was accustomed to making of herself. Ted did all the carrying up to the fourth floor, however, and a week after they had moved on February 1, Sylvia wrote to Aurelia about her "cheerful kitchen" filled with the smell of chicken stew and apfelkuchen. "Ted has just finished painting the living room walls white over the nice rough-textured linen paper. . . . We are going to have a lovely engraving of Isis from one of Ted's astrological books blown up to cover one of the side-wall panels."

Happy event followed happy event. On February 10, Sylvia signed a contract with William Heinemann Ltd. to publish *The Colossus and Other Poems*, the book manuscript she had submitted just a week earlier. Plans were for the book to appear in midfall. It seemed almost too easy. As she described the day (and herself "resplendent in black wool suit, black cashmere coat, fawn kidskin gloves from Paris [Olwyn's Christmas present] and matching calfskin bag [from Italy] . . . and of enormous and impressive size"), she signed the contract in the York Minster pub on Dean Street in Soho and then went with the publisher and Ted for a good lunch at a nearby Italian restaurant. A month earlier, she and Ted had lunched there, "homeless and cold and very grim." Things do improve, as Ted always told her. To remind Sylvia of the happy occasion, Ted bought for her the three-volume set of D. H. Lawrence's *Collected Poems*, which he inscribed, "February 10, 1960, London."

This was the beginning of a new phase in Sylvia's career as a writer. Just a few months earlier, she had written to Judith

Reutlinger, a New England acquaintance who had asked for a copy of her poem "Lament," that she had not yet published a book. She then added, "But I hope to manage this in a year or so if fates and editors are willing."

12

Babies and Bell Jars

1960-61

"The Old Dregs"

Despite her work on literary projects, most of Plath's energy and attention during the winter of 1960 were not going into her writing or publishing. Instead, she was preparing for motherhood. The most important news she sent home was information about her weight; her most interesting occupation was feeling the baby move. Listening to its heartbeat in early March was one of the high points of Sylvia's year.

From the time Ted and Sylvia had moved into their flat, various workmen were continuously on hand, remodeling the premises. After that work was finished, she and Ted settled in. They worked out a schedule whereby, for a time, each had one day a week in bed—being waited on, choosing menus, reading and writing, forgetting the outside world. Both were exhausted from the strain of coming to England, living out of suitcases, and spending nearly a month finding a flat. By late February, however, they began to take advantage of living in London, seeing movies and such plays as Ibsen's *Rosmersholm* and Brendan Behan's *The Hostage*. Both Ted and Sylvia loved Primrose Hill and the zoo in Regent's Park, and they took walks at night as well as during the day on the quiet streets.

Their move to London nearly coincided with the publication of *Lupercal*, Ted's second collection of poems (March 18 was the official publication date). His publishers, Faber & Faber, were also readying *Meet My Folks*, his children's book. On February 23, he received advance copies of *Lupercal*, which he took along for a poetry reading he was giving the next day at the Oxford Poetry Society. (He and Sylvia went to Oxford by train and, despite a cold rain, spent much of the day walking in the city.) On February 28, they went to a buffet dinner with the *St. Botolph's Review* editors—David and Barbara Ross, the Huwses, and Luke Myers, who was about to sail for New Orleans for the birth of his child. On March 1 Ted and Sylvia lunched at a Greek restaurant with Ted's editors, and the next day they had cocktails with John Lehmann, the editor of *London Magazine*, who had recently taken some of Sylvia's poems and her story about Mass. General, now titled "The Daughters of Blossom Street."

Even though she tried to keep up with a social life she thought was important to them as free-lance writers, Sylvia was increasingly tired in the last month of her pregnancy. She was also disappointed: she had written only one poem that she liked since moving to England. "You're," the series of metaphors describing the active child she was carrying, was little to show for three months' time. Her physical discomfort was also making her irritable. She insisted that she have the small apartment practically to herself. Number 3 Chalcot Square consisted of one small bedroom, a kitchen, a living room, and a bath. Like Ted, Sylvia felt physically inhibited by the tiny quarters, the narrow stairs, the low ceilings. Her weight was mounting toward 155 pounds. She used the living room as her study, leaving Ted to set up a card table in a small vestibule area as his workspace.

Sylvia's need for privacy is reflected in several of her letters home. In early March she wrote, "I really put my foot down about visitors now. I get tired easily and like the house to myself so I can cook, read, write or rest when I please. . . . I have no desire for people sleeping in my living room or causing me extra cooking or housework." A case in point was a London visit by Ted's sister Olwyn and her friend Janet Crosbie-Hill, who had been invited to the Hugheses' for lunch. Janet described the uncomfortable afternoon,

As Olwyn had spoken only with affection of both brother and sister-in-law, I was totally unprepared for the resentment our visit seemed to cause Sylvia. When, after a delayed and perfunctory lunch, W. S. Merwin arrived, Sylvia, who had been aggressively though quite uninterestingly rude hitherto, brightened visibly and offered Merwin the pleasure of taking herself and husband for a country run in his two-seater. This not materializing, there was a strained walk on Primrose Hill during which I was the unhappy witness of the sheer quantity of distress Sylvia was capable of causing her nearest and dearest. Her aggression was relentless and dominated the reactions of all present. Apologizing to me later, Olwyn attributed these astonishing effects to Sylvia's pregnancy.

This sort of scene, according to other observers, was not uncommon. Yet, inevitably, when Sylvia wrote home about an incident, she described her own long-suffering patience. Sylvia seemed to use her letters home to explain away her impolite behavior. It was as if her letters allowed her to fictionalize the real events of her life—Aurelia was far away and so she would never know the truth of Sylvia's stories.

Waiting for the baby to be born seemed interminable. But the wait brightened considerably when Ted won the Somerset Maugham Award for *The Hawk in the Rain*. This prize of £500 ($1400 at that time) was to be spent on travel abroad for three months, and could be spent any time during the next two years. The following Sunday, A. Alvarez, the important young literary critic, favorably reviewed *Lupercal* in *The Observer*, and on another page of the paper appeared a photo of Ted with the announcement of the Maugham award. He then received what Sylvia called "a flood of mail," including invitations to read and letters from old friends. In fact, Ted's mail was so heavy that on March 31, Sylvia wrote that she would type answers for him the next day or they would never get done.

But the next day Frieda Rebecca arrived. Born at 5:45 A.M. on April 1, Ted and Sylvia's first child was a healthy seven pounds, four ounces. She was named for Frieda Lawrence, D. H. Lawrence's widow and a woman the Hugheses much admired, and for Otto Plath's sister Frieda in California. Ann Davidow, Sylvia's friend from Smith, and the Merwins were the baby's godparents.

Sylvia was enthusiastic about Britain's national health service. She admired Sister Malti, the Indian midwife who delivered Frieda. She enjoyed her home delivery and was pleased that, because her labor had been a rapid four-and-a-half hours, she had been given no anesthesia. With Ted at her side, Sylvia had experienced natural childbirth. She wrote to Aurelia,

> I looked on my stomach and saw Frieda Rebecca, white as flour with the cream that covers new babies, little funny squiggles of hair plastered over her head, with big, dark-blue eyes. . . . The midwife sponged her beside the bed in my big pyrex mixing bowl, wrapped her up well, near a hot water bottle in the crib; she sucked at me a few minutes like a little expert and got a few drops of colostrum and then went to sleep. . . . I have never been so happy in my life.

Sylvia phoned her mother just a few hours after Frieda's birth and wrote to Marcia Brown later that same day.

Ted noticed that Frieda's birth seemed to be a turning point for Sylvia. He wrote that she had finally "received herself," arrived "at her own center of gravity." At times she was euphoric. But she was also overwhelmed with the changes in her life. Keeping to the orderly routine that had been so important to her was impossible. Though friends from these London years remember Sylvia's excitement about parenting, most of them did not see the erratic behavior that her physical weariness and what seems to have been postpartum depression led to. After the health service nurses stopped coming, Sylvia grew more and more tired. She tried to do everything she ordinarily would— such as taking Frieda to a "Ban-the-Bomb" march and rally when the child was only a few weeks old—but she was not up to her usual routines. She did have some help; Ted watched Frieda while Sylvia napped, and he did much of the laundry, shopping, and cleaning for a time. Dido Merwin brought in delicious meals.

Sylvia was soon accompanying Ted to social and literary events. Scarcely two weeks after Frieda's birth, they hired their first sitter in order to go to a Faber & Faber cocktail party, where they met Valerie and T. S. Eliot. The next night they had dinner in Soho with Lee Anderson, an American who was recording British poets for a Yale series of records. There were other lunches and dinners, as well as visits from Ted's family, from Mike Lotz, and from Ann Davidow and her fiancé, who was on a Guggenheim at Cambridge. With the latter couple, the three Hugheses drove to Stonehenge for what Sylvia called "an exquisite day." A few weeks later, Sylvia and Ted had dinner with the Eliots and the Stephen Spenders at the Eliot home. Sylvia wrote Wilbury Crockett a glowing description of that evening, during which time she was seated between Eliot and Spender. She and Ted also had dinner with Peter Davison, recently married to Jane Truslow, Sylvia's housemate at Smith. Davison was now an editor at *The Atlantic Monthly*.

With Ted's growing stature in poetry and work for the BBC, Sylvia was increasingly identified as Sylvia Hughes, Ted's wife. A. Alvarez described one embarrassing occasion around this time when he discovered Sylvia's dual identity:

> Ted went downstairs to get the pram ready while she dressed the baby. I stayed behind a minute, zipping up my son's coat. Sylvia turned to me, suddenly without gush.
>
> "I'm so glad you picked *that* poem," she said. "It's one of my favourites but no one else seemed to like it."
>
> For a moment I was completely blank; I didn't know what she was talking about. She noticed and helped me out.
>
> "The one you put in the *Observer* a year ago. About the factory at night."
>
> "For Christ's sake, Sylvia *Plath*." It was my turn to gush, "I'm sorry. It was a lovely poem."
>
> "Lovely" wasn't the right word, but what else do you say to a bright young housewife? . . .

As housewife-and-mother became Sylvia's identity in public, maintaining her identity as a writer at home was difficult. Someone had to watch the baby; that responsibility more and more often became Sylvia's. In early May Ted began working all day in W. S. Merwin's study. (The Merwins' apartment was occupied while they were in France for the summer, but the poet's study, which was kept locked, was not included in the occupancy. Merwin offered the study to Ted.) Evidently, Sylvia envied her husband the privacy and space, and by late June she had convinced Ted that he should share the borrowed study with her. She worked at Merwin's flat during the mornings while Ted took care of Frieda, and he worked there during the afternoons.

It was a bright spot in a period that was frequently marred by anxiety and anger. A friend remembers reports of quarrels, and Ted's coming to a pub even though Sylvia had been angry that he was going out. Ten weeks after Frieda's birth, Sylvia lamented, "I get tired so easily." "I am exhausted by noon." "The baby's feedings and keeping the house clean, cooking, and taking care of Ted's voluminous mail, plus my own, have driven me so I care only for carving out hours where I can start on my own writing." To Ann Davidow she wrote in June, "I am gradually getting my nose above crib-level." But to her mother, she blamed her bad temper on her own unease with a new period of writing, "I am at the depressing, painful stage of trying to start writing after a long spell of silence, but the mornings at the study are very peaceful. . . . I am infinitely lucky we can work things out so I get a solid hunk of time off, or rather, time on, a day."

As the summer progressed, Sylvia was once again worrying about money. She and Ted were trying to stretch his Guggenheim fellowship funds so that they would not have to look for jobs until fall. Ted sold the worksheets of the poems in his first two books to the Lilly Library at Indiana University for £160 ($450). He was writing prose as well as poetry regularly for the BBC: he recorded programs on May 8, May 20, June 26, August 2 (with Alvarez), and August 21. Although he and Sylvia had saved nearly $5000 from their year of teaching, they lived as though that money did not exist; it was earmarked for a house, the house that would have studies for each of them and ample room for children. Sylvia wrote to Aurelia early in July, "My own aim is to keep Ted writing full-time," but she also noted that one of them would have to take a job soon. "I am thinking of working myself, if Ted would just feed the baby her noon meal." Obviously, if Sylvia took an outside job, Ted would have to do much more than feed Frieda. The contradiction between Sylvia's wanting Ted to write full time and also be a househusband with a baby to care for seems to have escaped her.

Or she might have been posing for her mother's benefit, as she frequently did. Earlier in the spring, she had written confidentially to Aurelia that Ted was thinking of going back to school, this time to study toward a degree in zoology, given as an external course at the University of London. After Sylvia wrote to her mother about this notion, she instructed her to refer to it as The Plan if she mentioned it in subsequent letters. The sense of conspiracy between Sylvia and her mother suggests more than a little unhappiness with financial management. Mention of The Plan does not occur again.

Early in the summer Ted and Sylvia read their poems together at the Institute of Contemporary Arts following the Faber & Faber cocktail party at which the photograph of "Three Generations of Faber Poets" was taken: Ted Hughes with T. S. Eliot, W. H. Auden, Louis MacNiece, and Stephen Spender. In mid-July Sylvia, Ted, and Frieda went to The Beacon for a week's vacation, spending one of the days at Whitby, a seaside resort, which only made Sylvia homesick for Cape Cod. Once back in London, they continued to write at the Merwins', but leaving home became more difficult for Sylvia. During August Ted too stayed home to write, working in the attic apartment above theirs while that tenant was out for the day. On August 3, Harper's published *Lupercal* in the United States, again to good reviews. And at the close of summer, the three Hugheses returned to Yorkshire, this time for ten days of unwinding from what Sylvia called "months of half-fatigue."

September brought Londoners back to town, and Sylvia again raved about the "inexhaustible city" and her love for it. There was more socializing, and trips to museums and to the last day of the *Lady Chatterley* obscenity trial at the Old Bailey. Ted and Sylvia lunched with the Sweeneys, visiting from Harvard; went to more of John Lehmann's parties; and invited Thom Gunn, the British poet who later became Ted's friend, for lunch at their flat. Gunn remembers spending the afternoon taking a walk through the Primrose Hill area, thinking Sylvia "sensible, cheerful, considerate, obviously a careful and loving mother." Later she wrote to Aurelia that her October 27 birthday, her twenty-eighth, was the best she had ever known.

Ten days before that birthday, Sylvia had written a poem for

Ted called "Love Letter." One of her more relaxed, colloquial monologues, it described his drawing her away from a life of apathy to one of complete emotional fulfillment:

> Not easy to state the change you made.
> If I'm alive now, then I was dead,
> Though, like a stone, unbothered by it.

In the poem, what results from her emotional involvement is a nearly transcendent state, which Ted shares.

This was one of several good poems Sylvia wrote in the fall of 1960. Many of her spring and summer poems had been less fully realized (a short poem, "The Hanging Man," is an exception). She was once again aiming for sales to commercial magazines: an agent who had contacted her after "The Daughters of Blossom Street" appeared in *The London Magazine* was handling submissions. Sylvia finished three stories and continued to plan the novel about her college breakdown and recovery. Perhaps more important, she continued to write good poems. "A Life" and "Waking in Winter" are linked with "Love Letter" in that they use her past experiences as subject, and the lovely "Candles" draws on her grandparents' lives, juxtaposed with that of her infant daughter.

As a group, however, these fall 1960 poems show Sylvia's dissatisfaction with her life. Although Ted still made lists of topics for her to write about, she was more often using her writing to explore her psyche (one of her favorite words). "A Life" is a particularly bleak poem that moves from a description of an "ideal" family—the adjective used ironically—to a portrait of an isolated, sick woman who is "dragging her shadow in a circle." The woman has suffered "a sort of private blitzkrieg" and the only way she can exist after that experience is to live "quietly/ With no attachments, like a foetus in a bottle." Separate in her own bell jar, dead to all emotion, she has exorcized her grief and anger. The poem ends with a set of more desolate images: a crying seagull and a drowned man.

In the fall of 1960, Sylvia seemed to be restless. With her characteristic need for activity and change, she began making plans to find a house—and thinking as well of having a second child. Her incipient depression undercut what might have been a happy autumn for Sylvia: her child was healthy and intelligent; Sylvia was about to make her first appearance on the BBC; and on October 26, she mailed advance copies of *The Colossus and Other Poems* to her family and Mrs. Prouty. The latter in turn sent Sylvia a celebratory check for $150. Sylvia was grateful for the check. Her book had not been taken by an American publisher, nor had it won any prizes, so she knew she would make very little money from its publication.

Reviews of *The Colossus* were good. Sylvia read papers and magazines avidly and was pleased with the response, though it came slowly. Most of the better reviews came out in the winter —essays by John Wain, Roy Fuller, Geoffrey Dearmer. On December 18, 1960, she read the comment she had been watching for, the Alvarez review in *The Observer*. It was a highly favorable notice, but had one reservation—that Plath had not yet developed a consistent voice. When Sylvia saw him socially a month later, she told Alvarez that she agreed with his criticism, and that she was writing a new kind of poem. She was excited about the voice she was speaking in, which caught what she called her "humour and oddnesses" as well as her "realistic" view of human experience.

But even as Sylvia was enjoying her new poems, other problems arose. Frieda started teething, and "the long, wet, grey half-year" English winter seemed even bleaker than her memories of it. Though Sylvia hoped she was again pregnant, she began having attacks of sharp abdominal pains which her doctor called grumbling appendix. Later she had a series of sinus colds, complete with high temperatures. As she wrote to her mother on December 17, just before going to Yorkshire for Christmas, "We're both so tense we need to unwind for weeks."

Ted's fall had been busy with readings at universities, regular programs for the BBC, and a television appearance. His major interest, however, following his fascination with drama, was rewriting his libretto for the opera of the *Bardo Thödol*, the Tibetan Book of the Dead, which he was composing in collaboration with Chou Wen-Chung. The Hugheses had met and liked Professor Chou at Yaddo, and this project had grown from that acquaintance. Ted and Sylvia often discussed the text, which describes the progress of the soul during the forty-nine days between death and rebirth and also serves as a meditative guide to the Buddhist art of "dying" to the phenomenal world. Sylvia was intrigued by Ted's familiarity with non-Western cultures. The notion of reincarnation interested them both. In this opera project, on which Ted spent parts of the year, he was trying to re-create the imagery and language of the *Bardo Thödol* in comparable English, without literal translation.*

Plath's letters home late in 1960 spoke retrospectively of that year as one of struggle. During it, she said, she and Ted were deciding what direction their lives would take, and they had found that literary life had been draining their home. They wanted to live more simply—at least Sylvia said she did. She commented that Ted wanted to be "famous, a lion," and yet he also wanted to be a good husband and father. She might also have said that *she* wanted the same things Ted did: fame, accolades, a loving family (with children ranging in number from four to seven, depending on when she discussed the matter). Marriage might have been easier had either Ted or Sylvia been less ambitious, or had either of them been more willing to take on traditional gender roles. Ted's confidence that income from their writing would support them unnerved Sylvia, especially now that they had a family; she had been reared to think that husbands should be providers. The wife's having to assume the provider role was both unfair and inappropriate, in her judgment. With her journal dotted with accounts of "bloody private wounds," and of arguments over buttons and haircuts, Sylvia's married life had already known its share of regret and anger.

The Yorkshire holiday helped for a while. Sylvia and Ted took ten-mile walks. They slept deeply and had time for each other. The weather, however, was cold and damp, and Sylvia felt sick much of the time. When Sylvia returned to London, she applied for a copy-editing position with the book-publishing industry's trade magazine, *The Bookseller*. In this temporary job, she worked afternoons from 1:00 to 5:30, doing page layout and

---

* Ted's interest in drama occupied him for much of the 1960s. He wrote an adaptation of Seneca's *Oedipus* which Peter Brook directed at the Aldwych Theatre with Sir John Gielgud and Irene Worth. Then, also with Brook, Hughes wrote the largely non-verbal *Orghast at Persepolis* which was performed in Paris and Iran in 1970 and 1971.

editing for the special spring issue. On January 17 she and Ted recorded a "Poets in Partnership" program for the BBC, part of a feature series that focused on married couples who had the same occupation. On the program, Sylvia and Ted joked about their poverty (Sylvia wished for a new lamp). She also made the point that she was working outside the home, as well as being a mother, housewife, and writer. As a result of this broadcast later in January, they received much mail, including a kind letter from a woman named Elizabeth Compton, who invited them to share her Devon farmhouse. Her husband was also a writer.

Although they were now trying to avoid parties, on February 1 they attended one to meet Theodore Roethke. He suggested that Ted apply for a teaching job at the University of Washington, where Roethke had taught for many years. The three became friends. Sylvia's spring letter to Roethke, written to accompany a gift copy of *The Colossus*, expressed her admiration for his work and acknowledged his influence on her poetry, especially on "Poem for a Birthday." Her somewhat fawning tone in this letter is very different from that in the letter she wrote on February 5, 1961, to Anne Sexton. There Plath praised her friend's *To Bedlam and Part Way Back*, reminiscing about the Boston workshop where she had first seen some of the poems included in that book. She admonished Anne to write her a newsy letter, to tell Maxine Kumin that she admired her wry poem, written in an outspoken fraulein voice in *The New Yorker*, and closed by telling Anne about life in London, her wonderful comic child, and her equally wonderful husband.

And yet, only a few days before Sylvia wrote the Sexton letter, she had turned on Ted with fury. He had gone to the BBC to be interviewed by Moira Doolan about doing a series of children's programs. (Sylvia had disliked Doolan's voice on the phone, thinking she was a younger woman than she actually was.) The interview went well and lasted longer than Ted had expected. He got back late for lunch to find that Sylvia had burnt his notes and drafts of new work. A writer herself, Sylvia knew the best, or worst, way to retaliate.

Shortly after this episode, on February 6, Sylvia miscarried. The unexpected loss frightened and saddened her. Then, on February 28, as had earlier been planned, she had an appendec-

death - in life existence

tomy and was hospitalized two weeks. While in the hospital, Sylvia received a "first reading" contract from *The New Yorker*, which meant she was to send all her new poems first to that magazine. Having such a contract was an honor for a young writer, and Sylvia responded by writing some very good poems. She was writing more quickly now. Ted recalled that the poem "Tulips" was written like an urgent letter, without the use of a dictionary or a thesaurus. The ambivalence of "Tulips"—the woman's longing to stay in the hospital, to keep herself remote from even those who love her, set against the insistence that she recover and return home—perhaps reflected Sylvia's own ambivalence at the time. The poem continued the tone of "A Life" and foreshadowed many of Sylvia's late poems, in which unpleasant events were presented with equanimity, if not outright humor.

The speaker of "Tulips" is a woman who has been hospitalized for an operation. Her husband and their small child, whose photograph is beside her in the austere white room, have sent her vivid red tulips. The poem is an imagined dialogue between the woman and the flowers, as she accuses them of eating her oxygen. Surreal yet effective, Plath creates the woman's tranquil postoperative state as idyllic; she decides, momentarily at least, she wants to remain in the hospital.

pub. 1961

> I am a nun now, I have never been so pure.
>
> I didn't want any flowers, I only wanted
> To lie with my hands turned up and be utterly empty.

She thinks of her husband and child as antagonists. Their smiles in the photo are "hooks" that want to bring her back to a normal life.

The theme of "Tulips" was not an isolated sentiment in Plath's writing that spring. "I Am Vertical" explores even more directly the theme of leaving the hectic world of the living for the peaceful world of the dead. In Plath's poems, whatever offered tranquility, privacy, and some sure sense of self was positive—and in these poems, death seemed to provide that milieu.

Many of her other spring 1961 poems were about women or their children. "Barren Woman" and "Heavy Women" describe feminine fertility or its absence: Sylvia thought barrenness the worst possible condition for any woman. "Morning Song" is a poem of praise for an infant daughter. "Zoo Keeper's Wife" is a macabre account of a zoo keeper's courtship of his wife, which characterizes marriage as victimization of the woman. Since Ted had planned to study zoology, the poem has an ironic personal element. It is also the first of Plath's poems to suggest that what men are capable of doing to animals, they are capable of doing to women. It anticipates in many ways "The Rabbit Catcher," a powerful late poem on that theme.

Surely autobiographical, "Parliament Hill Fields," one of Plath's strongest poems of this period, describes a woman's grief over a miscarriage. Withdrawing from her family, she returns from a walk to see her healthy child getting ready for bed in a brightly-lit house. But even with that joyful sight, her depression continues: "The old dregs, the old difficulties take me to wife." With no explanation for the words "dregs" and "difficulties," the reader can only surmise that Plath was suggesting recurring withdrawal, if not depression.

The birth of one child and the loss of another brought Sylvia into a matriarchal world. Those experiences, coupled with her stay in the women's ward after her appendectomy, gave her a language that she used to express herself as a woman. Many of her 1961 poems ("In Plaster," for example) explore the emotions associated with women's experiences. At the same time, these were speaking poems, written in a more natural voice, regardless of whether the speaker was meant to be a Sylvia-like character or someone else.

Plath returned home from the hospital to the good news that Alfred A. Knopf had bought *The Colossus* for American publication. Knopf wanted to cut ten of the fifty poems which had appeared in the British book, unfortunately removing "Poem for a Birthday." Sylvia was elated, and was willing to do whatever Knopf requested. She seems not to have questioned the wisdom of deleting her best poem, although she later asked that two of its seven parts—"Stones" and "Flute Notes from a Reedy Pond" —be left in to close the book. She observed at one point that the collection had a theme, the person who is "broken and mended," beginning with the smashed colossus and ending with the self.

On the heels of this good news came word that Ted had won the Hawthornden prize for *Lupercal*. He had also been doing some BBC recording, and he and Sylvia made another joint appearance there, reading new poems and discussing their childhoods. Ted had also been commissioned to write a play for the London company of the Royal Shakespeare Theatre by its director, Peter Hall, clear indication that he was as highly thought of as a playwright as he was a poet.

Sylvia's letters home were ecstatic. What she was not writing to Aurelia, however, was even more exciting. With Knopf's acceptance of *The Colossus*, a deep frustration had dissolved, and she was now working "fiendishly" on her novel. Now called *The Bell Jar*, the book was written in the satirical voice of a Salinger or Roth character, who uses a mixture of wry understatement and comic exaggeration. The protagonist's interior monologue tells of her summer as guest editor at *Mademoiselle*, her first serious romance and its breakup, her depression, her attempted suicide, and—most important to Sylvia—her recovery.

Plath wanted to do more than write autobiographical fiction. She wanted her novel to speak for the lives of countless women she had known—women caught in conflicting social codes who were able to laugh about their plight. A central image of the book, the fig tree bearing ripe figs, depicts the female dilemma of the 1950s. No woman can have it all, but choosing is also difficult.

I saw my life branching out before me like the green fig tree. . . .

From the tip of every branch, like a fat purple fig, a wonderful future beckoned and winked. One fig was a husband and a happy home and children, and another fig was a famous poet and another fig was a brilliant professor, and another fig was Ee Gee, the amazing editor, and another fig was Europe and Africa and South America, and another fig was Constantin and Socrates and Attila and a pack of other lovers with queer names and off-beat professions, and another fig was an Olympic lady crew champion, and beyond and above these figs were many more figs I couldn't quite make out.

I saw myself sitting in the crotch of this fig tree, starving to death, just because I couldn't make up my mind which of the figs I would choose. I wanted each and every one of them, but choosing one meant losing all the rest. . . .

The protagonist's comic monologue is calculated to imply that a woman does not have to make that single choice. Her dilemma is entirely artificial. Only social pressure forces the choice.

Esther Greenwood, the narrator of the novel, appreciates the ridiculousness of her plight. Her perceptions set her outside society, but they do not free her from the pressures of that world. Plath carefully sets the story of Esther in the context of a political situation (not for nothing had she been reading Camus and Sartre), the controversial execution of Julius and Ethel Rosenberg. Esther's personal horror at what she finds in life is set against the horror of their executions.

Plath's choice of her grandmother's maiden name, Greenwood, was satisfying for both symbolic reasons and personal ones, and since the novel moves toward Esther's rebirth, the image is appropriate. In *The Bell Jar*, Esther is a survivor: she has a sense of humor, a cool if cynical view of life that colors the grim comedy of her descriptions. She is also—at the time she writes the story—a mother, a practical woman who has made the best of her life, and who tries to learn from it. Like Holden Caulfield in Salinger's *The Catcher in the Rye*, or Elizabeth in Shirley Jackson's *The Bird's Nest*, Esther is not ashamed of her descent into madness: she wants to tell about it, partly to rid herself of memories, partly to help other women faced with the same cultural pressure.

Writing *The Bell Jar* was a liberating experience for Sylvia. She went each morning to the Merwins' and wrote for three or four hours. For the first time in her life, her writing provided continuity for her. The long prose story had its own rhythm, its own demands. With poetry, when Sylvia had finished one poem, there was no reason to write any particular next poem; everything was separate, distinct. With a novel, everything could be used: the writer's life was fair game, including all the writer's experiences and certainly the writer's emotions, whatever had prompted them. And in writing this novel, Plath did draw on all her experiences. For example, she borrowed a sexual experience from a blind date during her freshman year at Smith, describing it as though it happened with Buddy Willard.

In many ways, *The Catcher in the Rye* was the model Plath was using for *The Bell Jar*. Sylvia turned to it for structure, and drew on it whenever she ran out of events that seemed to fit Esther's story. Holden meets a sailor and a Cuban; so does Esther. Holden walks forty-one blocks back to his New York hotel; Esther walks forty-eight. Holden looks as yellow in his mirror as Esther (looking Chinese) does in hers. He vomits before going to bed; in *The Bell Jar*, Doreen does that, but then Esther and the other guest editors share in another long purge after eating bad crab. Both books have a cemetery scene. *Catcher* has its violent and bloody suicide in James Castle's death, which becomes the suicide by hanging in *The Bell Jar*. Holden Caulfield wants to go West because he thinks that part of the country will save him. Esther wants to go to Chicago for the same reasons. The suggestion of sexual deviance in the subplot, too, echoes Holden's discovery of the homosexuality of Mr. Antolini, his friend and former teacher. That discovery precipitates Holden's breakdown. For Esther, however, the suspicion of her friend's sexual preference is much less important than the fact of her death.

Tone and mood in *The Bell Jar* change quickly. Plath opens with a flush of Esther's euphoric memories, painfully described yet distant enough to be harmless. This was a "comic" novel Sylvia was writing (she later called it "a pot-boiler"). Its outcome was to be positive: the rebirth of Esther, a woman who had come through both Dante's hell and her own, to find her fulfillment not in some idealized Beatrice, the unattainable woman/spirit, but in herself. *The Bell Jar* would reach beyond *Catcher*, because in that book Holden was telling his story to a sympathetic therapist and to his readers, but he was not yet free of the asylum or its stigma. For Esther, there was rebirth.

For Plath, too, a yearning for rebirth, for a clean start, seems to have dominated the spring of 1961. Now that her appendix had been removed, she could no longer blame her moods on health problems. The moods, however, remained and a vengeful anger periodically erupted through the calm surface of her life. It also erupted in her writing.

13

The Devon Life

1961-62

"The Shine of These Small Things"

ylvia's convalescence at home, following her miscarriage and her appendectomy, convinced her that she and Ted needed a house to themselves. Ted could not keep working in such a crowded space—his concentration at the mercy of every phone bell or caller—nor could she. (Sylvia's dream was an upstairs study for herself with a babysitter minding the children in a downstairs nursery.) As long as she and Ted used Merwin's study during his absences from London, they could manage, but they could not rely forever on their friend's generosity. Using the $1500 that Ted had earned from his BBC work in 1960, they bought a small Morris station wagon and, in late June of 1961, began driving into the London suburbs and to Devon, looking for appropriate and affordable houses.

Sylvia was writing *The Bell Jar* seven mornings a week at Merwin's study, where Ted worked every afternoon. Both were trying to finish projects during May because the Merwins would be back in London later that month, and then in mid-June Sylvia's mother was coming to visit. With the Merwins going to France for the summer, Aurelia would stay at their apartment most of the time.

Although her letters home that spring indicate that Sylvia was eager to see her mother and to show off her grandchild, once Aurelia arrived in London Sylvia could hardly wait to leave. She urged Aurelia to spend six weeks every summer visiting them in the future, saying nothing about things they might do together but only "then Ted and I could take an annual two-week holiday in the middle of your stay while you got re-acquainted with your grandchildren." Now a mother herself, Sylvia had a better understanding of the time and energy Aurelia had spent on her care. She realized that her debt to her mother was impossibly great, and a kind of desperation existed in that knowledge. She could never repay Aurelia. And, again, she felt that she could not live up to her mother's expectations—or what she thought were her mother's expectations—that she excel in everything she did, including motherhood. During this visit, Sylvia was afraid that she would be judged and probably found wanting. The anger growing out of Sylvia's feelings about her mother surfaced not only in *The Bell Jar* but in two poems, "Widow," written May 16, 1961, and "The Rival," written in July.

In *The Bell Jar*, Esther Greenwood's feelings toward older women are also ambivalent. As she says, "all the old ladies I ever knew wanted to teach me something." In her self-disgust, however, Esther cannot accept their teaching. The reader can see that many of these women characters would have been excellent role models for Esther, and would have helped her with her dilemma of life choices. In her present state, Esther cannot distinguish helpful people from conspirators. In her view, because she narrates the novel, all women act against her.

Esther's mother is cast as the chief villain. While she sleeps in the room she shares with her daughter, Esther considers strangling her mother, mostly because *she* can sleep while Esther cannot. In her depression, Esther cannot tolerate her mother's love for her. She experiences a second birth at the end of *The Bell Jar*, just as in effect she replaced her natural mother with her psychiatrist, Dr. Nolan.

Even though Sylvia enjoyed writing the book, and wrote her friend Ann Davidow that she had never been so excited about anything else she had written, she realized that the portraits of these women would hurt feelings. She told Ann that she would publish her "funny, and yet serious" novel under a pseudonym. Once past the glee of knowing that her novel was working—was coherent, interesting, even amusing in the gallows mode of humor she admired—Sylvia realized that the voice of *The Bell Jar* could also become a voice for her poetry. For the first time in her life, it was hard to stop writing each day.

Plath's depiction of her mother and other female characters may trouble the reader who knows her biography, but *The Bell Jar* is a fiction, and in fiction real people are transformed. Plath's caricatures helped to emphasize the torment of Esther Greenwood, the novel's protagonist, who sees herself as subject to external forces working against her. The "bell jar" of the title that encloses the heroine in an airless suffocation is one image of that external force.

Plath's novel is also a story of betrayal. Esther thinks that everyone she trusts has somehow disappointed her. For all his prudish talk, Buddy is not really a virgin. For all his sexual experience, Irwin botches her deflowering. For all her brilliance and insight, Jay Cee does not recognize Esther's talents. And even Esther's helpful mother brings the news that she has not been accepted into the Harvard writing class. People fail Esther; disappointments test her. She lives through it all, however, heading toward eventual rebirth and ironically living to reach the very goals she has seemingly rebelled against during her college years: she marries and becomes a mother.

In literary study, the classic betrayal is that of Judas betraying Jesus. Sylvia was a product of traditional literary study, and she used elements of the Christ legend throughout *The Bell Jar*— ironically. She reduced the number of *Mademoiselle* guest editors from the actual twenty to the religiously significant twelve; one —Doreen—is conspicuously different, i.e., evil—from the start. It is Doreen's influence that leads Esther to evil, and to her breakdown: she runs away from the Judas-like friend, takes scalding baths to purify herself, acts viciously against Doreen to escape her influence. But—the nature of evil being what it is— Doreen comes through victorious and it is Esther who nearly dies of severe food poisoning, a slick version of the Last Supper.

Esther's wandering in the "garden" of the Boston Common and being tempted by the sailor, and her three suicide attempts, are heavily ironic replications of Jesus's suffering. But these events are invested with deep irony: no mere young woman could attain the stature of a Jesus figure—not in "literature." No reader who had been trained as Sylvia had to identify religious allusions would have even tried to spot Jesus in Esther Greenwood, even though she carried the name of a noble Old Testament woman.

In most of Plath's writing, the intellectual component from the world of literature that she had studied was omnipresent. Young as she was, much of what she knew came from her studies, the books she had read. Still in her twenties, she was writing as much from literature as from life. The worksheets and manuscripts of all her work, *The Bell Jar* as well as the poems, are usually more explicit about these literary sources than are the finished works.

In June Aurelia arrived; she spent much time at Chalcot Square but lived in the Merwins' flat and toured London from there. As Sylvia had feared would happen, she and Aurelia had some arguments, but once Sylvia and Ted left for their French vacation in late June, Aurelia had her beautiful grandchild to herself. She moved into Chalcot Square for the two weeks that Sylvia and Ted were gone.

The vacation in France that Sylvia had looked forward to so eagerly was a disappointment. She and Ted returned home on July 13, after four or five days at the Merwins' farm in Lacam, and a few days later they, with Frieda and Aurelia, drove to Ted's family home in Yorkshire for another week of vacation. Sylvia was now in her third month of a new pregnancy. Aurelia, fascinated with the atmosphere and landscape, enjoyed Ted's parents and other relatives, and began a correspondence with Ted's mother that lasted many years.

The summer events had further convinced Sylvia that she and Ted needed to leave London, to find a simpler life where their family could flourish. Having a second child also added urgency to what she saw as their need for more livable space. In late July Ted and Sylvia drove to Devon and looked at eight properties they had chosen from real estate listings. All but one of the places were impossible, but it seemed perfect for them. The ancient ten-room house had a wine cellar and a small attic. The main house sat at the end of a gated lane, and its servants' cottage, the stable (which was also a garage), and the cobblestone court took up the front of the two-acre plot. The "wilderness" of a back yard contained seventy apple and cherry trees and blackberry and raspberry bushes. The yard adjoined the churchyard and cemetery, and a nine-foot stone wall surrounded the yard.

Both Sylvia and Ted were intrigued by the history of Court Green. The oldest walls in the house were three feet thick. The roof of both the main house and the cottage were of thatch. Beneath the ancient elm tree, about which Sylvia would write several poems, was the mound of a Roman fortress.

The house contained a small kitchen, a cold larder, a larger eating area, a living room, a small study with a tiny fireplace, and a long room that would become the children's playroom and Sylvia's sewing room. Upstairs, Sylvia would choose to have her study facing the front, beside their bedroom, and near Frieda's small bedroom, a guest room, one other bedroom, and the bath. Ted would take the peaked attic as his study.

For Sylvia, the move to Devon was crucial. It would provide necessary space for a growing family to live comfortably, and for both her and Ted to write. It would allow her to assume more fully the roles of mother, wife, and homemaker. In Devon she would have land, trees, flowers, and gardens. While she told friends that it was Ted who wanted to leave London, it seems clear that she thought living in Devon would benefit both of them and their work.

To buy the property they had to spend all they had saved. In August, Aurelia sent them a check for $5880 from their Boston savings. She added a loan of $1400 (charging three percent interest, at Sylvia's insistence), an amount Ted's mother matched with a gift. Though there would be furnishing and redecorating costs, Sylvia seemed to think that their writing incomes would sustain the enterprise.

In the month that remained before the move, they took care of business in London. They advertised and sublet their flat, resorting to some subterfuge so that David Wevill, a young Canadian poet, and his striking, somewhat older wife, Assia, could rent it. They saw friends—the American poet Ruth Fainlight and her husband, Alan Sillitoe, among them. Sylvia also called Clarissa Roche, who had finally arrived to join her husband Paul in London after years of living in Mexico. Sylvia and Clarissa, as Americans, often traded "Englishisms," anecdotes about the British customs they thought amusing. This time Sylvia told Clarissa about an English cafe that closed from noon to 2:00 P.M. so that the staff could have lunch.

Finally August 31 came. Ted and Sylvia had packed their books, records, clothes, and household and baby goods, and relinquished the image of themselves as Londoners, at least for a time. For Sylvia, the move to Devon was hopeful. It was the beginning of a new fantasy.

When the Hughes family and all their possessions arrived in a small moving van and their station wagon, they saw that the wonderful new home was dilapidated and in need of a great amount of work. Rose and Percy Key, near neighbors, brought in tea that day and helped set the tone of welcome in the midst of discouragement. Once again, Sylvia's American standards of living made it difficult for her to accept living in the ages-old house, despite its charm. By September 4, however, when she wrote home to Aurelia, she was careful to be cheerful: "My whole spirit has expanded immensely—I don't have that crowded, harassed feeling I've had in all the small places I've lived in before."

She loved the quiet center of the village, sitting on a slope so that the sidewalks that formed a triangle around it pitched at unexpected angles. She liked walking the short distance to the village over the cobbled pavement. (The narrow pitch cobblestones in her courtyard were like those of the nearby church floor, edges melted to a mosaic through centuries of wear.) She felt refreshed by the blue skies that seemed closer to earth here, and the fields that stretched away into a faint horizon, studded with clusters of shaggy sheep and a few scattered flowers. And she knew that if she found Devon peaceful, thinking of herself as an American "city" person, then Ted was enjoying it even more.

When Sylvia's brother Warren came for a week in September, Sylvia and Ted used his visit as an excuse to explore the new territory. They took picnics to the coast and tried out various

beaches, ate at the local inn, went for long walks, picked black-
berries, and met townspeople whenever possible. Warren helped
with various tasks, including the sanding of Sylvia's new writing
table (which was six feet long, one of her dreams) that Ted had
made for her. Once Warren had left, Sylvia and Ted settled into
what would be their Devon routine. On Tuesdays and Thurs-
days, Nancy Axworthy came to clean and iron. Each morning
Sylvia worked in her study; after lunch, Ted wrote while
Sylvia did the housework and took Frieda outside for yard
work and gardening. By the end of September, Ted had
recorded four BBC programs at Plymouth, a location closer
than London. He was finishing a new radio play for the Third
Programme.

It looked as if moving had been wise. Yet the physical work
of living in Devon was much greater for Sylvia, and now that
she was six months pregnant, she felt much pressure to attend
to household matters first. As she wrote to the Huwses in her
usual wry tone, the house was indeed "a very ancient manor,
with plaster crumbling ominously behind the wallpaper which
obviously holds it on . . . and nettles overall." She was writing
good poems, however. Part of the impetus for her writing was
the arrival of *American Poetry Now*, the supplement of contemporary American poems she had edited for the journal *Critical
Quarterly*. The booklet was eclectic, full of strong poems by
people who would nearly all become important poets. Robert
Creeley, Richard Wilbur, and Denise Levertov appeared with
Edgar Bowers, Barbara Guest, Louis Simpson, George Starbuck, Luke Myers, Dan Hoffman, Anthony Hecht, and Hyam
Plotzik. Plath included three poems each by Adrienne Rich,
William Stafford, and W. S. Merwin, and two by Howard
Nemerov, W. D. Snodgrass, and Anne Sexton. The Sexton and
Snodgrass poems close the volume, giving them an importance
that reflected Sylvia's opinion that the most interesting poetry
was that written out of personal experience. The process of
choosing these poems and editing the booklet gave her a better
understanding of her own Americanisms. Her voice in poems as
different as "Mirror," "Blackberrying," and "The Moon and the
Yew Tree" was a continuation of that strikingly real and unhappy voice in "Tulips." She seemed to be taking her poetry

more seriously; she dated each finished poem and saved the worksheets for it.

Most of the poems Sylvia wrote during September and October of 1961 still came from Ted's lists of subjects for her to write about ("Finisterre," "The Surgeon at 2 A.M." and "The Moon and the Yew Tree"), but each drew on sources of imagery that Sylvia had used throughout her writing. Many of the images appear first in *The Bell Jar;* others had been in other pieces: the moon as a source of mystery and chill; mirrors as reflections of souls; sinister landscapes; and a number of different uses of images of water, blood, hooks, stones, flowers, graves. Each image is enriched by her cumulative use of it throughout different poems.

The speaker's search for truth is one theme that dominates Plath's Devon poems. "The Moon and the Yew Tree" began as an exercise. It quickly became one of her strongest, most surprising and most intense poems. It begins with a description of her Devon yard and its proximity to the old church burial ground. She admits her ignorance about death ("I simply cannot see where there is to get to") and says specifically that the moon —for all its dominance in that shadowy landscape—is no answer. To her, the moon represents not beauty but "the O-gape of complete despair." (Plath used the coined word "O-gape" in other contexts to contrast with *agape*, the term for Christian love. She used it, too, to describe the elongated mouths seen in African sculpture and painting—figures in pain or abandonment.) In the midst of her relatively sonorous description of the Devon location, the speaker says sharply, "I live here." Or she attempts to exist here, grounded in the ancient culture and its graveyard, scrutinized by the moon, which reminds her of the scrutiny of her mother. Both moon and mother have no tenderness, the poem continues. The poem concludes with the image of "blackness—blackness and silence." "The Moon and the Yew Tree" expresses Plath's increasingly bleak sense of discomfort and foreboding in her Devon environs.

Images of blackness, fear, and hopelessness occur in many of Plath's 1961 poems. At the end of the bushes in "Blackberrying" is "nothing, nothing but a great space." In "Finisterre" the landscape is dominated by the Bay of the Dead.

Her 1961 poems also reflect some of her admiration for the work of W. S. Merwin. Merwin shared many of Ted's interests in myth, ritual, and anthropology (he had lived in Mallorca as a tutor to Robert Graves's son); but his macabre and existential vision was closer to Sylvia's. She admired his bleak, symbolic poems. By 1960, Merwin was building poems around a single image, or clusters of images, rather than writing narratives. He often jumped from one image to the next without transition. Thematically, in his poems, the common becomes the miraculous, and the rational is often eclipsed by the intuitive. His poems "In a Cloud of Hands," "My Friends," "The Annunciation" (in which tenderness is the essence of love), and "Departure's Girl-Friend," with its images of covered, shrouded mirrors, all influenced Plath.

One of her key poems during this early Devon period is "Last Words," a death poem with a strangely positive emphasis, whose mixed tones are reminiscent of Merwin's work. Here the poet asks for a burial with great ceremony, one in which her household objects—"things . . . warmed by much handling"—surround her, to bring her comfort. Emphasizing the artifacts of a woman's life as she does here suggests that Plath's life in Devon was giving her a sense of place and community she had not previously known. As she made bright curtains, baked whole wheat banana bread, and painted flowers on furniture, she was arriving at a different sense of her identity as woman. Whether her convictions came from Paul Radin's African legends and art, or from Robert Graves's *The White Goddess*, or from D. H. Lawrence or Carl Jung or Theodore Roethke, she was discovering that the objects and events of her daily life were the subjects she wanted to write about.

Sylvia tried to become part of the village life. She went to the church behind their house, where the music was wonderful but the sermons frustrated her. Together, the family went for long walks and to the meets organized by the local hunt. Although it was possible to travel into London by morning train and arrive before 10:00 A.M., Sylvia seldom made that trip. She did go in in late October, to attend the Guinness party where she collected a £75 poetry prize and read one of the prize-winning poems, as did Robert Graves. While she was in London, she went to see two Edward Albee plays, left some manuscripts with an agent who sold them for $280 to Indiana University, took new fiction to her literary agent, and spent the rest of the time with friends.

In early November, Sylvia received a Saxton grant of $2000. She and Ted had each previously applied for the funding and been turned down. The Saxton grant made possible child-care help while she finished *The Bell Jar* and was, therefore, "an absolute lifesaver." Also that autumn both Sylvia and Ted had been asked to judge writing contests, Ted the Poetry Book Society competition, Sylvia the Guinness Awards. Plath and Hughes would make close to $7000 from their writing in the year ahead, Ted earning the larger share. And Sylvia wrote that her "acquisitive soul" was happy because they were both reviewing children's books for *The New Statesman*. Of the fifty or sixty books sent to them, they chose ten to review and kept all the books. Their children's library was soon extensive.

But between early November, when they received news of the Saxton grant, and the Christmas holidays, Sylvia again went through the winter doldrums. England was beginning one of its coldest winters. Even with four heaters running, she could not heat the house much above fifty or fifty-five degrees. Without the heaters, the temperature stood at thirty-eight degrees in the master bedroom, Sylvia said.

She claimed, however, that what depressed her was the impact of several essays that had appeared in *The Nation*. These analyses of American foreign policy described the marriage of the military and big business; the bomb shelter craze; America's awarding medals to former German Army officers; and President Kennedy's warnings to the Soviet Union. As Sylvia wrote to her mother, "I began to wonder if there was any point in trying to bring up children in such a mad, self-destructive world. The sad thing is that the power for destruction is real and universal."

The holidays calmed her. She had made friends with the bank manager and his wife, the Tyrers, who had invited them to a New Year's Eve party. Even at close to 170 pounds in this ninth month of her pregnancy, Sylvia looked radiant. She spent the last weeks before Christmas busy around the house, cooking and decorating. She wrote to Aurelia that her turkey with dressing, chestnuts, and apple pies made a fine feast, and that Christmas of 1961 was "the happiest and fullest" she had ever known. Even though she thought of herself as an exile so long as she lived in England, Sylvia seemed—in her letters at least—to be very pleased with life in Devon.

Existence continued amazingly full with Nicholas Farrar's dramatic birth at five minutes before midnight on January 17, 1962. A more painful labor than her earlier delivery, this one ended with a gush of the birth waters, propelling the heavy baby explosively into the room. Winifred Davies, Sylvia's midwife and friend, had been with her since late afternoon; the doctor was just entering at the time of the baby's birth.

Even though Nick weighed nearly ten pounds, he ate often and, initially, cried a great deal. But with Sylvia and the baby in the upstairs guest room, Ted was less disturbed than he had been during Frieda's first weeks. Despite her physical weariness, Sylvia felt more relaxed: she knew what to expect. Most of the time, she enjoyed the night feedings, sitting by candlelight, looking out the upstairs windows at the great elm, silhouetted against the stark Devon landscape and moon. The only disappointment in the early months of Nick's care came ten days after his birth, when Sylvia had a severe attack of milk fever and ran a temperature of over 103° for several days.

Her annotated calendar for 1962 suggests that the postbirth period was not entirely happy. Adjoining each day's calendar space, Sylvia listed things she wanted to get done. The list for February 12, for example, reads, "Mending, Ted's story, Ted's BBC, scrapbooks, notebook, clean playroom, vac study." Only two items—"Ted's story" and "clean playroom"—are crossed off. The lists mushroom, items from a week before or a day before appearing repeatedly. She was trying to catch up, but the burden of caring for the large house with one child under two and a new baby was overwhelming. Yet her energetic activity went on. January 31, she sent in the income tax. The next week she cooked spaghetti, lemon pie, banana bread, stew, rhubarb, and cupcakes. Friends came to see the baby. On February 17, Ted's play *The Wound* was rebroadcast on the BBC and on the next day their friend Charles Causley came to dinner.

Somehow, Sylvia was also returning to writing. Her first project was a radio play. Called "3 Sisters' Exercise" in draft, it became "Three Women." Although Sylvia said that "Three Women" grew from the Bergman film of that title, and also was influenced by Virginia Woolf's novel *The Waves*, she drew as well on Dylan Thomas's *Under Milk Wood*, and on the emotions she had known during her two childbirths, her miscarriage, and her recovery from surgery in the hospital. The "three women" of the title have each just been through labor. One has had a son, another a miscarriage, and the third a daughter whom she will give up for adoption. The range of emotions—joy, guilt, shame and sorrow—allowed Plath to write new kinds of poetry, some lines ornate, others flat and distinct, as the characters tried to rein in their sometimes overwhelming feelings.

In an early version, the women had names, but in the final, Plath used the more formal "First Voice," "Second," "Third," to give the play a universal quality. Much of the text suggested Dylan Thomas's *Under Milk Wood*, which was subtitled *A Play for Voices*. Read by the author on his 1953 American tour (which Plath heard in Amherst), his work had been one of her earliest models of truthful, comic—sometimes bawdy—drama. What Sylvia attempted in "Three Women" was also a truthful and unconventional treatment of an equally unconventional literary subject—birth.

Her play of 378 lines is an alternating tapestry of the three voices but each speaker tells a dramatic tale complete in itself. The confident First Voice conveys some of Plath's humor ("I am slow as the world. I am very patient, / Turning through my time, the suns and stars / Regarding me with attention. . . . I am a great event") as it builds to the agony of the birth and the quiet of recovery. Some of the most beautiful writing is the mother's expression of her fears for the child:

How long can I be a wall, keeping the wind off?
How long can I be
Gentling the sun with the shade of my hand. . . .

In contrast, the Second Voice is anguished and angry; the Third, trapped in her guilt as she gives up her child ("I am a wound walking out of the hospital. / I am a wound they are letting go. / I leave my health behind").

After Sylvia finished "Three Women," she sent in her quarterly report to the Saxton foundation. She considered *The Bell Jar* already finished, except for minor revision. Then she began writing her second novel, one based on her "Falcon Yard" fiction in which she and Ted met at the *St. Botolph's Review* party. The book was to be finished for Ted's birthday in August. But she also wrote Aurelia, asking that she buy her some underwear and send it, because getting out to shop was so difficult. Sylvia was feeling the distance from London and the confinement of the responsibility for two children. She was also mired in what she called "the horrible winter," once again experiencing her own "megrims." Her spirits reached a new low when she discovered that much of her personal discomfort was from chilblains, stinging itchy sores that developed from extremely cold temperatures.

Part of her depression was a natural aftermath of the birth of a second child. Nicholas's birth had, in effect, re-created her own family situation as a child. Sylvia had been two and a half when her brother Warren was born; her children were somewhat closer in age, but the girl's birth first followed by the boy's set up the same kind of pattern she had known—and disliked—as a child. Psychologists now understand that giving birth does in most instances return the mother to her own childhood and makes a repetition of childhood emotions likely. Fragile as she was psychologically during this winter, Sylvia more than likely did not understand why she was so subject to fits of unrest and temper. Caring for two very small children was stressful, although Ted did help, lovingly, with both Frieda and Nicholas. As Sylvia wrote to Aurelia, she hoped that when her mother came for her summer visit, "We can give him a 6-week holiday from any baby care. He needs it. . . ."

Life in the Devon house—far from being the relaxed idyll Sylvia described to Aurelia in her letters home—was a frantic, sometimes sullen, race to keep up with the chores of caring for two small children. Diapers figure more prominently than writing schedules, and even with the cleaning help two days a week, chores were interminable. It may have looked as if Sylvia did those chores with enthusiasm, but her resentment that so much work existed underlay all her responses to any suggestion that they take a break, change routine, have some fun. Aside from the week Warren was visiting them in the fall of 1961, they did nothing to explore the area or to benefit from being in a new part of England. It could be said, though Sylvia never said it in her letters, that not only was the English winter grim but life in the Devon house shared that quality.

At least until March 12, when Sylvia picked the first bouquet of daffodils for Ted's tea tray. The Devon house soon had thousands of daffodils in bloom. That same day she wrote to Aurelia, "I have the queerest feeling of having been reborn with Frieda —it's as if my real, rich, happy life only started just about then." But soon after that she wrote to Clarissa Roche, emphasizing what a financial drain the house was (they were "broke," in her words), that the winter had been nothing but grim, and that she was making forays into the wild garden, trying to control pests with "lethal pellets of SLUGIT and SLUGDEATH." Abstractly, Sylvia may have loved all the parts of being a homemaker and mother; physically, to maintain home and family left her no time for herself, or for her writing, or even for her relationship with Ted.

Social life in the village had not helped to lighten her winter mood. Sylvia and Ted were not prominent there in any way. They were simply the young couple who had bought Court Green. They saw the Tyrers, Rose and Percy Key, Winifred Davies, and Sylvia's new acquaintances including Elizabeth and David Compton. The Tyrers' friendship quickly became a burden when they seemed to think the Hugheses should help educate their teenage daughter, Nicola. What resulted, according to Plath's journals, was an imposition—largely upon Ted—that Sylvia resented. She was clearly suspicious of Nicola's motives, noting that the girl's visits increased whenever Ted had gotten some publicity in the papers. Sylvia promised herself to be "omnipresent" whenever Nicola came around.

Her apparent jealousy about Nicola and Ted's friendship must have seemed a little unreasonable even to her; there is often some acerbic humor in what she writes about the girl. In one episode from Plath's journal, Nicola says that the film *The Seven*

Samurai bored her. Even though it is Ted's favorite movie, he agrees with her. Sylvia admits in her journal that she relaxed once the Tyrers had moved away, and she also admits that she and Ted needed time together, alone, without the children and all the responsibilities they created.

Part of Sylvia's uneasiness about Ted during that winter and spring stemmed from his moodiness and also from the bleak and introspective things he had been writing. Several of his stories and his play *The Wound* recounted death or near-death experiences. In his stories "The Rain Horse" and "Snow" the male protagonist is mysteriously hunted down and trapped by a female adversary. Because she usually typed his work, Sylvia could hardly ignore this distrust of—and anger toward—the feminine. Ted may not have consciously known what his writing suggested, but the fact that he was writing everything but the poetry he was known for might have hinted that he was in a period of transition. After his poem collection *Lupercal* was published in 1960, what poems he did write were either angry or oblique, eventually collected in a book called *Recklings* (the weakest animals of the litter) or, much later, in *Wodwo*.

Spring was bittersweet for Sylvia. She was not sure what was causing the distance between herself and Ted, but she knew that something was wrong. And while her infant son was growing rapidly, Percy Key, her good neighbor, was dying. The contrast between the healthy infant and the deteriorating man depressed Sylvia, and the rapidity of Percy's decline from what was evidently lung cancer gave her little time to accept his approaching death. "I find this difficult to believe," she wrote sadly in her journal. More important is what she was writing in her poems. Percy's impending death is the subject of several of her spring poems, as if it was standing for some ominous other happening as well that she did not yet want to recognize or even name.

Her dirge for Percy Key begins with "Among the Narcissi" and continues in the haunting poem "Pheasant," where the speaker tries to prevent a man's killing the bird. The poignancy of the speaker's plea for the kingly bird, its wonder and its easiness in life, all rest on a fear that the powerful hunter will not listen, contrasted with a reverence for the natural life that

202

deserves to exist. Manuscripts of the poem show that it is closely connected with Percy's death in its inception, and also with Sylvia's fears that her husband is instrumental in death of some kind.

Her poems "Elm," perhaps the greatest of her spring work, and "Berck-Plage" also stem from dismay over Percy's illness. Like "Three Women," "Elm" is written in a woman's voice, speaking a woman's wisdom and truth, unflinchingly. Like other 1962 poems, it is dedicated to a woman friend. On a May weekend visit from Alan Sillitoe and Ruth Fainlight, during which time the two women had breast-fed their infant sons together in the upstairs room that overlooked the elm, Sylvia read the poem aloud to Ruth. After that weekend Sylvia dedicated the poem to her.

As she had in Boston, Sylvia was seeking out women as friends. Winifred Davies was a mentor, but Sylvia's best friend became Elizabeth Compton, who had written while Sylvia and Ted were in London about their possibly living in the Comptons' Devon farmhouse. The Comptons came to tea in late winter. With her customary eagerness, Sylvia questioned Elizabeth, asking rapidly what her opinions were about this or that national and international event. When Elizabeth said she was a member of the Liberal party, Sylvia jumped up and said, "Thank God, a committed woman!" Their conversation ranged from armament issues and American big business to Sylvia's plans for expanding her family and the garden. Elizabeth thought that Sylvia's life was a seamless blend of the concrete and the abstract, joy about her children meshing somehow with worry about world issues. Sylvia gave the impression of wholeness, purposeful activity, and plans for a future that would be glorious.

The Hugheses then visited the Comptons at their farmhouse twenty-five miles away. Sylvia began calling Elizabeth "Earth Mother," as she had formerly called Clarissa Roche; she admired Elizabeth's ability to keep house and care for her children in the inconvenient home (smoky oil lamps were the only lights).

The Comptons and Ted and Sylvia became good friends that spring. Only gradually did Elizabeth notice that Ted was either off working or in London or Exeter much of the time. He had a series of dental appointments in Exeter; he was doing BBC broadcasts. Sylvia was the person hungry for friendships; she planned the family outings and celebrations (the children's christenings, Frieda's birthday). She also celebrated her friends' birthdays. Elizabeth recalled Sylvia and Ted's coming unexpectedly on her birthday that summer, bringing wine and a beautiful cake, complete with candles.

Initially, Elizabeth marveled at the closeness between Sylvia and Ted. It was as if they shared one attitude, one experience of life. But then Sylvia became more open with her friend and hesitantly shared some of her worries about Ted's apparent unhappiness. Other spring poems also reflected her anxiety: "Little Fugue" in particular speaks of a woman's anxiety, her fear of loss, and the figures of Otto Plath and Ted Hughes are merged in this poem as they would be in the later "Daddy." The male voice here gives "a yew hedge of orders," and the male figure is portrayed as a dark funnel, drawing the speaker (a child, "guilty of nothing") down and into an abyss of guilt she cannot get free of. The poem closes with the speaker fighting to stay far from the threats mentioned in the poem, trying to maintain some sense of normalcy, trying to survive.

> I survive the while,
> Arranging my morning.
> These are my fingers, this my baby.
> The clouds are a marriage dress, of that pallor.

Many of Sylvia's poems from April and May of 1962 are about marriage or about the female speaker's role as lonely, wistful wife. The comparatively obscure poem "An Appearance" was originally called "The Methodical Woman" and presents negatively the woman who can organize life. As with many of Plath's late poems, this one is much clearer in early drafts than in the final version. As she reworked her spring poems, Sylvia disguised their meanings—perhaps to keep Ted from knowing that she was uneasy, perhaps to keep herself from naming her suspicions.

For instance, even though the poem "Crossing the Water" appears to be about death in the abstract, in early drafts it too was about a marital relationship. In their boat, the man and woman, separated, float on a dark lake; the tone is ominous. The boat has "nothing to steer by." Asking whether the relationship is founded on luck or accident, the speaker trails her hand in the cold water. At the close of the poem, with no explanation, the woman's hand is dead.

By the time Sylvia had written this group of anxiety and death poems, it was the end of May 1962. Earlier that month David and Assia Wevill had spent a weekend, the last of several pairs of friends that had visited Devon in the spring. The day after they left, Sylvia wrote two angry, revealing poems, "The Rabbit Catcher" and "Event." It had been clear to Sylvia that Ted was either seeing Assia already or making plans to do so. The beautiful woman, whose present marriage was her third, made no secret of her admiration for Ted. She had boasted earlier to friends that she would seduce him, and had told Sylvia that her present marriage was "little more than a loving friendship."

The original draft of "The Rabbit Catcher" includes autobiographical details that Sylvia deleted from the final version. The young wife of the rabbit catcher dreams of an ideal marriage that will allow her freedom to become herself. Once married, however, she finds that her husband maintains rigid control over her life. In the poem, however, *she* does not complain. It is rather the husband who says that he is missing too much of life, that he is going to do and have whatever he chooses. In the drafts, the wife speaks of her "impotence" and his "morning anger." Titled "Snares" in draft, "The Rabbit Catcher" is both a cry for understanding and a lament for the wife's misconceptions. Now what she sees, in place of her ideal marriage, is the snare used for catching rabbits. Behind the snares are her husband's hands, taking pleasure in their power to deliver death. The poem closes with a line that identifies the wife with the rabbit: "Those hands / Muffled me like gloves."

The common tragedy of Plath's spring poems is that the woman speaker has come to realize what a trap her marriage is, now dramatically changed because of what seem to be changes in her husband. "Event," originally called "Quarrel," continued the narrative. It mourns, "I cannot see your eyes. . . . I walk with an absence." Filled with images of despair and loss, the poem closes with the speaker's admission, "I am appalled by the death smell of everything." Written a week later, Sylvia's poem "Apprehensions" tells the same story; the speaker states, "I am deserted." The desolation and the fear of these poems are the themes of her late June poem, "Berck-Plage." In these spring poems Plath had already written her text for the summer of personal discovery. It is evident in the poems that she suspected Ted of infidelity. But, perhaps worse in some ways, she also suspected him of not caring how much she needed their marriage to justify her existence as a woman—perhaps to justify her life. Infidelity was less the issue than was Sylvia's almost obsessive need to live the perfect life, love the perfect man, create the perfect household, as a means of proving that she was a success in all the areas women were supposed to excel in. Her marriage had been carrying the weight of this idealistic fabrication, as well as the stresses of both adults' being professional writers and working in a household with two very young children. Assia continued to pretend that she and Ted were only friends. As a thank-you gift for the weekend, Assia sent Sylvia a piece of needlepoint, the rose at its center already finished. Sylvia carefully worked the rest of the piece, until her own intuition about the nature of Assia and Ted's relationship made such activity impossible.

Besides writing her revealing poems, Sylvia survived early summer by working frantically to get the house and grounds ready for her mother's visit. She cleaned the barn and cottage, mowed the grass, painted, weeded. She tried to repress her anger at a series of mysterious phone calls for Ted, even though she was sure they were from Assia. On June 7, she and Ted went to a meeting of beekeepers. There she bought a hive; soon she was keeping bees. She found the satisfaction of this hobby another bond with her father.

On June 8, Alvarez and a friend visited the Hugheses on their way to Cornwall for a Whitsun holiday. Alvarez saw changes in Ted and Sylvia's relationship but attributed them to what he called Sylvia's new maturity:

No longer quiet and withheld, a housewifely appendage to a powerful husband, she seemed made solid and complete, her own woman again. Perhaps the birth of a son had something to do with this new, confident air. But there was a sharpness and clarity about her that seemed to go beyond that. It was she who showed me around the house and the garden; the electric gadgets, the freshly painted rooms, the orchard and the burial mound. . . . Ted, meanwhile, seemed content to sit back and play with little Frieda, who clung to him dependently. Since it was a strong, close marriage, he seemed unconcerned that the balance of power had shifted for the time being to Sylvia.

Alvarez's later explanation for the change was that Sylvia was confident because she was writing well again. In truth, in her anger and confusion, she was leading a comparatively independent life as a way of removing herself from her husband's authority. She was leaving no doubt in anyone's mind that—if necessary—she could survive alone.

On June 16, Sylvia cooked a quiet sixth anniversary dinner. June 21, Aurelia arrived. A few days later Sylvia went into London to record a BBC program and to sell books at a bookdealers. Then she returned to attend Percy Key's funeral on June 29. The next day she finished writing the sadly powerful long poem "Berck-Plage," with its concluding scene of the casket-bearers in the cemetery:

> Six round black hats in the grass and a lozenge of wood,
> And a naked mouth, red and awkward.

Other lines and images in the masterful work connect that poem with others Sylvia wrote during the spring, and those she would write later. A seminal poem, "Berck-Plage" opens with the poet acknowledging her "twangling apprehensions" and builds to a decidedly unromantic treatment of death. Although the polite on-lookers call death a blessing, the speaker disagrees emphatically. Death, even in what appears to be dignity, can be worse than the various indignities of life.

And the indignities of life fill Plath's summer poems. In them she wrote about lies ("Words heard, by accident, over the phone") and about her misery ("My heart is very quiet," the speaker says in a draft of "Poppies in July." The poem closes "I am unattached, I am unattached"). Yet on July 9, driving with her mother to Exeter to shop and have lunch, Sylvia told Aurelia how happy she was in her life with Ted and the children. Emotional truth surfaced in Sylvia's poems, whether or not she planned for it to; the rest of her life she lived as though it were some blueprint for a woman's fantasy. Like a child, Sylvia seemed to believe that pretending would make any situation improve.

The evening of July 9, however, Sylvia intercepted a mysterious phone call for Ted and when Ted's conversation was over, she tore the telephone wires from the wall. She turned her rage inward as she stoically, blankly, dressed Nick and carried him to the car. Leaving Frieda with Aurelia, she drove the twenty-five miles to the Comptons'. When she arrived, both Elizabeth and David were worried about her behavior; distraught, she wept and held on to Elizabeth's hands, begging "Help me, help me." After she talked openly to her friends, Sylvia fed Nick and the two of them spent the night in the Comptons' living room.

The next morning Sylvia returned home. That evening after dinner, she carried from Court Green various of Ted's letters, drafts of work, and papers, and the manuscript of what was to have been her second novel, the book about her great love for Ted. Dedicated to "Ponter," one of her nicknames for Hughes, the new novel was to have been his August birthday present. Aurelia, holding Nicholas and maneuvering to keep the inquisitive Frieda inside the house, tried to stop Sylvia, but she could not. Sylvia built and fed an eager fire with the torn pages of manuscript and correspondence. It was, in effect, a funeral pyre.

14

The *Ariel* Poems

1962

"I Am Myself"

After the evening of the bonfire, Aurelia moved to Winifred Davies's nearby house. Sylvia's mother realized that the Hugheses' marriage was "seriously troubled" and, even though Ted wanted her to stay on with them, she knew that Sylvia and Ted needed time to themselves. Over the next few weeks, Ted was living in London with friends some of the time, while Sylvia kept herself busy with housekeeping and the children. She wrote only two poems the rest of that summer. On July 20 she finished the elliptical "Poppies in July," with its frightening lines in the draft version, "I put my hands among the flames. Nothing burns. . . ." and on August 13 she completed "Burning the Letters," a long poem about the July scene in the yard. She wrote no more poems until September 26.

Sylvia was both angry and bewildered, but at this time she didn't show her true emotional state to anyone except Elizabeth Compton. She instead busied herself with activities directly related to her professional career. Early in July she went to London to see George MacBeth about her doing readings for the BBC programs in poetry and to have lunch with Douglas Cleverdon, Ted's BBC producer, who was directing her radio play "Three Women" for its August broadcast. On July 19 she went in to meet with Eric White, head of the London Arts Council, about her planning the American Poetry Night for the Royal Court Theatre's summer festival, and to tape a reading of her poem "The Surgeon at 2 A.M." for an August BBC broadcast. Between the two trips, she opened a separate bank account for her own earnings. There would be two more installments of the Saxton grant, at $520 each, and she wanted to be sure those funds were not eaten away by daily living expenses. She also worried that Ted would continue his habit of writing checks on their account without recording them.

With Aurelia in England, Sylvia was free to come and go as she wanted. July 25, her mother moved back into Court Green so that Sylvia and Ted could attend an arts festival in Wales, where they were scheduled to give poetry readings and discuss their work. On the way to Bangor, they spent the night with the Huwses, who had moved to Wales the previous year. Ted and Dan Huws went walking; Sylvia and Helga visited upstairs. Both Sylvia and Ted talked about the troubled marriage, and Helga could see how upset her friend was. Sylvia seemed distant, even hesitant; and she walked slowly, heavily.

Anthony Dyson and Brian Cox, the editors of *Critical Quarterly*, were the Hugheses' hosts in Bangor. Several times in the past these men had taken Sylvia and Ted to dinner in London; dinner in Wales was strained in comparison.

Once back in Devon, Ted and Sylvia helped Aurelia prepare for her return trip on August 4. As she looked from the train as it left the station, Aurelia was thoroughly depressed by her daughter and son-in-law's stony faces. It seemed clear that no reconciliation was near, and she feared for her daughter's ability to keep up with the life she had committed herself to, particularly if she were to have to handle the children and the house alone.

As soon as Aurelia was gone, Sylvia called Joan Webb, the wife of her Devon physician, about the riding lessons they had talked about taking. For the next few months, Sylvia and Joan rode twice a week, Sylvia on the reddish-brown Ariel, a gentle horse very different from the runaway Sam of Cambridge days.

Her riding, visits to the Comptons' and beekeeping helped to fill Sylvia's days. This summer and fall should have been a happy time professionally: May 14 had seen the American publication of *The Colossus,* and other of her new poems were appearing in *The Observer, Harper's, London Magazine, Poetry, The New States-man, The New Yorker,* and *Encounter.* But Sylvia took little plea-sure in these accomplishments now.

She did maintain a correspondence with Alvarez (she had sent him poems early in the summer, and in July she wrote that he should be honest in his comments, not just "nice"). And she was evidently reading a great deal, particularly during the evenings when the children had been put to bed and she was alone. She had found C. A. Robinson's translations of Greek plays and was drawing a great deal of her imagery for the summer poems from his rendering of Euripides' *Medea.* In "Burning the Letters," she used echoes of the Medea legend, echoes that would persist through her poetry from this point until she wrote her last poems. In the legend, Medea loses her husband, Jason, to a rival after helping him find the Golden Fleece (and losing her own family and country in the process). She kills her rival by giving her gifts, a poison crown and gold-embroidered cloak that ex-plode into fire when she puts them on. Medea later kills her own two children by Jason as the ultimate punishment for his having left her. Certainly Sylvia saw similarities in her situation, believ-ing as she did that Ted was attractive to other women because of his literary reputation, which she took some credit for. Like Medea, Plath used fire as a weapon against her husband when she burned his papers. In Euripides' drama, Medea is described as "subtle," a word Plath uses often in these poems. Medea is also described as a "lioness" in scathing lines spoken by Jason after he discovers his children's deaths. It might well be said that Plath used the Medea legend as scaffolding for her own poems of anger and that "Burning the Letters" was the first poem in her *Medea* cycle, which ended with her February 1963 poem, "Edge."

The year 1962 was important for Plath, because she began to develop her own aesthetic about writing. With *The Bell Jar* successfully completed and accepted for publication by Hei-nemann, she had confidence that she could write for the commercial market. As a fiction writer, she might be able to live from her writing. While she loved poetry and knew that her best work was in the writing of poems, she was pragmatic enough to realize that she had to make money as well as develop her talents. In 1962 she wrote book reviews of both children's and adult books, worked on essays for both the BBC and *Punch*, finished the radio play that paid substantially, and made plans to become a regular BBC contributor and reader. One of the essays Plath wrote early in 1962, "Context," defined what she saw as her role as a writer in clear and emphatic language. She described herself as a "political" poet:

> The issues of our time which preoccupy me at the moment are the incalculable genetic effects of fallout and a documentary article on the terrifying, mad, omnipotent marriage of big business and the military in America—"Juggernaut, The Warfare State," by Fred J. Cook in a recent *Nation*. Does this influence the kind of poetry I write? Yes, but in a sidelong fashion. I am not gifted with the tongue of Jeremiah, though I may be sleepless enough before my vision of the apocalypse.

According to Plath here, her role as a poet was to write about the real world, "the terrors of mass extinction" and the rest of life's problems, in ways that would create art. Even in a *New Statesman* review of children's books, where she lamented atmospheric contamination from bomb-test fallout, she stressed the artist's responsibility to be aware of practical concerns of life. The poet should be involved in all aspects of living.

That conviction, coupled with her immense knowledge of literature, gave Plath a number of options when she came to write the poems of the fall, which are often considered autobiographical. Some experience from the writer's life may serve as catalyst for the work; but the materials of fiction and poetry are often drawn from other experiences, other literatures, besides the obviously personal ones. Plath's 1962 poems are certainly about anger, about the complexities of the modern family structure, about women's roles in marriage and life. But they are about much more than Sylvia Plath's personal situation in 1962. As George Steiner said so perceptively, these 1962 poems of Plath's are comparable to Pablo Picasso's remarkable antiwar painting, *Guernica*.

One of the worst episodes of Plath's summer of heartbreak occurred on August 16 and 17, when Mrs. Prouty, her Smith benefactor, invited Sylvia and Ted to be her guests in London. Mrs. Prouty, who by this time cared deeply about both Sylvia and Ted, put them up in The Connaught. They went with her to dinner and breakfast, saw Agatha Christie's long-running play *The Mousetrap*, and talked about their writing, their Devon house, and the children. It was Ted's birthday, but he gave Sylvia a copy of Joseph Heller's *Catch 22*. Sylvia felt wretched because she and Ted were pretending to be a happy couple, but the pretense seemed kinder than disclosure would have been. And it continued: on September 9 Mrs. Prouty came to dinner in Devon so that she could see the children and the house.

In London with Ted, Sylvia was all too ready to think that physical closeness meant reconciliation. So her disappointment was enormous when they returned to Devon and Ted resumed his life of unexplained absences. Two days later Sylvia cooked an elaborate dinner of roast lamb in honor of the August 19 birthday of David Compton, who came with Elizabeth to the Hugheses' home for the meal. That evening was also the premier broadcast of Plath's "Three Women."

For all her apparent calm, Sylvia did not behave as though she was reconciled to a separation from Ted. There were long afternoons of crying and talking with Elizabeth Compton, and harsh self-scrutiny as wife and mother. Where had she gone wrong? What had she done that she should not have done?

Late summer brought evidence of Sylvia's confusion. On August 22, she bought an insurance policy on Ted's life. After she paid the £173 premium, she had only £10 left in their account. Yet on August 27, she wrote to Aurelia that she had decided to separate. In Sylvia's eyes, Ted had lied to her repeatedly, had betrayed her (that word from the past, which she used whenever a man disappointed her). She would prefer to live away from him. A few days after that, when she was driving the station wagon, she experienced the overwhelming realization that she would be raising her children alone, that her isolated life would go on and on, forcing her to cope, no matter what Ted did.

Years before she had written in her journal, "My tragedy is to have been born a woman." Circumstances were bearing out her worst fears. While driving in Devon one day, Sylvia let the car go off the road.

On September 5, she was fined £1 for her traffic offense. Otherwise there was no aftermath, no drama. The accident was minor and she was not hurt. Ted spoke to Alvarez about it, and Alvarez remembered Ted's mood as well as the facts of the event itself. "Driving on her own, Sylvia had some kind of accident: apparently she had blacked out and run off the road onto an old airfield, though mercifully without damaging herself or their old Morris station wagon. His [Ted's] dark presence, as he spoke, darkened an even deeper shade of gloom." Later, in her poem "Lady Lazarus," Sylvia wrote about the accident as if it had been comparable to her 1953 suicide attempt.

But in September Sylvia was not writing, nor was she eating. She was merely enduring in Devon, bothered by the presence of friends in the guest room who had overstayed their welcome. She was worried about money and about the future. Once again she was ill with her high-temperature flu, as were the children. She was losing weight and relying on sleeping pills, a practice that added to her depression. (There is some evidence as well that her depression alternated with a manic side: her boundless energy, her insomnia, her sometimes erratic decisions were all marks of that.) At the advice of her solicitor, Sylvia took up smoking cigarettes. Finally, she wrote to Ruth Beuscher, her Boston therapist. She felt that life was droning on unbearably, that something decisive was going to have to happen.

Earlier in the summer, Sylvia had planned a trip to Ireland. On one of Ted's stays at home, he evidently agreed to the trip, and so she immediately jumped at the chance. Perhaps she thought a vacation would mean reconciliation. They traveled to Connemara in Galway, planning to meet their Harvard friends Jack and Moira Sweeney there, and to visit Yeats's tower, Bal- lylea. But the vacation was shortened when Ted departed abruptly for London. According to Sylvia, Ted lied about his plans, saying he was going grouse hunting for the day while she sailed—and then never returning. According to other accounts, the two had an irreconcilable argument. And still another ver-

sion recounts a mysterious tale of Ted and Sylvia in a large room
at the tower, watching a portrait hanging there as its face
changed to resemble Ted's. In any case, Sylvia remained several
days longer, enjoying the sea, the beauty of the coast, the seafood.

Once she returned to Devon, she found a telegram from Ted
saying that he was staying in London for another few weeks.
Her anger knew no bounds. She went to Winifred Davies, and
spent three hours that night mulling over the choices open to
her. She decided that she had to separate from Ted. She could
no longer stand the indecision of the situation. She had convinced herself that his behavior meant she and her writing might
be unsafe. Now she made an appointment to see a London solicitor on September 25.

Sylvia's determination may have stemmed in part from the
reassurance she received in a letter from Ruth Beuscher. Dated
September 17, 1962, Beuscher's warm reply offered Sylvia all
the possible support a friend could give. She said that she
(Beuscher) was "furious" with Ted and his immature behavior.
She could not be impartial but neither could she take Sylvia on
as a patient by mail (which Sylvia had evidently suggested).
Sylvia, however, should count on her as a close friend, and she
offered her love and support throughout the coming hard times.
The important thing, according to Beuscher, was that Sylvia
should keep control of her life in her own hands. If living with
Ted in this divided way was impossible, then Sylvia should not
continue to do it.

Sylvia replied quickly, explaining what she had done and
what she planned, which at this time was to get a legal separation. But in Beuscher's next letter, dated September 25, she
urged Sylvia to get a divorce instead of a separation. She thought
that a divorce would be better legally and financially. To that
end, she warned, Sylvia should not be intimate with Ted because then she could not use adultery as grounds for a divorce.
Neither should she take the children to their grandparents' home
until custody had been decided. Again, Beuscher's primary admonition was that Sylvia take charge, that she make a plan and
stick to it.

The last days of September continued to be erratic for Sylvia.

Letters to both Aurelia and Mrs. Prouty (who had by this time been told the truth) repeat what was becoming a litany: Ted was immature, selfish, cruel; he lied, ruining the most important quality of their marriage, trust; he spent money that belonged to the family on himself and his pleasures. But especially in Sylvia's letters to Mrs. Prouty, there is also the statement of her immense grief at losing her husband: "I loved the man I have lived with 6 happy years with all my heart, but there is *nothing* of this left. . . . Luckily Dr. Beuscher and my stay at McLean's gave me the strength to face pain and difficulty."

Sylvia may have been remembering her years of therapy because, according to her letters, Ted was taunting her with her earlier suicide attempt, saying that if she were to repeat that action, everything would be simpler for him. He called her a "hag" in a world of beautiful women. He described himself as being dragged down by her—or so Sylvia's letters say. Her correspondence with her mother and with Mrs. Prouty recounts incredible happenings: jealous and angry insults; a fight between Ted and David Wevill. In the past, Sylvia's letters had created a fabrication of the ideal. Might they now portray situations that would evoke sympathy for the young mother and her two children? In the case of Plath's earlier letters, one can compare this correspondence with her private journals to discern the truth. However, the journals from this period of her later life have disappeared—according to Ted Hughes—so comparing accounts is impossible. In her own mind, certainly, Sylvia saw her position as bleak and thought of herself as Ted's victim.

She became acutely aware of her own needs. She insisted that she must have time for her own writing, that she must have a nanny for the children. Yet even as she wrote Aurelia that she and Ted were finished, she explained that she would never return to America to live. She felt at home in England. In London she could make her living as a writer.

Winifred Davies's advice may have saved Sylvia from more depression during the fall. Because Sylvia could not sleep well and was waking very early, Winifred suggested that she use that time to write. Beginning in late September, Sylvia did just that, starting with a few pages of a new novel, her third, only recently begun. By the 29th she was writing poems once more. "A Birthday Present," that stark demand for truth, was dated September 30, 1962. This was the beginning of an astonishingly productive period during which Sylvia wrote most of the poems in her *Ariel* collection: "The Detective" on October 1; "The Courage of Shutting-Up" the next day; the five magnificent "bee" poems during the following week, ending with "Wintering" on October 9. It is the cutting, wry voice of the defensive and tormented wife that gives these October poems their strength. Especially notable is the raucous gallows humor of the detective who finds a crow in the last line of "The Detective," and the blunt insistence of the speaker in "The Courage of Shutting-Up."

The most important of these October poems is Plath's bee sequence, her survival poetry. Expert and complicated poems, the series of five bee poems describes the joy of creation, the role in the bee community of the old queen who fights against dispossession by the more beautiful queens, and survives. "Winter is for women," Plath wrote. Women survive together. As winter approaches, the community that endures is female:

> They have got rid of the men
> The blunt, clumsy stumblers, the boors.

Much of Plath's effect in these poems stems from the racy rhythm—noun after noun, phrase after phrase. These are poems written, as she said, "for the ear, not the eye: they are poems written out loud."

Sylvia had found those same speechlike qualities in Anne Sexton's second book of poems, *All My Pretty Ones*, which she had received from Sexton on August 17. In a letter thanking Anne, Sylvia said that she was "absolutely stunned and delighted" because the book was not only masterful but "womanly in the greatest sense" and "so blessedly unliterary." Plath listed a dozen of her favorites from the book but closed by saying, "Hell, they are all terrific." She asked to see new poems and a newsy letter. She closed wishing her friend "more power—although you seem to need nothing—it is all there." It was reaffirming for Sylvia to read consummate poems about women's subjects, observed through a woman's eyes and told with a woman's voice. Her aim, like Sexton's, was to write about things that interested her, which more and more were "womanly." Ever since "Three Women," that had become a rich direction for her, and it was a route that was quickly leading to some of her best poems.

The bee poems spoke about domestic and womanly topics, but they were very much poems about power as well. From the first fairly literary poem, "The Bee Meeting," with its echoes of Hawthorne's story "Young Goodman Brown," through the magnificent "Stings," with its fearless female speaker ("I am in control . . . I / Have a self to recover"), Plath moved farther and farther from the literary mainstream and further into her own mythic world. As in "Lady Lazarus" and "Purdah," the woman avenger in "Stings" is also lionlike, red, winged, and powerful. Egyptian, African, and Grecian, Sylvia's lioness not only escapes her painful life but sends tribulation on her enemies. She is a world force, a moral and corrective force. Sylvia's use of the lioness image recalls Jason's calling Medea a lioness. It also usurped Ted's astrological identity as a Leo, the lion.

As she finished these poems on October 9, Sylvia's personal situation hit rock bottom. It became clear that Ted was going to move out. Even though Sylvia had seen a lawyer and had discussed separation, she was not ready for this complete break. Her October 9 letter to Aurelia was distraught. She was vindictive, reciting stories about Ted and his lover—spiteful, angry, bitter tales. She was pathetic: "In Ireland I may find my soul, and in London . . . my brain, and maybe in heaven what was my heart." But she also wrote in some parts of the letter with the comic exaggeration that was customary for her: "Everything is breaking—my dinner set cracking in half, the health inspector says the cottage should be demolished. . . . Even my beloved bees set upon me today . . . and I am all over stings."

By October 12, when she again wrote to her mother, she was even less composed. Ted had moved out on October 11. In her subsequent fear and panic, Sylvia wrote Aurelia that she did not see how she could go to court and testify, portraying herself as the abandoned wife, or how she would live through the winter without a babysitter. She begged for someone from home to come and live with her for six weeks, but she insisted that the help must be either Aunt Dot, her mother's sister, or Maggie, Warren's new wife, whom Sylvia had not yet met. On October

13, however, in another letter, she swung into her familiar take-charge voice. There she wrote about her financial affairs, giving her mother information about the ways she would manage, faced as she was at that time with another bout of flu and more weight loss.

In the midst of this emotional storm, however, Sylvia finished "The Applicant" and wrote "Daddy," poems that are clear testimony to the power of art to transform. The fury that she had managed to keep more or less in check all summer burst loose, and more fiery poems appeared—"The Jailer," "Purdah," "Ariel," "Lady Lazarus." Some of Sylvia's finest poetry poured out in the weeks following Ted's departure.

The artistry evident in the poems of October 1962 was the fruit of years of Sylvia's studying her craft. Because of her daring, her reckless willingness to put words to emotions new to her, she found the form for the sorrow and anger she felt. The artist in Sylvia shaped the feelings that the wife could only begin to express. Meanwhile, the daughter wrote about those same feelings in her letters, the raw recital of facts from which the poetry would grow.

On October 16, Sylvia wrote to Aurelia that she had the flu again and was running a temperature of over 101 degrees. That same day, she wrote the bitterly accusatory poem that was called in draft "Mum: Medusa" about her mother's supposedly harmful influence on her. Even as she documented her dependency on her mother with a stream of intimate letters home, she reproached herself in the poem for that dependency. As had been the case since childhood, Sylvia desperately needed her mother. And, as since childhood, Aurelia responded. Reacting to that October 16 letter, she wired Winifred Davies to hire someone to stay with Sylvia ("salary paid here" the telegram instructed).

Sylvia continued to write out her vengeance. On October 17, she wrote "The Jailer," the most vindictive of her late poems. In it, the male protagonist treats the speaker like a slave. She is worn to exhaustion. His rejection of her turns her to a skeleton. "My ribs show. What have I eaten? / Lies and smiles." She can see the futility of thinking she is in any way necessary to his life; she says sadly, "I am myself. That is not enough." Much angrier than "Medusa," "The Jailer" ironically reflects the same kind of dependence, this time on a husband. In the poems themselves, Sylvia was attempting to free herself of artistic dependence. Before these October poems, she had usually written on topics Ted suggested. Now she was writing poems of her own devising.

Compared to "The Jailer," Plath's poem "Daddy," which she wrote on October 12, is a nearly reasonable hate-chant that draws much of its power from its ironic tone and its form and movement. "Daddy" is a highly controlled narrative about her father's effect on her, which then merges with the influence of her husband. Her anger at Ted was the fuel for this and for many of her other October poems. "Stopped Dead," written on October 19, and "Amnesiac" and "Lyonnesse," both written on October 21, continue the description of her estranged husband. The "high cold masks of amnesia" that Sylvia referred to in "The Jailer" remain his most hurtful trait: how can a man deny what his family has meant to him, she asks. But as Sylvia's thirtieth birthday approached on October 27, she speculated about her future. In quick succession, she wrote four of her strongest poems: "Fever 103°," "Ariel," "Purdah," and "Lady Lazarus." In each poem a betrayed woman—sick, sexually abused, even dead—survives, and survives to mete out vengeance.

In "Ariel" the subject of the poem finds herself through the expansion of her spirit as she rides a beloved horse in early morning. The physical and emotional pleasure allows her to "unpeel," to lose what she calls "dead hands, dead stringencies." In her new-found freedom from male surveillance, she takes on all the independence, the aggression, that her culture had attempted to deny her. "I / Am the arrow" is the key image, recalling a speech of Mrs. Norton's in which she had said that men are arrows and women are the places they fly off from. In "Ariel" the woman is the arrow—but she is also a lioness. Through her insight and understanding, she has become "God's lioness," and "Ariel" in Hebrew means just that. ("God's Lioness" was the title of a draft version of the poem.)

"Fever 103°" portrays illness as a purifying event. Plath uses an image of sexual purity as a desirable quality for a woman. She imagines that her fevers have burned her out so that she is now "too pure" for everyday life. Yet her incorporation of the image of the leopard at Hiroshima, burned to white ash in the radiation, keeps the poem ironic and tells the reader that such sacrifice is never desirable.

The image of the lioness returns in "Purdah" as the woman with power becomes a Medea-like avenger, intent on punishing the unfaithful husband. Its tone is more sinister, and more sexual, than that of "Lady Lazarus," written at nearly the same time. In "Lady Lazarus," which is similar to "Daddy" because of its tight control and the macabre rhythm that Sylvia called "light verse," the speaker's guilt and anger have turned to pride. She is good at her profession (which is attempting suicide), and in a society that allows women so few distinctions, hers is significant. The poem ends with a phoenixlike image of rebirth that gives way to vengeance:

> Out of the ash
> I rise with my red hair
> And I eat men like air.

In one sense, this is the ending of Plath's long and debilitating saga of pain. By the end of October, she had reached a kind of reconciliation with herself, though she was worn and anguished from the struggle. It had gone on since early spring, over seven months, and it had become her life.

As she wrote to her mother on October 16, the writing that had come from the pain of those months was almost worth the suffering. "I am a writer . . . I am a genius of a writer; I have it in me. I am writing the best poems of my life; they will make my name." But at the end of that same letter, Sylvia added, almost wildly, "I am . . . full of plans, but do need help for the next two months. I am fighting now against hard odds and alone."

15

Resolution

1962 - 63

"I See by My Own Light"

Winifred Davies found a wonderful young nurse who was willing to work for Sylvia. From October 21 to December 11, Susan O'Neill-Roe came at 8:30 A.M. and stayed until 6:00 P.M. Soon after Susan had begun caring for the children, Sylvia wrote her mother that she felt like a new person. She was writing each day until late in the morning and was thinking of continuing her new novel as well as working on her exciting poems. Susan agreed to stay overnight when Sylvia went out of town, so she planned her first trip to London since Ted had left. London, for Sylvia, was a cultural home. Devon, in contrast, was isolated and lonely, its rich fall harvest rotting in the forgotten gardens, its townspeople giving Sylvia a wide berth because word was that Ted had left her.

Although the Webbs invited Sylvia for tea on October 26, she had no plans for her birthday the following day. She inscribed John Berryman's poem collection, *Homage to Mistress Bradstreet*, with that date as if she had bought the book as a present; and she had been annotating poems from D. H. Lawrence's *Collected Poems* with October dates ("The Mess of Love" is dated October

22, for example). She was reading Blake, Yeats, Woolf, and Dylan Thomas (whose birthday she shared) during those fall nights after the children were in bed. Her household calendar for her birthday was completely blank, but she was not idle: on that day she finished the poems "Ariel" and "Poppies in October."

Susan had stabilized the household so Sylvia was free to concentrate on writing what she called her "dawn" poems. On a drive to attend a Bach concert with Elizabeth Compton, Sylvia had used that phrase, telling her friend she was writing "dawn poems in blood." Elizabeth thought Sylvia looked ill. She was thin, coughing, running a low temperature, trying to recover from still another bout of the flu—but flushed with the joy of successful work.

Other friends remember Sylvia's frantic need to talk, her nonstop delivery of story after story, as she adopted the raconteur stance once more, just as she had after her 1953 breakdown and recovery. Clearly she needed someone to listen. She was also ready to take on whatever adventure might occur, especially after her year of living quietly in Devon. On October 25 she wrote an admonitory letter to her mother. Contrasted with the panic-filled letters of earlier October, this one is a model of confidence:

> For goodness sakes, stop being so *frightened* of everything, Mother! Almost every other word in your letter is "frightened!" One thing I want for my children to have is a bold sense of adventure, not the fear of trying something new. . . . If I chained myself to my Bendix I would never see the world. . . .

Responding to her own advice, Sylvia packed a literary world into her trip to London on October 29 and 30. She met with Peter Dickinson about the summer American Poetry Night at the Royal Court Theatre, recorded her poem "Berck-Plage" for the BBC, and went to Al Alvarez's studio and read him the new October poems. Because he was recently divorced, Sylvia confided to him that she and Ted were separated. She attended a play and a PEN party in Chelsea where she and Dan Huws talked about Frieda's development, the child's regression since Ted had left, and Sylvia's consequent fear that her daughter might have emotional difficulties. As good friends, they also talked about the possibility of divorce. Dan, who was a Catholic, said, "You know what we believe—till death do us part." Sylvia, with great intensity, agreed, "Yes, yes, that's what I believe too."

The next day Sylvia had lunch with the BBC producer Peter Orr before taping the interview with him and reading from her new poems. In the interview, Plath spoke about herself as an American poet (though an old-fashioned American, one morally upright and traditional) and about the vitality of some recent American poetry. She admired the fact that it drew on "interior experiences" and on "private and taboo subjects," as did the work of Robert Lowell and Anne Sexton. She criticized British poetry for its gentility and praised American poetry for its immediacy. She stated that the subjects of the best poems must be both real, based on genuine emotion, and relevant, "relevant to the larger things, the bigger things such as Hiroshima and Dachau and so on." "I'm a rather political person," she concluded.

Certainly the poems that Sylvia had just been writing and that she read for Orr evidenced the aesthetic she described in the interview. They were drawn from her own life, but they opened to universal interpretation. Except for "The Rabbit Catcher," all the poems Sylvia read had been written during October, and three of them—"Nick and the Candlestick," "Lady Lazarus," and "Purdah"—were dated October 29, the previous day. She raced emphatically through "Cut," "Medusa," "Amnesiac," "Fever 103°," "The Applicant," "A Birthday Present," "Stopped Dead," "Daddy," and "A Secret," reading with an intense and sure speed and inflection that suggested ample practice. Plath's expert reading gave further credence to her comment that these poems were written for the ear rather than the eye, and that she said them aloud to herself as she wrote them.

Sylvia returned to Devon, triumphant, flooded with compliments from friends and acquaintances about her appearance and her work. On November 2, she wrote an exuberant letter to Mrs. Prouty. Prouty had evidently told Sylvia that she must return to London for the winter. (Sylvia had been considering

going to either Ireland or Spain, but childcare was a problem.)
Now Sylvia agreed. Contrasted with daily life in Devon, London was brilliant. People there wanted to know her. She may have received more attention, in fact, because she was separated from Ted. For whatever reasons, Sylvia seemed sure that living in London would continue to be exciting. She would settle in, if she could find a flat, and have wonderful salons. She would have friends, good schools for the children, accessible plays and films, and opportunities to record for the BBC and write for the London magazines. Sylvia's tendency to idealize circumstances was again operating in full force.

Once home from her London trip, congratulating herself on coming through in good form, Sylvia began her search for a London flat. November 5, the following Monday, she repeated her trip, this time staying two days and scouring the city for apartments. Ted helped her part of the time, but she found the vacancy at 123 Fitzroy Road on her own. She had returned to the Primrose Hill area where she and Ted had lived so happily in 1960 and 1961. To her amazement, she noticed a "To Let" sign just around the corner from 3 Chalcot Road, their former address. The flat to be rented was the top two floors of "Yeats's house," so indicated by the blue historical marker above the front door. Sylvia had just visited Yeats's tower in Ireland. She had recently been reading a great deal of his work and, of course, she had long admired him. Finding this flat was beyond her wildest hopes. Three rooms on the top floor and as many on the second meant she would have space enough for a live-in girl. She was elated as she began a siege to get the flat. Single women were considered bad credit risks, so she and Ted went to the agent's together. The flat had been tentatively promised to Professor Trevor Thomas, an art historian who had asked the agents to reserve the maisonette just two days earlier. In return for a pledge of a year's rent paid in advance, Ted and Sylvia were given the flat and Thomas was given the lower floor. He was not inclined to like the Hughes family after what he considered their trickery in getting the more desirable apartment.

From 123 Fitzroy Road Sylvia walked to Alvarez's studio for a drink and a talk, happy that she would most likely be moving to London. She had become even more friendly to him since the publication of his anthology, *The New Poetry*, with its introduction critical of much contemporary British poetry. He, in turn, enjoyed her as she clinked the ice in her drink, saying that ice was all she missed about America. She read him more poems. He told her—again—that she was the most interesting woman poet since Emily Dickinson.

The next week Sylvia went on a clothes shopping spree in Exeter. She came home with a camel suit and matching sweater, a blue and black tweed skirt and a black sweater, and a green cardigan and red wool skirt. Later, in St. Ives, Cornwall, she bought a pewter bracelet, hair clasp, and earrings, and a blue enameled necklace. She wrote to Mrs. Prouty—whose birthday check she had been spending—that she had had few new clothes since her Smith days. Now her new London life could "begin over from the skin out."

Sylvia felt new confidence partly because she was looking better. Her new shorter hair style left bangs to frame her face, and her new clothes transformed her. She wrote proudly to her mother that men stared at her in the street. She also had a new correspondent. Father Bart, a young Catholic priest studying literature at Oxford, had begun writing to her about poetry. They exchanged poems, and she asked him questions about his faith—a topic of increasing interest to her—and answered his questions about modern and contemporary poetry. After Sylvia had read some of his poems, her advice to him reflected what she was accomplishing in her October poems: "Speak straight out . . . let the world blow in more roughly."

Sylvia's exuberance colored some of her November poems. There are moments of joy, although the tenor remains dark. On November 4 she wrote the gnomic "The Couriers," a poem about signs and portents that seem to be based on Robert Graves's *White Goddess* symbology. After the speaker sorts through possible alternatives for her life, she comes to the celebration of the last line (more explicit in draft than in the final version), "Love, love, it is my season." As Sylvia's visits to London seemed to prove, it *was* her season.

She began getting ready physically, psychologically, and professionally for the move to London. In mid-November she assembled a second book of poems. She first called it *The Rival and Other Poems*, then *A Birthday Present*, then *The Rabbit Catcher*, then *Daddy*, and finally *Ariel*. Her first idea was that the enemy suggested by "the rival"—whether mother, sister, lover, or the self as double—was the dominant theme. Then she focused on the issue of truth, the heart of the enigmatic "A Birthday Present." With the choice of both "The Rabbit Catcher" and "Daddy" as title poems, she was emphasizing Ted's control of her life and what she saw as his abandonment. It was only with "Ariel," God's lioness, that she chose a rich enough image to free the reader's imagination: androgynous power, animal made human and spirit, the whimsicality of Shakespeare's character in *The Tempest*. Sylvia chose a title that stressed her affinity with a liberating imagination and thereby drew a portrait of the woman as artist. The magic of Plath's collection occurs because domestic events are transformed by art. Sylvia, too, was an Ariel, using "art to enchant" and earning her freedom through truthfulness. As she had told Ted of her October poems, "They saved me."

Dedicated to Frieda and Nicholas, the book as Plath arranged it began with "Morning Song" and ended with "Wintering." (In the published version, Hughes included many more late poems, omitted many of those Plath had wanted to include, and rearranged everything.) Plath's *Ariel* included poems from early in 1960 through "Death & Co.," written on November 14, 1962. Starting with the word "love" and ending with "spring," the book plunged through her most anguished and vituperative poems to end with the emotionally positive bee sequence. She did not order the poems chronologically; for instance, "Tulips," a 1961 poem, was placed directly after "Lady Lazarus," a late October poem. With her arrangement, she was telling a story, the story of her life as artist and married woman, and the dissolution of that life. But she let the sequence build and look ahead to spring, just as in *The Bell Jar* she implied a healthy rebirth with her ending.

In *Ariel* as Sylvia arranged it, there is also a tone of spirituality, which was to become more obvious in her poems from December, January, and February. Renunciation and transcendence began to replace the angry chastisement and name-calling of the October poems. Plath had been shaken to the core by the events of the summer of 1962, and it took her some time to recover her sense of self. "Letter in November," written on November 11, shows Plath's complex emotional state at the time. Walking in the Devon orchard, the speaker is "stupidly happy" because "This is my property. / Two times a day / I pace it." Although she relies on sleeping pills, although her present life seems far from happy, she still loves and finds pleasure in her surroundings, her "wall of old corpses," the sense of history the house exudes, and the seventy wonderful fruit trees. An image of a golden apple leads to the turn in the magnificent poem, however, because it is from the speaker's recollection of the fantastic golden fruit, brimming with promise, that the poet faces reality. She has won the battle, but the skirmish has nearly destroyed her.

Plath's late fall poems suggest that she was now relying on her own belief system, a system increasingly developed from contacts with other women. Her dependence on Ruth Beuscher, her admiration for Winifred Davies, her rapport with Elizabeth Compton, Ruth Fainlight, Susan O'Neill-Roe, and Clarissa Roche—as well as her continued intimacy with Ann Davidow and Marcia Brown—showed that Plath recognized what comfort and wisdom her women friends could provide. She was trying to broaden that circle: she wrote an admiring letter to British poet Stevie Smith, asking to meet her; and she grew closer to Olive Higgins Prouty, the older woman who had survived a breakdown and the struggle to write despite social pressure.

Thematically, too, many of Sylvia's later poems were concerned with the beauty of the maternal. Her positive descriptions of women as robust and life-giving (as in "Heavy Women" and "Morning Song") contrast the negative imagery of women as thin and unproductive ("Munich Mannequins," "Barren Women"), and in her letters home Sylvia frequently identified Ted's new women friends with the second group. In her late 1962 poems, she describes her rival as having "a womb of marble," makes pointed references to abortion, and in another poem laments, "Barren, the lot are barren!" Sylvia increasingly took pleasure in her role as mother of children, a pleasure her poems reflected.

On November 17, Clarissa Roche—whom Sylvia in the past

had called "earth mother"—arrived in Devon with her five-week-old daughter. During the past year Sylvia had been inviting Paul and Clarissa to visit Devon, most recently in her October 19 letter in which she said she was living "without access to friend or relative." She painted a pathetic picture of herself and so, although it had been nearly five years since she had seen Sylvia, Clarissa could not deny her. In the foggy, rainy night, Sylvia—a shadowy figure holding a large umbrella—hugged Clarissa repeatedly, saying, "You've saved my life." Clarissa felt she was not joking.

The Devon house struck Clarissa as cold and forbidding, and there were signs that Sylvia was distraught. She talked incessantly, composing bitterly amusing stories out of the terrible marital scenes of the past summer and fall. "All experience is grist for the novelist," she said, but the pain and embarrassment of some of the happenings tore through her pretense of distance. Clarissa heard about the summer bonfire; the curses Sylvia and Ted exchanged; the letters from Father Bart, the poet-priest from Oxford; the good times in London. Clarissa struggled along with Sylvia to see what shape her life would take on. She could see how frightened her friend was to face the future, despite her façade of bravado; how weary she was bearing the full responsibility for the children; how ill she had been, having lost twenty pounds during the summer and fall. Yet great, gusty laughter ricocheted through the house during the long weekend, for Sylvia was a good comic story teller. The laughter, sometimes, seemed almost desperate.

There were signs that Sylvia's mood was erratic. Between October 19, when she had written to the Roches about their coming, and November 17, when Clarissa arrived, Sylvia had made important decisions. She had found the flat in London and had immersed herself in Yeats's writing. She saw only promise ahead, once she left Devon. She told Clarissa that on the day she had returned from London with the promise of the flat, she had taken Yeats's collected plays into her lap—by candlelight—and opened the book at random, to find the lines, "Get wine and food to give you strength and courage, and I will get the house ready." For Sylvia, it was a sign that she was in touch with good spirits. Just as she was obsessed with the idea of herself being reborn, and the rebirth she had seen as the only possible solution to her breakdown in 1953, now she felt so alone and insecure that she again sought external assurance. No one was able to convince her that she had not needed rebirth but just needed some counseling.

A November letter from Sylvia to Ruth Beuscher prompted Dr. Beuscher to consider whether she should ask Sylvia to come to America and stay with her. Professional ethics dictated that a therapist not become so involved in a patient's life, but Beuscher was sure that Sylvia needed a confidante. A later letter from Plath reassured Beuscher that she was coping with the changes and that she was intent on making a new life for herself and the children in London.

More confident because Clarissa's visit had given her some relief from her anxiety, but depressed because Susan was taking a week off, Sylvia immersed herself in activity. She invited Winifred Davies for dinner on November 21. Although the next day was Thanksgiving in America, an important family holiday in the Plath home, Sylvia and the children celebrated alone. She wrote to Aurelia that she was sick, worn out from handling all the work while Susan was gone. But in the same letter Sylvia recovers her sense of humor enough to announce, wryly:

Boy, when I get to be 50 and if I'm famous, there will be no tributes to "The loving husband without whose help I would never have succeeded etc. etc." Everything I have done I have done in spite of Ted. . . .

Within a few days, Sylvia had again invited Winifred—this time with her son Garnett, an apprentice police officer visiting from London, and Susan O'Neill-Roe—for a special dinner. She was trying to keep up her spirits and her confidence.

On December 3, Sylvia went to London once more, this time signing the lease and arranging for a gas stove, electricity, and a telephone. London was shrouded in a terrible fog; as a result, there was no public transportation, and getting around in the city was nearly impossible. Instead of being discouraged, however, Sylvia thought the weather was a kind of personal challenge. She saw Alvarez, had lunch to discuss a poetry reading she was to give in early spring, and worked further on the American Poetry Night. Then she returned to Devon and spent four hectic days packing and loading the car (one entire day was spent stringing onions from her garden and packing honey, apples, potatoes, and holly). Then she, the children, and Susan drove to London.

Her checkbook testifies to the amount of purchasing she was doing. Some painting was done, and carpets were laid in the bedrooms. Her bedroom was decorated in what she called "bee" colors, white, yellow, and black. She put a deposit down on the telephone, although she was told that getting one could take months. Without a phone, making the professional and social contacts she had planned was difficult. Every few days she tried to get to a public phone, but dressing both children and timing such expeditions on cold days was frustrating. And once Sylvia had called people, they had no way to get back in touch with her. Sylvia was living in London, but she was nearly as isolated as she had been in Devon.

The coming Christmas holiday complicated matters further. People were busy with their own family plans. Few cared to invite Sylvia's young family to their celebrations. Most of the people Sylvia did reach seemed glad that she had moved back to London, but they put her off, saying they would call her after the first of the year.

Being in London meant that Ted could see the children, and he came frequently to take them to the zoo or for walks. Seeing him was difficult for Sylvia, but she tried to pretend that she was busy and happy to be living in the city. When she had first moved to Fitzroy Road, she was thrilled that shopkeepers remembered her. As soon as December 20, she was having tea with Katherine Frankfort, a neighbor, and then going to see Ingmar Bergman's film *Through a Glass Darkly*. Doris Bartlett, a sitter Frieda remembered, cared for the children. Sylvia had also been lucky in being able to buy what she needed without worrying about money; before she had moved from Devon, her beloved Aunt Dot had sent her a check for $700.

As was customary, Sylvia wrote to her mother that she was exuberant with the move. "Well, here I am! Safely in Yeats' house! I can just about allow myself time for a cup of tea and a bit of letter writing after the immensity of the move. . . . I can truly say I have never been so happy in my life. I just sit thinking, Whew! I have done it! And beaming. Shall I write a poem, shall I paint a floor, shall I hug a baby?" She wrote to Aurelia, "Everything is such fun, such an adventure."

Professor Thomas, Sylvia's downstairs neighbor, did not see much evidence of that fun in his various meetings with her. She appeared elegant and composed, usually wearing a long, lightweight coat, her hair braided and coiled around her head. And she was usually quite somber, worriedly maneuvering the children and a large, old-fashioned perambulator, and often carrying packages—taking out trash, more often carrying in food. The children were unnaturally quiet, he thought, and Sylvia herself seemed, in his words, "erratic" one day, "charming" another, and "bad tempered" and "pathetic" as well. She appeared to be busy. She invited friends for tea and dinner—Alvarez for the 24th (but he stopped only long enough for a drink); the Frankforts for the 26th; a guest known only as "Colin" for the 27th; Garnett Davies for the 30th. She shopped for dressy clothes in fake fur and velvet, and spent Christmas with some friends. Assia and her friends donated bits of furniture for the flat. But the days were long and the week before Christmas, London was once again buried in fog. The children were ill, too, and on December 28, Sylvia went to see her former physician, Dr. Horder, about the children's health and her own weight loss and insomnia. She needed more sleeping pills.

At the same time she was experiencing mixed success professionally. On December 21, *The Atlantic* had accepted two of the longer "bee" poems, and she was asked to judge the Cheltenham poetry contest again. But she seemed to be battling with *The New Yorker*. Because of her "first reading" contract, she had to send all her poems there first. Yet beginning in June of 1962, Howard Moss, the poetry editor, rejected nearly all her work. Sylvia's records show that she sent Moss ten large groups of new poems from October 1962 to February 4, 1963. Of all that work Moss accepted only the second part of "Amnesiac," saying the opening of that poem was not related to the rest. Sylvia counted on *The New Yorker* as a source of steady income. Was she going to have to change her style to please that magazine?

These wholesale rejections of her current poems were both puzzling and enervating. Sylvia was excited about these poems, and she knew that Alvarez, Ted, and Douglas Cleverdon, the BBC producer, admired them. Cleverdon had asked her to get a program of new poems ready for a BBC reading. She had herself developed enough confidence in her own critical judgment to know how good her new work was, but at times she was insecure enough to need confirmation.

The confusion *The New Yorker* rejections created was intensified in early January when Sylvia received a rejection letter from Judith Jones, her Knopf editor of *The Colossus*, to whom she had submitted *The Bell Jar* for American publication. Dated December 28, 1962, Jones's letter criticized the manuscript for its unbelievable point of view, saying that Plath's use of the college girl's voice did not prepare the reader for the seriousness of her illness or for her suicide attempt.

Sylvia quickly submitted the novel to Harper & Row, eager to find an American publisher before Heinemann brought out the book in England on January 14, 1963. Even though she had earlier referred to *The Bell Jar* as a "pot-boiler" and would be publishing it under a pseudonym ("Victoria Lucas"), her attitude about the novel had changed. Reading it in proofs, Sylvia realized what she had accomplished. *The Bell Jar* was a good, crisp, funny, and yet poignant book. It spoke with the voice of an over-aged Smithie, reminiscent of the cynical Smith voice that colored the campus newspaper and year book. It was a 1950s voice, a 1950s attitude, just as it was supposed to be.

Any rejection was painful at this time, however, because Plath was staking everything on her identity as a writer. She had moved back to London because she needed to have contacts for free-lance work. She intended to show people that Ted's leaving her had not demolished her life, though it had come close to doing that. But her first few weeks in London had not been reassuring, either socially or professionally. She had not been asked to do anything she could not have done in Devon, and socially she sensed that she was being kept at a distance. Her experience with Alvarez—who had been an interested and attentive literary friend in the months before she finally settled in London—was repeated with other acquaintances. Although Alvarez had come for a drink on Christmas Eve, she did not see him again.

Hurt by what she considered rejections of various kinds, Sylvia wrote to her former confidants. On January 2, 1963, to Marcia Brown, she told the story of her losing twenty pounds during the summer and said that she almost died with the flu, in the midst of herculean labors and the stress of Ted's leaving.

> I have been so utterly *flattened* by having to be a business-woman, farmer—harvesting 70 apple trees, stringing all my onions, digging and scrubbing all my potatoes, extracting and bottling my honey, etc.—mother, writer *and* all-round desperado that I'd give anything to be alone. I feel like a very efficient tool or weapon. . . .

She urged Marcia and her husband to come for a spring visit, saying that she and the children were very lonely.

To the Huwses she wrote that she was happy to be away from Devon (where people suggested, once Ted had left, that she and he were never married because so much of her mail came to "Sylvia Plath"), but that she was lonely in London. She continued her conversation with Dan about what she called "Frieda's awful regression" without Ted in the household, and referred to herself as a "desperate mother." The purpose of her letter, however, was to ask the Huwses to replace the Merwins as Frieda's godparents. She added that Ted joined her in asking them. Ted had been living in Dido Merwin's mother's flat in London, and during the weeks Sylvia was in London she thought Dido had slighted her several times. She therefore wanted to make this change in the relationship.

January was a depressing month. It began for Sylvia with a chest X-ray. She was sick again, running intermittent high temperatures. She and the children were trading colds. And at the beginning of their illnesses came the worst snowfall in London in 150 years. Because of consistent difficulty starting the car, Sylvia and the children were at times completely housebound.

On January 3, Clarissa Roche and her two youngest children came to visit. Having recently spent time with Sylvia, Clarissa knew what to look for. The kitchen was immaculate. Menus were written out on the counter—but, she asked Sylvia, had anyone been eating anything? Sylvia ate the porkchops and frozen corn Clarissa cooked for her and admitted that it was all too much trouble, everything was too much trouble. Going outside, going shopping, any outing meant getting everyone dressed, worrying about slipping on the snow and ice. None of it was possible any longer.

Clarissa put Sylvia to bed for the afternoon. It was clear that her friend was sick. She was despondent, she hardly knew the difference between night and day. Later, Paul came with the two older children and Sylvia joined everyone downstairs. She made plans to go with Clarissa and Paul on February 13 to see Paul Scofield in *King Lear*. She also gave them the galleys of *The Bell Jar*, now dedicated to the Comptons, asking them to return the proofs to her with their comments. She promised that she would dedicate her next book to them: they were her good friends, friends that bridged the Atlantic, who had known Smith and her place in it. In retrospect, Smith seemed to Plath the heart of stability. It was clear that England was not the refuge Sylvia had hoped it might become.

Although Paul and Clarissa urged Sylvia to come back to Kent with them, she declined. She thought she could cope with the London winter. But conditions grew much worse. Thaws caused ice to layer over the accumulations of snow. More and more damage occurred, and power cuts were frequent. Stores sold out of candles. Sylvia, sick and worried over the intolerable conditions—and fearful without heat and light—was genuinely afraid for her children's well-being. "Snow Blitz," the wonderfully comic essay she wrote about it all for *Punch*, was misleading, another example of her ability to retell her experiences for whatever effect she chose. In truth, the weather had trapped her. As Trevor Thomas commented on Plath's "Snow Blitz" essay, "In reality she was anything but the brave little woman of her apocalyptic account. She was frightened and pathetic as she appeared at my door all muffled up with scarves and dressing gown."

Despite her poor health and the weather, however, Sylvia was trying to maintain a regular writing schedule. She had enrolled Frieda in a nursery school for three hours every weekday morning. While she was gone, Nick napped. During these mornings Sylvia wrote the poignant "Ocean 1212-W" for the BBC and her scathing exposé of American public education, "America, America!" She worked on her new novel, now titled *Double Exposure*, about the gradual corruption of a naive American girl who revered honesty by a powerful and inherently dishonest man. As in her other writing, the theme came directly from her life. She also wrote a story called "A Winter's Tale," echoing Shakespeare's play. Clearly intended for women's magazines, the story describes the numb emotional state of its protagonist, Kate, a widow. "I had come to savor loneliness," Kate explains, though she admits she is becoming "too broody" since she began living alone.

> I didn't believe in mending. If the heart was fragile, like a porcelain cup, and a great loss shattered it, all the time and kindness in the world couldn't hide the ugly cracks. Once the precious liquid of love had seeped away, you were left dry. Dry and empty.

Echoing Sylvia's words to Elizabeth Compton during the summer, when she lamented the loss of her husband, the images in this passage would appear as well in her February poems.

But January was dominated by illness, not writing. Early in the month she and the children ran what she called "scalding fevers." Sylvia had blackouts. Frieda developed an allergy to penicillin and had hives. The three of them lived on boiled eggs and chicken broth. By January 10, when Sylvia wrote a thank-you note to the Roches, she was in bed under doctor's orders. Dr. Horder was looking for a nurse for her and the children. She got out of bed that night to do a live broadcast about Donald Hall's anthology of American poetry for the BBC, but quickly returned home.

That week of recuperation brought some good news. A cheerful letter from Ruth Fainlight in Morocco announced that she and Alan Sillitoe would be back in England in March and that she would visit Sylvia immediately. "I'm so glad you're in your flat, back in society, and off the blasted heath. . . . I'm looking forward very much to being in London and, as you say, going to the theatres and movies together with you, and talking, talking, talking." Tony Dyson wrote that *Critical Quarterly* would pay Sylvia from £3 to £5 for any poem she cared to give the journal, and he was looking forward to taking her to dinner over Easter vacation. Charles Osborne of *The London Magazine* wrote that he was looking forward to seeing her soon, and in reply she wrote that she was "writing by candlelight with cold fingers, a sinister return to Dickensian conditions." On January 13, "Winter Trees," one of her new poems, appeared in *The Observer*. January 14, *The Bell Jar* was officially published and available. But on January 16, the live-in nurse Dr. Horder had found left, and a few days later Sylvia received a letter from Elizabeth Lawrence of Harper & Row rejecting *The Bell Jar*. Addressing Sylvia as "Mrs. Ted Hughes," the editor complained that the breakdown remained only "a private experience." The novel did not work, she said.

When Nicholas turned a year old the same week, Sylvia spent the day reflecting on the many changes the year had brought. She wrote several beautiful poems about the children, but she could see ahead only endless days of chores, demands, tasks that tested both her physical and psychological strengths.

On January 25, two reviews of *The Bell Jar* by the unknown "Victoria Lucas" appeared. Robert Taubman, writing in *New Statesman*, thought the novel was excellent and that "Lucas" was a female J. D. Salinger. *The Times Literary Supplement* was less excited about the book but still reviewed it favorably. Although the reviews were very good, Sylvia was frustrated: they seemed to have missed the point of the ending, the affirmation of Esther's rebirth.

She was so upset, in fact, with such a need to talk to somebody that she went downstairs to Professor Thomas, weeping uncontrollably. He asked her in and, alternating between grief and resentment, she gave free rein to her anger against her husband and the other woman, her frustration at being chained to the house and the children when she wanted to be free to write and become famous. Asking for a Sunday paper, she pointed to a poem in *The Observer* and said it was by her husband. Then turning to a review of *The Bell Jar* by Victoria Lucas she disclosed that she, Sylvia Plath, was Victoria Lucas, and said that she did not want to die. Thomas tried to console her. He asked why she had not thought of getting a divorce. She told him she had reluctantly signed the divorce papers the previous week. She thanked Professor Thomas and said he reminded her of her father.

Recovered from the flu, Sylvia again tried to find an au pair and, by the week of January 22, had hired a Belgian girl to live with her and the children. The girl—boy crazy and food fussy—lasted until February 8. While she was there, Sylvia wrote more poems: four on January 28, two on January 29, three on February 1. She wrote one more on February 4 and two on February 5. With another bout of the flu, in addition to her growing depression, Sylvia was again at the edge of physical and emotional exhaustion. Her handwriting in the worksheets from some of these late poems—small, angular, almost scratchy—suggests that she was writing under extremely difficult circumstances, or that she was either terribly fatigued or terribly distraught, or both.

Sylvia's late winter poems continued using the mother-and-child themes from her November and December poems, such as the Pietà and its religious connotations. In her last poems, however, she concentrated on the living, the real, the day-to-day beauty of children and their innocence. She was impatient with abstractions. "Eternity bores me, / I never wanted it," she wrote in "Years." What she did want was reassurance. The Sylvia Plath who looked out at the world during the winter of 1962–63 was relentlessly critical of herself ("People or stars / Regard me sadly, I disappoint them") and thoroughly convinced of the evil of the world. She feared for her children, especially for Nick since, as a boy, he might be asked to fight for those very abstractions she could no longer bear. In "Mary's Song" she described him as "the golden child the world will kill and eat." The only power a child's mother had was to pray, as in her poem "Brasilia": "leave / This one . . . safe." Whatever her reasons, Plath was now willing to bow to the power of religious belief, perhaps because she had herself become so powerless.

In late January and early February, Sylvia wrote three joyful poems about childhood. "Child," "Kindness," and "Balloons" describe the kind of happy lives Sylvia wished for her children.

But these poems contrast sharply with most of her late work. Such poems as "Totem," "Paralytic," and "Mystic" draw on several belief systems to express the sense that death is a reasonable alternative to life. "Totem" describes the "same self" unfolding like a suit from a bag: "There is no terminus, only suitcases." In "Paralytic," the paralyzed speaker is a "buddha, all / Wants, desire / Falling from me." And in "Mystic," the speaker asks directly, "Once one has seen God, what is the remedy?" A later line in the poem responds to that question with another question, "Is there no great love, only tenderness?"

Sylvia's late poems drum on, describing her consciousness of —even obsession with—death. Her last poems are increasingly gnomic, sharing in the long tradition of religious poetry that does not verbalize ideas some readers might reject. Plath kept each poem carefully arranged with its worksheets, dated, filed separately from the poems intended for the *Ariel* collection. That book was finished. These late poems were for another book, as yet incomplete and untitled.

On February 4, Plath wrote "Contusion," a poem that is apparently about a bruise, but which contains imagery suggestive of death, including the closing line, "The mirrors are sheeted." In many cultures, after there has been a death in the house, mirrors are covered so that no other souls can be taken away. What "Contusion" presents, then, is a glimpse of a household in mourning. It was an eerie foreshadowing.

Similar in tone was Plath's ominous last poem, "Edge": "We have come so far, it is over." That poem describes a woman who is now "perfect" because she has died. Called "Nuns in Snow" in an early draft, "Edge" places the woman's death in the tradition of "Greek necessity"—a reference to the belief that suicide is an honorable way out of dishonor. But it also forces the reader to reflect on the way nuns—or any Catholic, and the oblique reference to Aurelia's early Catholic rearing is relevant—would react with disapproval to the woman's suicide. A strange mixture of cynicism and pathos, the poem presents the dead woman as wearing "a smile of accomplishment." She is finally a woman the critical world might approve, now that her independent and sometimes vengeful character has been tamed. Dead, that headstrong woman is no threat.

As with her October poems, Plath's last poems are interrelated. Some of the central imagery of "Edge," and its title, occurred first in a draft of the poem "Mystic." "Mystic" contains references to the monastic order of St. Teresa (the bare-footed) and the lives of sacrifice nuns were expected to live. Plath weaves imagery of transcendence, or of the visionary, throughout her last poems.

Among Plath's papers are notes on St. Thérèse, St. Teresa, St. John of the Cross, and other Christian mystics. Because of her acute empathy and what she regarded as her natural psychic powers, Sylvia felt keenly the possibility of various visionary experiences. Once she found for herself the mysticism about which she wrote (Ted Hughes reported that she had told him she had seen God several times during January and February), perhaps the immediate frustrations of her life seemed pointless.

Perhaps this new attitude explains the cool, objective tone she chose to use in "Edge," a poem about a woman's suicide as the end of a life spent striving for success. The poem ends with the moon icily observing the dead woman. The distant, uncaring moon observes; neither life nor death occasions comment from it. The moon is the kind of feminine being a sensual, living woman would not want to mirror. Yet the always wry Plath cannot help but show the comic side of human beings thinking their lives are worth comment. The ambivalent moon, dressed in what she elsewhere called "snazzy blacks," remains a chilling part of every woman's world, a world replete with unexpected distance and contradictions.

February began with a kind note from David Machin, Sylvia's editor for *The Bell Jar* at Heinemann, asking her to get in touch with him about having a celebratory lunch. He had tried to call and had found that she still had no telephone. He was pleased with the reviews. (On January 31 Lawrence Lerner had written favorably about the book in *The Listener*, describing it as a political novel. And on the same day, *Time & Tide* gave it a good review.) A few days later, Sylvia heard again from Ruth Fainlight, who said that they would be back at Pembroke Crescent in March and that she and the baby planned to go to Devon with Sylvia in April. Marcia Brown and her husband were also going to visit London, and on February 4 Sylvia wrote to her old friend, "Dearest Marty, . . . Everything has blown and bubbled and warped and split." Life was suspended. Sylvia felt herself "in limbo between the old world and the very uncertain and rather grim new." She told Marcia that she was lonely, "cut off" from friends and relatives and torn with the sad knowledge that her beautiful and dear children would live without a father.

Sylvia's letter to Aurelia written the same day repeated the word "grim" but spoke more directly about her pain. Sylvia wrote that her present unhappiness stemmed from "seeing the finality of it all." Moving to London had not brought her reconciliation with Ted, or professional acclaim, or new friendships. Although she had been living in London less than two months, with her characteristic impatience she was ready to make another change. She was becoming depressed, partly with the realization of what faced her: she would live as a single parent, with these two wonderful children, for the rest of her days. Though she did not say it, she would live the life her own mother had led, a life that Sylvia had often criticized for its self-sacrifice and dedication.

Aurelia had suggested flying Frieda to America by jet, so that she could spend some time with the Plath family there. Sylvia would not hear of this. She pointed out that her children had no stability in their lives and needed her desperately now. "The children need me most right now, and so I shall try to go on for the next few years writing mornings, being with them afternoons and seeing friends or studying and reading evenings." As for Frieda specifically, Sylvia wrote, "I am her one security and to uproot her would be thoughtless and cruel." She mentioned that Dr. Horder, whom she was seeing frequently for her depression, was planning for her to consult a woman doctor. Meanwhile, the letter closed, "I shall simply have to fight it out on my own here."

On February 4, 1963, Plath mailed another group of new poems to *The New Yorker*, and in a letter to Father Bart spoke of writing poems "in blood, or at least with it." She wrote that she had recovered from the flu and was making curtains once again, Sylvia's "normal" life continued. She called David Machin and set a lunch date for the following Monday, February 11, arranging for Katherine Frankfort to babysit on that day. About this same time, Sylvia received letters from several poetry magazines, asking her to send poems, and from other literary admirers. On February 7 she wrote letters to both Nancy Axworthy, who was taking care of the Devon house, and Elizabeth Compton, telling them what joy it would be to come back to Devon in the spring. "Thank God you are there," she wrote to Elizabeth. "I long to see my home," she closed. It was a letter filled with plans.

Sylvia was experiencing wide mood swings during the winter of 1963. She was seeing Dr. Horder frequently. He prescribed for her an antidepressant drug, which would take from ten to twenty days to become effective.

On February 8, Sylvia saw Dr. Horder several times. He continued to be alarmed at her state—thin and anxious, she was visibly unable to cope with the many problems of her present life. She had fired her au pair, refusing to pay her. Sleeping pills did not work any longer. The new drug had not yet begun to alleviate her depression. Horder tried to find Sylvia a bed in a hospital for the weekend. None was available in two locations; a third seemed unsuitable. Sylvia's fears of electroconvulsive shock treatments made her unwilling to be hospitalized. She had said repeatedly ten years before that she would not go through such treatment again. By the time Horder talked with her later on that Friday afternoon, Sylvia assured him that she was better and that she had made plans to take the children to friends' for the weekend. Dr. Horder set up appointments to see Sylvia on both Saturday and Sunday.

She kept her appointments and continued taking the antidepressant medicine. On Sunday her doctor thought she was beginning to respond to the medication. But sometimes when a depressed patient becomes capable of increased activity, the depression is still in place; if the patient acts, it may be to carry out a plan for suicide created in the depths of the illness.

At 11:45 P.M. on Sunday evening, Sylvia went down to Professor Thomas's flat to buy postage stamps from him. He was happy to provide them and told her she need not pay him at that late hour. She insisted, saying, "Oh! but I must pay you or I won't be right with my conscience before God, will I?" Dr.

Thomas thought Sylvia looked very ill, and he suggested that he call her doctor. She refused and implied she was returning to her flat. Ten minutes later Professor Thomas opened his door again, and she was still standing as if in a trance in the hall. As Professor Thomas recalled the scene, "I said, 'You aren't really well, are you? . . . Let me call the doctor.' She said no again and that she was having a wonderful dream, a marvellous vision. I urged her to go back upstairs out of the cold. Twenty minutes later I looked again and she had gone. I could not sleep and I heard her walking to and fro on the wood floor. . . ."

It was the night of February 10, 1963, just three years to the day since Sylvia had signed the contract for her first book, *The Colossus*. So much, both good and bad, had happened in those short years. Sylvia had learned a great deal. She had become a mother and a homeowner; she had learned to share her life, and she had come into her own as a woman. In so doing, she had become a stronger writer. She knew that it would do no longer to write poems that were only exercises. Poems, like life, had to be honest and direct, arrowlike in their aim, relentless in their intensity.

Sylvia had learned to write those poems—without advice, criticism, or lists of suitable subjects. She had learned to take the fury and the joy, the feelings she could both deny and boast of, and from them create art that spoke powerfully to readers. And just when she was at the height of these accomplishments, because of changes in her personal life that revived earlier fears and depressions, her momentum stopped. The woman who had wanted nothing else but to write wondered why she had worked so tirelessly. "Words dry and riderless," finally, seemed not to be a way out of her dilemma—at least not while she struggled under the weight of acute depression.

Early on the morning of February 11, 1963, Sylvia Plath knelt beside the open oven in the second-floor kitchen of her Primrose Hill flat and turned on the gas. She had left cups of milk beside the children's beds. She had put tape around the doors and had shoved towels under them to protect the children from escaping fumes. She had taken a quantity of sleeping pills, and had left a note, asking that her doctor be called. The nurse who was to arrive early came around 9:30 A.M. Sylvia was dead. The police were called, as was Dr. Horder. At 10:00 A.M., Katherine Frankfort arrived to babysit. Ted came soon after.

On February 15 an inquest was held. The following day, the death of Sylvia Plath Hughes was ruled a suicide.

Afterword

Assuming that writers find immortality through the life of their work, a kind of second existence began for Sylvia Plath shortly after her death. On February 17, 1963, in *The Observer*, A. Alvarez published a memorial essay, "A Poet's Epitaph," in which he said of Plath's death, "The loss to literature is inestimable." Along with his essay, Alvarez published "Edge" and three of Plath's other late poems.

Other notices and publication of more late poems appeared during the coming year. In 1965, Faber & Faber brought out *Ariel*, the collection of her late poems as chosen and edited by Ted Hughes. (It included fewer fall poems than Plath had chosen for the book, and those poems were arranged differently; it added many of her very late poems.) In 1966 Harper & Row published *Ariel* in the United States, with an introduction by Robert Lowell.

By 1968 Faber & Faber had printed over 10,000 copies of *Ariel* in hardcover and more than 122,000 in paperback. Figures about United States sales are unavailable, but the book sold much more widely in America than it did in England. There were several printings of *Ariel* in both hardcover and paper in both countries.

In 1967, *The Bell Jar* was reissued in England, this time under Sylvia Plath's name. In 1971, the novel appeared in the U.S. Published by Harper & Row, *The Bell Jar* included a biographical essay and reproductions of some of Plath's ink drawings. Translated and published in many countries, *The Bell Jar* has sold even more widely than Plath's poetry, and each year in the U.S. alone sells between 80,000 and 100,000 copies.

In 1971 Ted Hughes brought out two other collections of Plath's later poetry, *Crossing the Water* and *Winter Trees*. In the U.S., *Crossing the Water* was published in 1971, and *Winter Trees* the following year. At least 60,000 copies of each title were sold in England alone.

In 1975 Aurelia Plath edited and published a large collection of her daughter's letters—written to herself and her son Warren—as *Letters Home by Sylvia Plath, Correspondence 1950–1963*. The book received wide notice. Literary rights to all of Plath's work are controlled by Ted Hughes, who gave Aurelia Plath permission to publish the letters.

In 1977, Hughes issued a collection of some of Plath's published and unpublished short stories, essays, and journal entries under the title *Johnny Panic and the Bible of Dreams and Other Prose Writings*. A somewhat fuller selection was published under the same title in the U.S. in 1979. Plath's unpublished fiction and poetry is available to scholars and students in the two manuscript collections at the Lilly Library, Indiana University, and at Smith College.

In 1981 Plath's long-awaited and long-promised *Collected Poems* was published, again edited by Ted Hughes. It was a stunning book, filled with more poems—more different kinds of poems—than anyone might have predicted. *Sylvia Plath, The Collected Poems* won the 1982 Pulitzer Prize for Poetry, an award seldom given posthumously.

In 1982, excerpts from Plath's journals appeared in the U.S., edited by Frances McCullough, with Hughes as "Consulting Editor." (This book was not published in England.) Its publication—with Hughes's admission that he had destroyed one of the volumes of Plath's journals—created some furor. Several reviewers condemned Ted Hughes for irresponsibility in not preserving Plath's writing. Reviewers also complained about the many omissions in the text, and about the fact that some omissions were not clearly indicated.

Sylvia Plath's critical reputation has grown and changed many times since the original publication of *The Colossus and Other Poems* in 1960, and of *Ariel* in 1965. Plath has been championed, deified, criticized, and gossiped about, but her work continues to attract readers and to move them with its power and finesse, its technical range, and its strong, independent voice. As Plath had prophetically written in a 1958 journal entry,

> the coming again to make and make in the face of the flux; making of the moment something of permanence. That is the lifework. . . . My life, I feel, will not be lived until there are books and stories which relive it perpetually in time.

But even now, Plath's reputation as a writer is incomplete. Her later journal and the partial draft of the last novel that she was writing have yet to be recovered. Numerous short stories and poems remain uncollected; many of these have never been published. Only when all of Plath's work is accessible will the full impact of her art during the last years of her life be felt; only then can the distinction of her work be fully evaluated.

Plath is buried in Yorkshire, in an unremarkable grave in the Heptonstall churchyard near Hebden Bridge. Her grave is not far from the graves of other members of the Hughes family. In death, as in life, Sylvia Plath is something of an American in exile.

Notes on Sources

PREFACE

Page 13 "disappeared somewhere around": Hughes's "Introduction" to *Johnny Panic and the Bible of Dreams, Short Stories, Prose and Diary Excerpts* (New York: Harper & Row, 1979), p. 1. Hereafter cited as *JP*.

"Two more notebooks": Hughes's "Foreword" to *The Journals of Sylvia Plath*, ed. Frances McCullough (New York: The Dial Press, 1982), p. xiii. Hereafter cited as *J*. In a longer version of the foreword, which was published as an essay in *Grand Street* and then reprinted as "Sylvia Plath and Her Journals" in *Ariel Ascending, Writings About Sylvia Plath*, Paul Alexander, ed. (New York: Harper & Row, 1985), p. 152. Hereafter cited as Alexander. Hughes uses the phrase, "disappeared more recently (and may, presumably, still turn up)."

CHAPTER ONE, CHILDHOOD, 1932–40

Page 15 "The Center of": *JP*, p. 23, "Ocean 1212-W."

Page 20 "We worked together": Aurelia Plath, *Letters Home by Sylvia Plath, Correspondence 1950–1963* (New York: The Dial Press, 1975), p. 12. Hereafter cited as *LH*. Much information about Plath's childhood has come from her mother, friends, and teachers.

"At the end": *LH*, p. 13.

Page 22 "A baby. I": "Ocean 1212-W" from *JP*, p. 23.

"The road I": *JP*, p. 22.

Page 23 "I am so": Aurelia Plath to Sylvia Plath (hereafter cited as SP), Wednesday afternoon, 1939, Plath letters, Lilly Library, Indiana University. Hereafter cited as Lilly.

NOTES ON SOURCES

Page 28 "When he buys": *LH*, p. 24.
"I'll never speak": *LH*, p. 25.
Page 30 "You will be": *The Collected Poems, Sylvia Plath* (New York: Harper & Row, 1981), p. 205. Hereafter cited as *CP*.
"*In the beginning*": *JP*, pp. 306–12.

CHAPTER TWO, ADOLESCENCE, 1940–47
Page 31 "Once I Was": *CP*, p. 133, "Maenad," "Poem for a Birthday."
Page 33 "*All* the girls": SP to Aurelia Plath, July 18, 1943, Plath letters, Lilly.
Page 37 "We had no": Aurelia Plath, notes about SP, Smith Plath Collection, Smith College. Hereafter cited as Smith.
Page 39 "Lunch—two bowls": SP to Aurelia Plath, July 5, 1945, Plath letters, Lilly.
Page 40 "I was not": Plath, Poems, Lilly.
Page 41 "For your self-aggrandisement": Aurelia Plath, notes about SP, Smith.

CHAPTER THREE, BRADFORD HIGH SCHOOL, 1947–50
Page 42 "The Rich Junk"; *JP*, p. 63, "A Comparison."
Page 44 "joy, bounce, and": Wilbury Crockett, interview Aug. 23, 1984.
Page 47 "Never never never": *LH*, p. 40.
Page 48 "1948–49—Boys": Plath papers, Lilly, 1949.
Page 51 "the two alternating": Hughes, "Introduction," *JP*, p. 4.
"It was good": "The Dark River," Plath, Fiction, Lilly.
Page 52 "She reached out": "East Wind," Plath, Fiction, Lilly.

CHAPTER FOUR, BEGINNING SMITH COLLEGE, 1950–51
Page 55 "Blameless as Daylight": *CP*, p. 109, "The Eye-Mote."
"At home on": p. 16, unpublished journal, 1950, Smith.
Page 56 "something vital": Ibid.
Page 57 "this game of": *J*, pp. 9, 15.
Page 58 "I not only": Ed Cohen letters to SP, Sept. 15, 1950, Lilly.
"It is quite": Ed Cohen to SP, Sept. 28, 1950, Lilly.
"telling me that": Ed Cohen to SP, Sept. 2, 1950, Lilly.
"My father is": SP to Cohen, Aug. 6, 1950, Lilly.
Page 59 "A red-blooded": SP to Cohen, Aug. 11, 1950, Lilly.
"You're a Communist": SP to Cohen, late August, 1950, Lilly.
Page 60 "Spare me from": quoted in *LH*, p. 40.
"I've so much": SP to Aurelia, Oct. 10, 1950, Lilly.
Page 61 "Girls are a": *LH*, pp. 46, 48.
Page 62 "I get a": *LH*, pp. 53, 57.
"God, who am": *J*, p. 17.
Page 65 "Life is loneliness": *J*, p. 19.
"What is my": p. 79, unpublished journal, 1950, Smith.
Page 67 "I hate you": p. 77, unpublished journals, 1950, Smith.
"I need someone": *J*, p. 16.

"Dear Cousin": Richard Norton–Sylvia Plath correspondence, Lilly. All excerpts that follow are from this extensive collection.

Page 69   "Girls look for": *J*, p. 23.

Page 70   "would marriage sap": *J*, pp. 23–24.

"as I look": *LH*, p. 67.

Page 71   "I wish I": SP to Aurelia Plath, May 1, 1951, Plath letters, Lilly.

CHAPTER FIVE, CONQUERING SMITH, 1951–52

Page 73   "Eating the Fingers": *CP*, p. 133, "Maenad," "Poem for a Birthday."

Page 74   "Being born a": *J*, p. 30.

"Once a woman": p. 77, unpublished journals, 1950, Smith.

"Everything but: what": p. 325, unpublished journals, Smith.

Page 75   "religion *was* life": Plath, papers for Religion 14, Plath Collection, Lilly.

Page 76   "My *own* philosophy": marginal notes from Ortega y Gasset's *The Revolt of the Masses*, SP's collection of her books, Lilly.

"striving always for": paper on Thomas Mann, Plath Collection, Lilly. See also her paper on Dostoevsky, Ibid.

"the misfits are": marginal notes from SP's copy of Margaret Mead's *Male and Female*, Lilly.

Page 77   "I can whittle": p. 212, unpublished journals, 1951, Smith.

"I am vain": *J*, p. 35.

Page 78   "It was not": Robert Gorham Davis, correspondence, Sept. 25, 1984.

Page 80   "You might as": Ed Cohen to SP, Sept. 16, 1951, Plath letters, Lilly.

Page 82   "a potential": *LH*, p. 81.

"Henry started out": *LH*, p. 87.

Page 83   "Last spring": all manuscripts of "Sunday at the Mintons' " are in Fiction, Lilly. The published text is included in *JP*, pp. 295–305.

Page 84   "To the gal": Plath Collection, Smith.

Page 85   "I took the": *LH*, p. 91.

CHAPTER SIX, JUNIOR YEAR, 1952–53

Page 86   "The Doomsday of": *JP*, p. 310, "Among the Bumblebees."

"God, those first": SP to Warren Plath, Sept. 28, 1952, Lilly.

Page 88   "He often wrote": all material mentioned is available at the Plath Collection, Lilly.

"lying up there": *J*, p. 60.

"God, if ever": *J*, pp. 59–60.

Page 89   "I am afraid": *J*, p. 60.

"Oh, Mother, I": *LH*, p. 98.

Page 90   "I hope you're": SP to Aurelia Plath, Nov. 6, 1952, Lilly.

"One column was": Plath Collection, Smith College memorabilia, Lilly.

Page 91   "the agitation, the": Ed Cohen to SP, Jan. 2, 1953, Plath letters, Lilly.

Page 92   "Break break break": *LH*, pp. 101–02.

Page 93   "I'm sorry I": SP to Aurelia Plath, Jan. 8, 1953, Plath letters, Lilly.

Page 94 "Do I want": p. 364, unpublished journals, 1953, Smith.
"to live hard": p. 405, unpublished journals, 1953, Smith.
Page 95 "I wasn't anybody": "Dialogue," Plath, Fiction, Lilly.
Page 96 "Today I bought": p. 410, unpublished journals, 1953, Smith.
Page 97 "one of the": I am indebted to the recollections of Madelyn Mathers, Neva Nelson, Ann Shawber, Laurie Totten, Carol LeVarn, Leslie Westoff, and especially Janet Wagner for the events of the *Mademoiselle* month.
Page 98 "Somehow I can't": *LH*, pp. 117–18.
Page 101 "I didn't pay": Janet Wagner to author, May 23, 1985.
"Dating Gordon Lameyer": I am indebted to Gordon Lameyer's recollections and his unpublished memoir for these accounts, and subsequent ones.
Page 102 "an Over-grown,": *J*, p. 82.
"You are so": *J*, p. 85
Page 103 "Stop thinking selfishly": *J*, p. 87.
" 'I just wanted' ": *LH*, p. 124.
"By the roots": "The Hanging Man," *CP*, p. 141.

CHAPTER SEVEN, SMITH, A CULMINATION, 1954–55
Page 105 "I Shall Be": *CP*, p. 137, "The Stones," "Poem for a Birthday."
Page 106 "It was my": *LH*, p. 126.
"Although Mrs. Plath": various letters between Olive Higgins Prouty and Aurelia Plath, Plath letters, Lilly, chart these months. Interview with Wilbury Crockett, correspondence with Ruth Beuscher.
Page 107 "I want you": Plath letters, from Evelyn Page and others, Lilly.
"she was caught": *JP*, pp. 261–68.
Page 109 "There was no": *JP*, pp. 261–68; here p. 265.
"I need more": *LH*, pp. 131–32.
Page 111 "Her photographs are": *A Closer Look at Ariel: A Memory of Sylvia Plath* (New York: Harper's Magazine Press, 1973), pp. 40–41.
"everything hurt": conversations with Ellie Friedman, July 14, 1984, and Feb. 28, 1986; see also her essay "A Friend Recalls Sylvia Plath" (Klein) in *Glamour* (Nov. 1966), pp. 168–84.
Page 112 "One friend": Constance Taylor, conversation, June 20, 1985.
"George Gibian": correspondence, Sept. 27, 1984, and Sept. 24, 1985.
Page 113 "I did not": "The Devil's Advocate," course paper for Professor Gibian, Lilly.
"symbol of god": Plath scrapbook, Smith years, Lilly.
Page 114 "Weekend in NYC": Plath, scrapbook, Smith years, Lilly.
Page 115 "Nancy Hunter remarked": See her *A Closer Look at Ariel*, pp. 52–53.
Page 116 "She simultaneously maintained": I am indebted to Gordon Lameyer's recollections and his unpublished memoir for this account, and subsequent ones. See also Sylvia's letters to Lameyer, privately held.
Page 117 "I could not": Hunter, *Closer Look*, p. 75.
"play daddy": Sassoon to SP, Plath letters, Lilly.

Page 118 "great works of": Plath, notes from Alfred Kazin's course in Modern American Fiction, Lilly.

"I keep reading": SP to Lameyer, quoted in Lameyer, "Letters from Sylvia," *Smith Alumnae Quarterly*, 67, pp. 3–10.

Page 119 "We will work": Plath, application for *Mademoiselle* College Board editorship, *Mademoiselle* file, Lilly.

CHAPTER EIGHT, ENGLAND, 1955–56

Page 120 "In the Sun's": *CP*, p. 268, "Mystic."

"If only I": *LH*, p. 148.

Page 122 "The roof slants": Ibid.

"her impersonal appetite": Peter Davison, *Half-Remembered, A Personal History* (New York: Harper & Row, 1973).

Page 124 "There would be": Hilary Bailey, letter to the author, Jan. 30, 1985.

"she was almost": Christopher Levenson, letter to the author, Oct. 27, 1984.

Page 125 "Jane Baltzell, a": see her memoir, as Jane Baltzell Kopp, in *Sylvia Plath: The Woman and the Work*, Edward Butscher, ed. (Baltimore: Johns Hopkins Press, 1979), pp. 61–81.

"Sylvia's classes at": information from letters of Dorothea Krook, July 28 and Aug. 5, 1985.

Page 126 "did not feel": Campbell memoir in *The Art of Sylvia Plath, A Symposium*, Charles Newman, ed. (reprinted from *Tri-Quarterly*) (Bloomington: Indiana Univ. Press, 1970), pp. 182–86.

"I felt the": Krook memoir, in Butscher, pp. 49–60.

Page 127 "I wear about": *LH*, p. 217.

Page 128 "Her letters to": see Elinor Friedman Klein's account in *Glamour*.

"We crouched by": Hilary Bailey, letter to the author, Jan. 30, 1985.

"According to Philip": see Gardner's *Dalhousie Review* essay and letter, Sept. 11, 1985.

Page 129 "men (Richard gone)": *J*, p. 103.

"Dear Doctor, I": Ibid.

"My God, I'd": *J*, p. 109.

Page 130 "then he kissed": *J*, p. 112, and unpublished journal, Smith.

Page 131 "In the last": *LH*, p. 233.

"She had difficulty": Hughes's letter to SP, Plath letters, Lilly.

"I flew back": SP to Marcia Brown, December 15, 1956, Smith.

Page 132 "talk, song, and": Daniel Huws, memoir, Feb. 16, 1986.

"In fact, the": Bertram Wyatt-Brown, letter to author, Jan. 24, 1987.

Page 133 "the only man": *LH*, p. 240.

"ruthless force": SP to Olive Higgins Prouty, Letters, Lilly.

"You don't really": Prouty to SP, June 3, 1956, Letters, Lilly.

Page 134 "I have become": *LH*, p. 243.

Page 135 "fantastically matched; both": *LH*, p. 261.

"The hurt going": *J*, p. 146.

NOTES ON SOURCES

CHAPTER NINE, MARRIAGE, 1956–57
Page 136 "I Am Learning": *CP*, p. 160, "Tulips."
Page 137 "Imagine yourself on": *LH*, p. 269.
Page 138 "as if an": *J*, p. 128.
"better team than": *LH*, p. 280.
Page 139 "a hectic suffocating": unpublished section, *LH*, p. 281.
"Both of us": *LH*, p. 281.
"How I long": *LH*, p. 285.
Page 140 "It is heaven": *LH*, p. 289.
"wandering around the": Sue Weller, letter to the author, Apr. 23, 1985.
Page 141 "she had a": Campbell memoir in Newman.
"shut off like": *J*, p. 164.
Page 143 "like Kafka, simply": *J*, pp. 166, 169.
"*love, a falcon*": *J*, p. 162.
Page 144 "Make her a": *J*, p. 168.
"I have never": *J*, p. 171.

CHAPTER TEN, MARRIAGE IN AMERICA, 1957–59
Page 146 "I Boarded Your": *CP*, p. 155, "Zoo Keeper's Wife."
Page 147 "I am middling": *J*, p. 176.
Page 148 "a being who": *J*, p. 176.
"could not sleep": *J*, p. 175.
Page 150 "This one I": *J*, p. 186.
"I've been through": p. 25, unpublished journals, 1957–58, Feb. 4, 1958, Smith.
"Work redeems": p. 12, unpublished journals, 1958–59, Smith.
"a grim grind": p. 26, unpublished journals, 1957–58, Feb. 4, Smith.
Page 151 "I have served": *J*, p. 234.
Page 152 "I felt sicker": *J*, pp. 249, 251.
Page 153 "composed, perfect and": *J*, p. 248.
"the world of": Adrienne Rich, letter to the author, Aug. 1, 1986.
Page 154 "And what is": conversation with Myron Lotz, Aug. 24, 1985.
"I have a": *J*, pp. 237–38.
"Ted insisted that": Interview with Clarissa Roche, June 26, 1985. Ted Hughes denies that this incident took place.
Page 155 "I feel my": *J*, p. 263.
"If I am": *J*, p. 266.
"I get very": *J*, p. 267.
"the Writer and": *J*, p. 273.
Page 156 "What is my": *J*, p. 186.
"Sylvia asked Rich": Rich, letter to the author, Aug. 2, 1986.
"Charles Doyle, a": Doyle, letter to the author, Oct. 20, 1973.
"women and women-talk": *J*, p. 295.
Page 157 "a depressing sight": *J*, p. 247.
Page 158 "Kathleen Spivack": in various memoirs; see bibliography. Also letters to the author from Spivack, Donald Junkins, others.

" 'Reminds me of' ": Spivack, "Lear in Boston: Robert Lowell as Teacher and Friend," *Ironwood*, Spring, 1985.

Page 159 "Kumin (who, with)": Maxine Kumin, letter to the author, June 28, 1984; see also Anne Sexton's memoir in Newman, pp. 174–81.

Page 160 "lack of technical": *J*, p. 306.

"A happier sense": *J*, p. 309.

CHAPTER ELEVEN, *THE COLOSSUS AND OTHER POEMS*, 1960

Page 162 "A Dawn of": *CP*, p. 240, "Poppies in October."

Page 163 "I have never": *LH*, p. 353.

"Sylvia usually walked": letter to the author from Sonia Raiziss, Oct. 20, 1985. Several long letters to the author from Pauline Hanson were invaluable to this section of the book.

Page 164 "already almost dark": May Swenson, letter to the author, July 10, 1984.

"full of them": *J*, pp. 314–15.

"the old fall": *J*, p. 315.

Page 165 "then invent on": *J*, p. 320.

"to be honest": *J*, p. 325.

Page 166 "I shall never": *CP*, p. 129.

Page 169 "The December London": Hughes's "Sylvia Plath and Her Journals" in *Ariel Ascending, Writings About Sylvia Plath*, Paul Alexander, ed. (New York: Harper & Row, 1984), pp. 159–60.

Page 170 "never—even when": Helga Huws, letter to the author, Feb. 16, 1986.

"cheerful kitchen": *LH*, p. 365.

"resplendent in black": *LH*, pp. 365–66.

Page 171 "But I hope": SP to Judith Reutlinger, Nov. 23, 1959, privately held.

CHAPTER TWELVE, BABIES AND BELL JARS, 1960–61

Page 172 "The Old Dregs": *CP*, p. 153, "Parliament Hill Fields."

Page 173 "I really put": *LH*, p. 368.

Page 174 "as Olwyn had": Janet Crosbie-Hill reminiscence, in Olwyn Hughes, letter to author, March 24, 1986.

Page 175 "I looked on": *LH*, p. 374.

"received herself": Hughes in memoir, Newman, pp. 192–93.

Page 176 "Ted went downstairs": A. Alvarez, *The Savage God* (New York: Random House, 1972), p. 8.

Page 177 "I get tired": *LH*, pp. 381–84.

"I am gradually": SP to Ann Davidow, June 29, 1960, Smith.

"I am at": *LH*, pp. 386, 387.

"My own aim": *LH*, p. 389.

"I am thinking": *LH*, p. 388.

Page 178 "sensible, cheerful, considerate": Thom Gunn, letter to the author, Sept. 21, 1984.

Page 179   "Not easy to": *CP*, p. 147.
  "dragging her shadow": *CP*, pp. 149–50.
Page 180   "We're both so": *LH*, p. 402.
Page 183   "I am a": *CP*, p. 161.
Page 184   "The old dregs": *CP*, p. 161.
  "broken and mended": SP to Judith Jones, referred to in Jones's Mar. 29, 1961, letter to SP, Smith.
Page 185   "I saw my life": *The Bell Jar* (New York: Harper & Row, 1971), pp. 84–85.

CHAPTER THIRTEEN, THE DEVON LIFE, 1961–62
Page 188   "The Shine of": *CP*, p. 152, "Last Words."
Page 189   "then Ted and": *LH*, p. 419.
Page 190   "funny, and yet": SP to Ann Davidow, April 27, 1961, Smith.
Page 193   "Englishisms": conversation wtih Clarissa Roche, June 26, 1985.
  "My whole spirit": *LH*, p. 428.
Page 194   "a very ancient": SP to Helga and Dan Huws, Oct. 31, 1961, privately held.
Page 196   "things . . . warmed": *CP*, p. 172.
Page 197   "I began to": *LH*, p. 438.
Page 198   "Her annotated calendar": For the year 1962, Smith.
Page 199   "How long can": *CP*, pp. 176–88, ms. of "Three Women," Smith.
Page 201   "I have the": *LH*, p. 450.
  "lethal pellets of": SP to Clarissa Roche, Mar. 12, 1962, privately held.
Page 202   "I find this": *JP*, p. 75.
Page 203   "Thank God, a": Sigmund memoir, in Butscher, p. 100.
Page 205   "she had boasted": Julia Matcham, letter to the author, Feb. 2, 1987.
  "little more than": Olwyn Hughes, letter to author, April 15, 1987.
  "Those hands/Muffled": *CP*, p. 194; ms. for "The Rabbit Catcher," Smith.
  "I cannot see": Ms. for "Event," Smith.
Page 206   "As a thank-you": Clarissa Roche, letter to author, April 1, 1987.
  "No longer quiet": A. Alvarez, *The Savage God*, p. 13.
Page 207   "Six round black": *CP*, p. 201.
  "My heart is": Ms. for "Poppies in July," Smith.
Page 208   "Help me, help": Sigmund memoir, in Butscher, p. 104.

CHAPTER FOURTEEN, THE *ARIEL* POEMS, 1962
Page 209   "I Am Myself": *CP*, p. 226, "The Jailer."
  "I put my": Ms. for "Poppies in July," Smith.
Page 210   "Aurelia was thoroughly": *LH*, p. 458.
Page 212   "The issues of": *JP*, p. 64.
Page 214   "My tragedy is": *J*, p. 30.
  "Driving on her own": A. Alvarez, *The Savage God*, pp. 13–14.

"And still another": Clarissa Roche, letter to the author, April 1, 1987, and June 26, 1985, interview.

Page 215   "Once she returned": SP to Aurelia Plath, Sept. 23, 1962, omitted portion of letter that is published in *LH*, p. 461; Plath letters, Lilly. Ted Hughes denies having sent this telegram.

Page 216   "I loved the": SP to Olive Higgins Prouty, Sept. 29, 1962, Plath letters, Lilly.

"Sylvia may have": SP to Aurelia Plath, Oct. 16, 1962, omitted portion of letter that is published in *LH*, p. 468; Plath letters, Lilly; and SP to Warren Plath, Oct. 18, 1962, omitted portion of letter that is published in *LH*, p. 472; Plath letters, Lilly. Ted Hughes denies having said this.

Page 217   "Winter is for": *CP*, pp. 218–19.

"absolutely stunned and": SP to Anne Sexton, Aug. 21, 1962, Univ. of Texas Humanities Center.

Page 218   "I am in": *CP*, pp. 214–15.

"In Ireland I": *LH*, p. 465.

Page 219   "My ribs show": Ms. of "The Jailer," Smith; *CP*, p. 226.

Page 220   "high cold masks": *CP*, p. 226.

Page 221   "Out of the": *CP*, p. 247.

"I am a": *LH*, p. 469.

CHAPTER FIFTEEN, RESOLUTION, 1962–63

Page 222   "I See by": *CP*, p. 132, "Dark House," "Poem for a Birthday."

Page 223   "For goodness sakes": SP to Aurelia Plath, Oct. 25, 1962, Plath letters, Lilly.

Page 224   "You know what": Dan Huws, letter to the author, Feb. 16, 1986.

"I'm a rather": Oct. 31, 1962, interview with Plath, Credo Records.

Page 226   "begin over from": SP to Olive Higgins Prouty, Nov. 20, 1962, Plath letters, Lilly.

"Speak straight out": SP to Father Bart, Nov. 23, 1962, privately held.

"Love, love, it": Ms. of "The Couriers," Smith.

Page 227   "They saved me": Hughes's memoir, in Alexander, p. 163.

Page 228   "This is my": *CP*, pp. 253–54.

Page 229   "You've saved my": Clarissa Roche memoir, Butscher, pp. 81–96.

"Clarissa heard about": conversation with Ms. Roche, June 26, 1985.

Page 230   "Boy, when I": SP to Aurelia Plath, Nov. 1962, omitted portion of letter that is published with *LH*, p. 481; Plath letters, Lilly.

Page 231   "Well, here I": *LH*, p. 488.

Page 232   "erratic": Trevor Thomas, letter to author, Feb. 11, 1987.

Page 234   "I have been": SP to Marcia Brown, January 2, 1963, Smith.

"Frieda's awful regression": SP to Daniel and Helga Huws, Jan. 1, 1963, privately held.

Page 235   "As Trevor Thomas": Thomas's memoir, p. 6, March, 1987.

Page 236   "I had come": Plath, "A Winter's Tale," unpublished story, Smith.

"I'm so glad": Ruth Fainlight to SP, Jan. 12, 1963, Smith.

Page 237 "writing by candlelight": SP to Charles Osborne, Jan. 9, 1963, Univ. of Texas Humanities Center.

"She was so": Trevor Thomas, telephone conversation, Jan. 25, 1987; also his memoir, Mar. 1987, and his letter to the author, Mar. 9, 1987.

Page 238 "Eternity bores me": *CP*, p. 255.

("People or stars": *CP*, p. 262.

"the golden child": *CP*, p. 257.

"leave/This one": *CP*, p. 259.

Page 239 "There is no": *CP*, p. 264.

"buddha, all/Wants": *CP*, p. 267.

"Once one has": *CP*, pp. 268–69.

"The mirrors are": *CP*, p. 271.

"We have come": *CP*, pp. 272–73.

Page 240 ("Ted Hughes reported": Judith Kroll, *Notable American Women* essay on Plath, Smith; and *Chapters in a Mythology* (New York: Harper & Row, 1976), p. 177.

Page 241 "Dearest Marty": SP to Marcia Brown, Feb. 4, 1963, Smith.

"seeing the finality": *LH*, p. 498.

Page 241 "in blood, or": SP to Father Bart, Feb. 4, 1963, privately held.

Page 242 "Thank God you": SP to Elizabeth Compton, Sigmund memoir, Butscher, p. 106.

"She had fired": Professor Thomas's memoir, p. 14, Mar. 1987.

"At 11:45 P.M.": Trevor Thomas, letter to the author, Feb. 11, 1987, and memoir, p. 15.

AFTERWORD

Page 245 "The loss to": Alvarez, "A Poet's Epitaph," *The Observer*, Feb. 17, 1963.

Page 247 "the coming again": p. 11, unpublished journals, 1958–59, Smith.

Major Sources
and Acknowledgments

I. MAJOR COLLECTIONS OF SYLVIA PLATH PAPERS
Code letters for these collections are given in parentheses. Particulars of individual correspondence may be found in II, following.

The Lilly Library, Indiana University (I)
The most extensive collection of Plath materials was purchased from her mother, Aurelia Schober Plath, in 1977. This collection includes nearly 2000 letters, many from Sylvia to her family, others to her from a variety of correspondents. (The full manuscript of Mrs. Plath's *Letters Home*, much of which was not included in the 1975 book, is also here.) The holdings include Plath's annotated photograph albums, high school and college year books and memorabilia, drawings, handmade paper dolls and costumes, her baby book and other materials of the family's, papers she wrote in high school, college, and her two Fulbright years at Cambridge, and early diaries.

The collection holds over 150 of Plath's personal books, many with underlinings and annotations (see III, following), application materials for various awards and admissions, notes from classes at Smith and Newnham College, and notes for her own teaching at Smith during 1957–58.

It also contains over 200 poems, many unpublished and some with worksheets; 60 works of fiction, many unpublished; and 15 pieces of nonfiction; and publication records and scrapbooks. The collection in total runs to 3324 items and is housed in 15 boxes and 11 oversize containers.

The Neilson Library, Rare Book Room, Smith College (S)
Purchased from Ted Hughes in 1981, this collection comprises much of Sylvia Plath's late correspondence, writing, and book holdings. It includes approxi-

mately 4000 pages of Plath's manuscripts and typescripts, among those 850 pages of journal material and the successive drafts and worksheets of more than 200 poems. Fragments of Plath's novel, *The Bell Jar*, occur on the backs of some of the 1962 poems.

Also found in the Smith collection is extensive correspondence, a folder of Ted Hughes's lists of subjects to write poems about, her extensive records of poems submitted to magazines and their acceptances, her financial records (checkbooks, lists of expenses), notes for BBC broadcasts, drawings, and a quantity of miscellaneous material. There are some photographs, address books, college year books, a calendar from 1962, and other notes connected with her writing.

Mrs. Plath has added materials to those purchased from Ted Hughes, some concerning herself, others concerning Sylvia. Clippings about many of the stage, music, and dance performances of Plath's work are also present.

I am, of course, grateful to the excellent staff at both the Lilly Library (especially Saundra Taylor), and the Smith (especially Ruth Mortimer), and grateful as well to the following libraries and their responsive research librarians: The Pennsylvania State University Library; The Spencer Library, University of Kansas; the University of Illinois Library; the Houghton Library at Harvard University; Michigan State University Library; the Olin Library, Washington University; the Humanities Research Center, University of Texas at Austin; the Suzallo Library, University of Washington; Worcester Polytechnic Institute; the Berg Collection of English and American Literature at the New York Public Library; the University of Liverpool Library; and The British Library. Thanks are also owed to the libraries at the University of Kentucky, Louisiana State University, Southern Illinois University, Carnegie-Mellon University, The University of Michigan, Yale University, Princeton University, University of Georgia, Northern Illinois University, University of Wisconsin, Dartmouth College, University of Minnesota, Radcliffe College, Cornell University, University of North Carolina, Temple University, University of California at Los Angeles, Duke University, Rutgers University, Northwestern University, State University of New York at Buffalo, Amherst College, University of Massachusetts, University of New Hampshire, and University of Hawaii; and to the Archives Division, The Commonwealth of Massachusetts; The Huntington Library; The Newberry Library; The Rosenbach Museum and Library; and the Boston Public Library.

II. INDIVIDUAL CORRESPONDENCE, SYLVIA PLATH
Selected. S, Smith; I, Indiana

Abels, Cyrilly. *I.*

Alvarez, Alfred. *S.*

Anderson, Lee. Washington University, 2 letters with 13 poems enclosed.

Arvin, Newton. *I.*

Atlantic Monthly, The, magazine file. Begins in 1954.

Benotti, Dorothy Schober. *I.*

Beuscher, Ruth. *S.*

Bowen, Elizabeth. *I*.
Brown, Marcia. *S*.
Cleverdon, Douglas. *S*.
Cohen, Edward M. *I*.
Cohn, Leonie. *S*.
Compton, Elizabeth. *I*.
Cox, Brian, *Critical Quarterly*.
University of Kansas. 10 letters
from SP, 1960–61.
Crockett, Wilbury A. *I*.
Davidow, Ann. *S*.
Davies, Winifred. *I*.
Davis, Hope Hale. *I*.
Davis, Robert Gorham. *I*.
Davison, Peter. *I*. And see *Atlantic
Monthly, The*.
Drew, Elizabeth. *I*.
Dunn, Esther Cloudman. *I*.
Dyson, Anthony. *S*.
Epstein, Enid. *S*.
Fainlight, Ruth. *S*.
Farrar, Hilda A. *I*.
Fisher, Alfred Young. *I, S*.
Geissler, Ruth Freeman. *I*.
Goodall, Cathy. *I*.
Hall, Donald. University of New
Hampshire. From SP, 1961.
Heinrichs, Frieda Plath. *I*.
Horder, John P. *I*.
Horovitz, Michael. *I*.
Hughes, Carol Orchard. *I*.
Hughes, Edith Farrar. *I*.
Hughes, James Edward (Ted). *S, I*.
Hughes, Olwyn. *I*, Washington
University Libraries, SP to OH,
1958, 1960, 1962.
Jones, Judith. *S*. See Knopf, Alfred
A., Inc.
Kassay, Allan Attila. *I*.
Kazin, Alfred. *I*, Berg Collection,
New York Public Library. SP to
AK, 1961.
Knopf, Alfred A., Inc. Humanities
Research Center, University of
Texas. 1960–62, correspondence

and *The Bell Jar;* 1963–65, with
Ted Hughes regarding *Ariel*.
Koffka, Elisabeth Ahlgrimm. *I*.
Lameyer, Gordon Ames. *I*. Private
holdings, July 23, 1953, to Mar.
18, 1956, 53 letters from SP.
Lawner, Lynne. *I*.
Lawrence, Elizabeth. *S*.
Lehmann, John. Humanities
Research Center, University of
Texas, 1955–60.
Little, Marybeth. *I*.
Lotz, Myron. *S, I*.
Machin, David. *S*.
McCurdy, Philip. *S* (as of spring,
1985).
Moore, Marianne. *S*.
Moss, Howard. *S*.
Neupert, Hans Joachim. *S*.
Norton, Charles Perry. *I*. Private
holdings, SP to CPN, Oct. 13,
1952, and Dec. 5, 1952.
Norton, Mildred. *I*.
Norton, Richard Allen. *I*.
Norton, William B. *I*.
Osborne, Charles. Humanities
Research Center, University of
Texas. SP to CO, 1961–63.
Page. Evelyn. *I*.
Pearson, Norman Holmes. *I*.
Plath, Aurelia Schober. *I, S*.
Plath, Margaret Wetzel. *I*.
Plath, Warren Joseph. *I*.
Prouty, Olive Higgins. *I, S*.
Randall, Helen. *I*.
Reutlinger, Judith. Private holding,
SP to JR, Nov. 23, 1959.
Richardson, John. *S*.
Roche, Clarissa. Private holdings,
SP to CR, 1961–63.
Roethke, Theodore. University of
Washington, SP to TR, poem
enclosures, 1961.
Sassoon, Richard L. *I*.
Schober, Aurelia Greenwood. *I*.
Schober, Frank. *I*.

Schober, Frank Richard. *I.*
Scott, Ira O. *I.*
Sexton, Anne. Humanities
Research Center, University of
Texas, SP to AS, 1961, 1962;
*Anne Sexton, A Self-Portrait in
Letters,* ed. Linda Gray Sexton
and Lois Ames. Boston:
Houghton Mifflin, 1977, pp.
261–62, 274, 307.
Smith, Stevie. *S,* quoted (from SP)
in "Introduction" to *Me Again,*

Uncollected Writings of Stevie Smith,
ed. Jack Barbera and William
McBrien. London: Virago, 1981.
Stetson, Mary. *S.*
Vendler, Helen Hennessy. *I.*
Weeks, Edward. *I,* see *Atlantic
Monthly, The,* file.
Wertz, Richard Wayne. *I.*
Woody, J. Melvin. *I.*
Wunderlich, Ray. *I.*

III. SYLVIA PLATH'S PERSONAL LIBRARY: BOOKS
Selected. S, Smith; I, Indiana.

Aeschylus. *The Oresteian Trilogy. S.*
Aristotle. *The Ethics of Aristotle* and *Aristotle's Politics. S.*
Auden, W. H. *The Collected Poetry of W. H. Auden. S.*
Augustine, Saint, Bishop of Hippo. *The City of God* and *The Confessions. S.*
Baudelaire, Charles. *Les fleurs du mal. S.*
Berryman, John. *Homage to Mistress Bradstreet and Other Poems. S.*
Blake, William. *The Portable Blake. S.*
Chaucer, Geoffrey. *The Poetical Works of Chaucer. S.*
cummings, e. e. *Collected Poems* and *i, six nonlectures. S.*
Dick-Read, Grantly. *Childbirth Without Fear. S.*
Dostoevsky, Fyodor. *The Brothers Karamazov* and *The Short Novels. S.*
Eliot, George. *Middlemarch* and *The Mill on the Floss. I.*
Eliot, T. S. *The Complete Poems and Plays. S.*
Euripides. *The Bacchae and Other Plays. S.*
Faulkner, William. *The Sound and the Fury. S.*
Fitzgerald, F. Scott. *Tender Is the Night. I.*
Frazer, James George. *The Golden Bough. S.*
Freud, Sigmund. *The Basic Writings of Sigmund Freud. S.*
Fromm, Erich. *Escape from Freedom. I.*
Frost, Robert. *Complete Poems of Robert Frost. S.*
Hawthorne, Nathaniel. *The Complete Novels and Selected Tales. I.*
Hemingway, Ernest. *The Sun Also Rises. I.*
Huxley, Aldous. *Heaven & Hell. I.*
Ibsen, Henrik. *Eleven Plays. S.*
James, Henry. *The Ambassadors, The Golden Bowl, The Portrait of a Lady, Selected
Short Stories,* and *What Maisie Knew. S.*
James, William. *The Varieties of Religious Experience. S.*
Jarrell, Randall. *Poetry and the Age. I.*
Joyce, James. *Chamber Music, Dubliners, Finnegans Wake,* and *Ulysses. S. The
Portable James Joyce,* ed. Harry Levin. *I.*

Kafka, Franz. *Selected Short Stories.* S.

Langer, Susanne K. *Philosophy in a New Key.* S.

Lawrence, D. H. *Aaron's Rod, The Complete Poems, The Complete Short Stories, Lady Chatterley's Lover, The Plumed Serpent, The Rainbow, Selected Essays, Sons and Lovers, Studies in Classic American Literature,* and *Women in Love.* S. *D. H. Lawrence* by F. R. Leavis. *I.*

Lieder, Paul Robert, ed. *Eminent British Poets of the Nineteenth Century, II. I.*

Lowell, Robert. *Imitations* and *Lord Weary's Castle.* S.

Mann, Thomas. *Death in Venice and Seven Other Stories.* S. *Tonio Kröger. I.*

Mead, Margaret. *Male and Female: A Study of the Sexes in a Changing World. I.*

Moore, Marianne. *Collected Poems* and *Predilections.* S.

Nietzsche, Friedrich W. *Thus Spake Zarathustra.* S.

Ortega y Gasset, José. *The Revolt of the Masses. I.*

Patch, Howard Rollin. *On Rereading Chaucer. I.*

Plato. *Five Dialogues, Plato, with an English Translation, Plato's The Republic.* S.

Riesman, David. *The Lonely Crowd.* S.

Rilke, Rainer Maria. *Der Ausgewahlten Gedichte erster Teil* and *Sonnets to Orpheus.* S.

Rimbaud, Jean Nicolas Arthur. *A Season in Hell.* S.

Saint Exupéry, Antoine de. *Wind, Sand and Stars.* S.

Salinger, J. D. *Nine Stories.* S.

Sexton, Anne. *All My Pretty Ones.* S.

Shakespeare, William. *The Complete Plays and Poems.* S.

Sitwell, Edith. *The Canticle of the Rose.* S. *The Complete Poems. I.*

Sophocles. *Electra and Other Plays* and *The Theban Plays.* S.

Spock, Benjamin. *Baby and Child Care.* S.

Stevens, Wallace. *Collected Poems.* S.

Strindberg, August. *Eight Famous Plays.* S.

Synge, John Millington. *Collected Plays.* S.

Teasdale, Sara. *Dark of the Moon. I.*

Tillich, Paul. *The Courage To Be. I.*

Thomas, Dylan. *In Country Sleep and Other Poems* and *Under Milk Wood.* S.

Tolstoi, Leo. *Ivan Ilych and Hadji Murad.* S.

Williams, Tennessee. *Camino Real.* S.

Wilson, Edmund. *Axel's Castle.* S.

Woolf, Virginia. *Between the Acts, A Haunted House and Other Short Stories, Jacob's Room, Mrs. Dalloway, A Room of One's Own, The Voyage Out, The Waves, The Years.* S.

Yeats, W. B. *The Collected Plays* and *The Collected Poems.* S.

IV. BIBLIOGRAPHY OF SOURCES, PRIMARY AND SECONDARY

PRIMARY

(See Gary Lane and Maria Stevens, *Sylvia Plath: A Bibliography* [Metuchen, N.J.: Scarecrow, 1978] for essays, single poems, and stories)

Ariel. New York: Harper & Row, 1966.

The Bell Jar. New York: Harper & Row, 1971.

Between Ourselves, Letters Between Mothers & Daughters, ed. Karen Payne. Boston: Houghton Mifflin Co., 1983.

The Collected Poems, ed. Ted Hughes. New York: Harper & Row, 1981.

The Colossus and Other Poems. New York: Alfred A. Knopf, 1962.

Crossing the Water. New York: Harper & Row, 1971.

Johnny Panic and the Bible of Dreams, Short Stories, Prose and Diary Excerpts. New York: Harper & Row, 1980.

The Journals of Sylvia Plath, ed. Frances McCullough. New York: Dial Press, 1982.

Letters Home by Sylvia Plath, Correspondence 1950–1963, ed. Aurelia Schober Plath. New York: Harper & Row, 1975.

Winter Trees. New York: Harper & Row, 1972.

SECONDARY
Collections of Essays on Sylvia Plath's Work

Because of the great number of essays and books on Sylvia Plath's work, I have limited this listing to items *not* covered by Lane and Stevens, *Sylvia Plath: A Bibliography*. The five collections of essays on Plath's work listed below are the places for beginning readers to start; each contains valuable material, most of it not available elsewhere.

Ariel Ascending, Writings About Sylvia Plath, ed. Paul Alexander. New York: Harper & Row, 1984. Includes new and reprinted essays about both the person and the work.

The Art of Sylvia Plath, A Symposium, ed. Charles Newman (reprinted from *Tri-Quarterly*). Bloomington: Indiana Univ. Press, 1970. Includes writings by Plath, a bibliography of secondary material, and essays on both the person and the poetry.

Critical Essays on Sylvia Plath, ed. Linda W. Wagner. Boston: G. K. Hall, 1984. Includes essays and reviews.

Sylvia Plath, New Views on the Poetry, ed. Gary Lane. Baltimore: Johns Hopkins Press, 1979. Largely new essays on Plath's poetry and fiction.

Sylvia Plath: The Woman and the Work, ed. Edward Butscher. New York: Dodd, Mead, 1977. Includes largely new essays on both Plath and her writing.

ADDITIONAL SECONDARY SOURCES

Andreasen, Nancy C. *The Broken Brain, The Biological Revolution in Psychiatry*. New York: Harper & Row, 1984.

Atkinson, Michael. "After Twelve Years, Plath Without Tears: A Look Back at 'Lady Lazarus,' " *A Book of Rereadings in Recent American Poetry—30 Essays*, ed. Greg Kuzma. Lincoln, Neb.: Pebble Press, 1979.

Auerbach, Nina. *Woman and the Demon*. Cambridge, Mass.: Harvard Univ. Press, 1982.

Axelrod, Steven Gould. "The Mirror and the Shadow: Plath's Poetics of Self-Doubt," *Contemporary Literature*, 26 (Fall 1985), 286–301.

Banner, Lois W. *American Beauty*. New York: Alfred A. Knopf, 1983.

Bennett, Paula. *My Life a Loaded Gun, Female Creativity and Feminist Poetics*. Boston: Beacon Press, 1986.

Berman, Jeffrey. *The Talking Cure: Literary Representations of Psychoanalysis*. New York: New York Univ. Press, 1985.

Bernard, Caroline King. *Sylvia Plath*. Boston: Twayne, 1978.

Besdine, M. "Jocasta Complex, Mothering and Women Geniuses," *Psychoanalytic Review*, 58 (1973), 51–74.

Biller, H. B. and S. D. Weiss. "The Father-Daughter Relationship and the Personality Development of the Female," *Journal of Genetic Psychology*, 116 (1970), 79–93.

Bollobàs, Eniko. "Woman *and* Poet? Conflicts in the Poetry of Emily Dickinson, Sylvia Plath and Anne Sexton," *The Origins and Originality of American Culture*, ed. Tibor Frank. Budapest: Akademiai Kiado, 1984, 375–83.

Bradford, The (Wellesley, Mass.), 1947–50. SP co-editor, Vol. 6, 1949–50.

Broe, Mary Lynn. *Protean Poetic, The Poetry of Sylvia Plath*. Columbia: Univ. of Missouri Press, 1980.

———. "A Subtle Psychic Bond: The Mother Figure in Sylvia Plath's Poetry," *The Lost Tradition: Mothers and Daughters in Literature*, ed. Cathy N. Davidson and E. M. Broner. New York: Frederick Ungar, 1980, 217–30.

Bundtzen, Lynda K. *Plath's Incarnations: Woman and the Creative Process*. Ann Arbor: Univ. of Michigan Press, 1983.

Chodorow, Nancy. *The Reproduction of Mothering, Psychoanalysis and the Sociology of Gender*. Berkeley: Univ. of California Press, 1978.

——— and Susan Contratto, "The Fantasy of the Perfect Mother," *Rethinking the Family: Some Feminist Questions*, ed. Barrie Thorne with Marilyn Yalom. New York: Londman, 1982, 54–71.

Christ, Carol. *Diving Deep and Surfacing: Women Writers on Spiritual Quest*. Boston: Beacon, 1980.

Cox, C. B. "*Critical Quarterly*—twenty-five years," *Critical Quarterly*, 26 (Spring and Summer, 1984), 3–20.

Davison, Jane Truslow. *The Fall of a Doll's House, Three Generations of American Women and the Houses They Lived In*. New York: Holt, Rinehart and Winston, 1980.

Dinnerstein, Dorothy. *The Mermaid and the Minotaur: Sexual Arrangements and Human Malaise*. New York: Harper Colophon, 1976.

DuPlessis, Rachel Blau. *Writing Beyond the Ending, Narrative Strategies of Twentieth-Century Women Writers*. Bloomington: Indiana Univ. Press, 1985.

Ehrenreich, Barbara and Deirdre English. *For Her Own Good, 150 Years of the Experts' Advice to Women*. Garden City, N.Y.: Doubleday, 1979.

Gelpi, Barbara Chatsworth. "A Common Language: The American Woman Poet" in *Shakespeare's Sisters, Feminist Essays on Women Poets*, ed. Sandra Gilbert and Susan Gubar. Bloomington: Indiana Univ. Press, 1979, 269–79.

Gilbert, Lynn and Gaylen Moore. *Particular Passions, Talks with Women Who Have Shaped Our Times*. New York: Clarkson N. Potter, 1981 (see interviews with Gloria Steinem, Shirley Hufstedler, and Elisabeth Kübler-Ross).

Gilbert, Sandra. "A Fine, White Flying Myth: The Life/Work of Sylvia Plath," *Shakespeare's Sisters*, 245–60. See also Gilbert and Susan Gubar's introduction, "Gender, Creativity, and the Woman Poet" in that collection.

———. " 'My Name Is Darkness': The Poetry of Self-Definition," *Contemporary Literature*, 18 (1977), 443–57.

——— and Susan Gubar. "Ceremonies of the Alphabet: Female Grandmatologies and the Female Autograph," *The Female Autograph*, ed. Domna C. Stanton and Jeanine Parisier Plottle. New York: New York Literary Forum, 1984, 23–54.

———. *The Madwoman in the Attic: The Woman Writer and the Nineteenth-Century Literary Imagination*. New Haven, Conn.: Yale Univ. Press, 1979.

Gilligan, Carol. *In a Different Voice, Psychological Theory and Women's Development*. Cambridge, Mass.: Harvard Univ. Press, 1982.

Graves, Robert. *The White Goddess*. New York: Farrar, Straus, 1948.

Hankoff, L. "Poetry, Adolescence, and Suicide," *The Pharos* (publication of Alpha Omega Alpha), Spring 1984, 7–12.

Hawthorn, Jeremy. *Multiple Personality and the Disintegration of Literary Character, From Oliver Goldsmith to Sylvia Plath*. New York: St. Martin's Press, 1983.

Heller, Shirley H. *20th Century American Women Authors, A Feminist Approach*. New York: Simon & Schuster, Monarch Notes, 1975.

Homberger, Eric. *The Art of the Real, Poetry in England and America Since 1939*. Totowa, N.J.: Rowman and Littlefield, 1977.

Huf, Linda. *A Portrait of the Artist As a Young Woman: The Writer As Heroine in American Literature*. New York: Ungar, 1983.

Juhasz, Suzanne. *Naked and Fiery Forms, Modern American Poetry by Women: A New Tradition*. New York: Harper Colophon, 1976.

Kaladin, Eugenia. *Mothers and More, American Women in the 1950s*. Boston: Twayne, 1984.

Karl, Frederick R. *American Fictions, 1940–1980, A Comprehensive History and Critical Evaluation*. New York: Harper & Row, 1983.

Krasne, Betty. "Conformity and Diversity: The Paradox of the Fifties," *Mount Holyoke Alumnae Quarterly* (Spring 1985), 25–27.

Kroll, Judith. *Chapters in a Mythology, The Poetry of Sylvia Plath*. New York: Harper & Row, 1976.

Ladies' Home Journal, 1949–55.

Leonard, Linda Schierse. *The Wounded Woman: Healing the Father-Daughter Relationship*. London: Shambhala, 1983.

Libby, Anthony. *Mythologies of Nothing, Mystical Death in American Poetry, 1940–70*. Chicago: Univ. of Chicago Press, 1984.

Lord, Mae Masket and Carole Stone. "Fathers and Daughters: A Study of Three Poems," *Contemporary Psychoanalysis*, 9 (August 1973), 526–39.

Mademoiselle 37, No. 4 (August 1953).

Malmsheimer, Lonna M. "Sylvia Plath," *American Writers*, ed. Leonard Unger. Supp. I, Pt. 2. New York: Charles Scribner's Sons, 1979, 526–49.

Martin, Elaine. "Mothers, Madness and the Middle Class in *The Bell Jar* and *Les Mots pour le Dire*," *French-American Review*, 5 (Spring 1981), 24–47.

Miller, Alice. *The Drama of the Gifted Child (Prisoners of Childhood)*. New York: Harper & Row, 1981. Trans. Ruth Ward.

————. *For Your Own Good: Hidden Cruelty in Childrearing and the Roots of Violence*. New York: Farrar, Straus and Giroux, 1983.

Moers, Ellen. *Literary Women*. Garden City, N.Y.: Doubleday, 1976.

Mossberg, Barbara. "Back, Back, Back: Sylvia Plath's Baby Book," *Coming to Light: Women Poets in the Twentieth Century*, ed. Diane Middlebrook and Marilyn Yalom. Ann Arbor: Univ. of Michigan Press, 1986.

————. "A Rose in Context: The Daughter Construct," *Historical Studies and Literary Criticism*, ed. Jerome J. McGann. Madison: Univ. of Wisconsin Press, 1985, 199–225.

Oberg, Arthur. *Modern American Lyric—Lowell, Berryman, Creeley, and Plath*. New Brunswick, N.J.: Rutgers Univ. Press, 1978.

Orgel, Shelley. "Sylvia Plath: Fusion with the Victim and Suicide," *Psychoanalytic Quarterly*, 43 (1973), 262–87.

Ostriker, Alicia. "The Thieves of Language: Women Poets and Revisionist Mythmaking," *Signs: A Journal of Women, Culture and Society*, 8 (Autumn 1982), 68–90.

Pearson, Carol and Katherine Pope. *The Female Hero in American and British Literature*. New York: R. R. Bowker, 1981.

Perloff, Marjorie. "The Two Ariels: The (Re)Making of the Sylvia Plath Canon," *American Poetry Review*, 13 (Nov.–Dec. 1984), 10–18.

Plath, Otto Emil. *Bumblebees and Their Ways*. New York: Macmillan, 1934.

Pope, Deborah. *A Separate Vision*. Baton Rouge: Louisiana State Univ. Press, 1984.

Pratt, Annis. *Archetypal Patterns in Women's Fiction*. Brighton, Sussex: Harvester, 1982.

Ratner, Rochelle. "Sylvia Plath: Beyond the Biographical," *American Writing Today*, ed. Richard Kostelanetz. New York: America/Forum Editions, 1982.

Rich, Adrienne. "Blood, Bread and Poetry: The Location of the Poet," *Massachusetts Review*, 24 (Autumn 1983), 521–40.

————. "Issues of Feminine Survival," *Radcliffe Quarterly* (March 1979, 69–71.

————. *Of Woman Born, Motherhood as Experience and Institution*. New York: W. W. Norton, 1976.

Ries, Lawrence R. *Wolf Masks, Violence in Contemporary Poetry*. Port Washington, N.Y.: Kennikat, 1979.

Rosenblatt, Jon. *Sylvia Plath: The Poetry of Initiation*. Chapel Hill: Univ. of North Carolina, 1979.

Rosenthal, M. L. and Sally Gall. " 'Pure? What Does It Mean?' Notes on Sylvia Plath's Poetic Art," *American Poetry Review*, 7 (1978), 37–40. *The Modern Poetic Sequence: The Genius of Modern Poetry* (New York: Oxford Univ. Press, 1983) contains parts of that essay.

Sanazaro, Leonard. *Sylvia Plath: The Dark Repose* (radio play), University of Nevada, 1984.

Sang, Barbara E. "Women and the Creative Process," *The Arts in Psychotherapy*, 8 (1981), 43–48.

Sarot, Ellin. "To Be 'God's Lioness' and Live: On Sylvia Plath," *Centennial Review*, 23 (Spring 1979), 105–28.

Shainess, Natalie. *Sweet Suffering: Woman as Victim*. New York: Bobbs-Merrill, 1984.

Showalter, Elaine. *The Female Malady*. New York: Pantheon Books, 1985.

———. *A Literature of Their Own*. Princeton, N.J.: Princeton Univ. Press, 1977.

Sigmund, Elizabeth. "To the Editor: *The Bell Jar*," *Times Literary Supplement*, Nov. 30, 1973, 1477.

Simpson, Louis. *A Revolution in Taste: Studies of Dylan Thomas, Allen Ginsberg, Sylvia Plath, and Robert Lowell*. New York: Macmillan, 1978.

Smith-Rosenberg, Carroll. *Disorderly Conduct*. New York: Alfred A. Knopf, 1985.

Sophian, The, 1950–55 and 1957–58.

Steinem, Gloria. *Outrageous Acts and Everyday Rebellions*. New York: Holt, Rinehart, and Winston, 1983.

Stewart, Grace. *A New Mythos, The Novel of the Artist as Heroine 1877–1977*. Montreal: Eden Press Women's Publications, 1981.

Stone, Carole. "Three Mother-Daughter Poems: The Struggle for Separation," *Contemporary Psychoanalysis*, 11 (Apr. 1975), 227–39.

Uroff, M. D. "Sylvia Plath and Confessional Poetry: A Reconsideration," *Iowa Review*, 8 (Winter 1977), 104–15.

———. *Sylvia Plath and Ted Hughes*. Urbana: Univ. of Illinois Press, 1979.

Van Dyne, Susan R. "Double Monologues: Voices in American Women's Poetry," *Massachusetts Review*, 23 (Autumn 1982), 461–85.

———. "Fueling the Phoenix Fire: The Manuscripts of Sylvia Plath's 'Lady Lazarus,' " *Massachusetts Review*, 24 (Winter 1983), 395–410.

Waggoner, Hyatt H. *American Visionary Poetry*. Baton Rouge: Louisiana State Univ. Press, 1982.

Wagner, Linda W. "45 Mercy Street and Other Vacant Houses," in *American Literature, The New England Heritage*, ed. James Nagel and Richard Astro. New York: Garland, 1981. 145–65.

———. "Modern American Literature: The Poetics of the Individual Voice," *Centennial Review*, 21 (Fall 1977), 333–54.

———. "Plath on Napoleon," *Notes on Contemporary Literature*, 15 (Mar. 1985), 6.

———. "Plath's *The Bell Jar* as Female Bildungsroman," *Women's Studies*, 12, 55–68.

———. "Plath's *Ladies' Home Journal* Syndrome," *Journal of American Culture*, 7 (Spring–Summer 1984), 32–38.

———. "Sylvia Plath's Specialness in Her Short Stories," *Journal of Narrative Technique*, 15 (Winter 1985), 1–14.

Wallace, Ronald. *God Be With the Clown, Humor in American Poetry*. Columbia: Univ. of Missouri Press, 1984.

Williamson, Alan. *Introspection and Contemporary Poetry*. Cambridge: Harvard Univ. Press, 1984.

Yalom, Marilyn. *Maternity, Mortality, and the Literature of Madness*. University Park, Pa.: The Pennsylvania State Univ. Press, 1985.

V. BIOGRAPHY OF SYLVIA PLATH, RELEVANT PUBLICATIONS

Alvarez, Alfred. *The Savage God: A Study of Suicide*. New York: Random House, 1972.

Ames, Lois, "Notes Toward a Biography" in *The Art of Sylvia Plath, A Symposium*, ed. Charles Newman (reprinted from *Tri-Quarterly*). Bloomington: Indiana Univ. Press, 1970, 155–73. Hereafter Newman.

————. "Sylvia Plath: A Biographical Note," *The Bell Jar*. New York: Harper & Row, 1971, 203–16.

Butscher, Edward. *Sylvia Plath: Method and Madness*. New York: Seabury Press, 1976.

Campbell, Wendy. "Remembering Sylvia" in Newman, 182–86.

Christiaen, Chris. "Poet on College Time," *Mademoiselle*, 41 (Aug. 1955), 49, 52, 62.

Davison, Peter. *Half Remembered, A Personal History*. New York: Harper & Row, 1973.

Gaebler, Max D. "Sylvia Plath Remembered" (Mar. 14, 1983), in Smith Archive.

Gardner, Philip. " 'The Bland Granta': Sylvia Plath at Cambridge," *Dalhousie Review*, 60 (Autumn 1980), 496–507.

Hamilton, Ian. *Robert Lowell, A Biography*. New York: Random House, 1982.

Hughes, Ted. "Foreword," *The Journals of Sylvia Plath, 1950–62*, ed. Frances McCullough and Ted Hughes. New York: Dial Press, 1982.

————. "Introduction," *The Collected Poems of Sylvia Plath*, ed. Ted Hughes. New York: Harper & Row, 1981.

————. "Introduction," *Johnny Panic and the Bible of Dreams, Short Stories, Prose, and Diary Excerpts*. New York: Harper & Row, 1979.

————. "Note," introducing 10 poems by Plath, *Encounter*, 21 (Oct. 1963), 45.

————. "Notes on the Chronological Order of Sylvia Plath's Poems," in Newman, 187–95.

————. "Sylvia Plath," *Poetry Book Society Bulletin*, 44 (Feb. 1965).

————. "Sylvia Plath and Her Journals," in *Ariel Ascending, Writings About Sylvia Plath*, ed. Paul Alexander. New York: Harper & Row, 1984. 152–64.

————. "Sylvia Plath's *Crossing the Water*: Some Reflections," *Critical Quarterly*, 13 (Summer 1971), 165–72.

————. "*Winter Trees*," *Poetry Book Society Bulletin*, 70 (Autumn 1971).

Kazin, Alfred. *New York Jew*. New York: Alfred A. Knopf, 1978.

Klein, Elinor. "A Friend Recalls Sylvia Plath," *Glamour* (Nov. 1966), 168–84.

Kopp, Jane Baltzell. " 'Gone, Very Gone Youth': Sylvia Plath at Cambridge," in *Sylvia Plath: The Woman and the Work*, ed. Edward Butscher. New York: Dodd, Mead, 1977, 61–80. Hereafter Butscher.

Krook, Dorothea. "Recollections of Sylvia Plath," in Butscher, 49–60.

Lameyer, Gordon. "Letters from Sylvia," *Smith Alumnae Quarterly*, 67 (Feb. 1976), 3–10.

———. "Sylvia at Smith," in Butscher, 32–41.

———. "Who Was Sylvia? A Memoir of Sylvia Plath," unpublished.

Middlebrook, Diane. "Housewife into Poet: The Apprenticeship of Anne Sexton," *New England Quarterly* (Dec. 1983), 483–503.

Morris, Irene V. "Sylvia Plath at Newnham—a Tutorial Recollection," *Newnham College Roll: Letter*, 1975, 45–47.

Plath, Aurelia Schober. *Letters Home by Sylvia Plath, Correspondence 1950–1963*. New York: Harper & Row, 1975. (Introduction and continuity; also different versions of each in Lilly Library Plath collection, unpublished.)

———. "Authors' Series Talk," Mar. 16, 1976, Wellesley College Club (in Smith Plath Archive).

——— and Robert Robinson. "Sylvia Plath's *Letters Home:* Some Reflections by Her Mother," *The Listener*, 95 (Apr. 22, 1976), 515–16.

Robins, Corinne. "Four Young Poets," *Mademoiselle*, 48 (Jan. 1959), 34–35, 85.

Roche, Clarissa, "Sylvia Plath: Vignettes from England" in Butscher, 81–96.

Rosenstein, Harriet. "Reconsidering Sylvia Plath," *Ms.*, 1 (Sept. 1972), 45–51, 96–99.

Sachar, Neva Nelson. "What's Going On/People," *Mademoiselle* (Mar. 1979), 112, 114.

Sexton, Anne. "The Barfly Ought To Sing" in Newman, 174–81.

Shook, Margaret. "Sylvia Plath: The Poet and the College," *Smith Alumnae Quarterly*, 63 (Apr. 1972), 4–9.

Sigmund, Elizabeth. "Sylvia in Devon: 1962" in Butscher, 100–07.

Spivack, Kathleen. "Lear in Boston: Robert Lowell as Teacher and Friend," *Ironwood* (Spring 1985), 76–92.

———. "Poets and Friends," *Boston Globe Magazine*, Aug. 9, 1981, 10–12, 35–42.

———. "Robert Lowell: A Memoir," *The Antioch Review*, 43 (Spring 1985), 183–93.

———. *Robert Lowell and the Teaching of Poetry, Boston/Cambridge, 1959–77*, unpublished manuscript.

Steiner, Nancy Hunter. *A Closer Look at Ariel: A Memory of Sylvia Plath*, introduction by George Stade. New York: Harper's Magazine Press, 1973.

Stoianoff, Ellen A. "Sylvia Plath: Three Poems and a Remembrance," *Mademoiselle*, 73 (Sept. 1971), 160–61.

VI. AUTHOR'S SOURCES

Grateful thanks are extended to the following for the many interviews and letters: Daniel Aaron, Al Alvarez, Judith Anderson, Nina Auerbach, Hilary Bailey, Shirley Baldwin, Ruth Barnes, Charles Bell, Ruth Beuscher, Mary Bonneville, Philip Booth, Marie Borroff, Vance Bourjaily, Ann Boutelle, Gerald Brace, Loring Brace, Joan Bramwell, Henry Braun, Marcia Brown, Lynda Bundtzen, Anne Burnside, Edward Butscher, Elizabeth Carter, Charles Causley, Edward Cohen, Malcolm Cowley, Brian Cox, Wilbury A. Crockett, Janet Crosbie-Hill, Marcia Damon-Rey, Ann Davidow, Hope Davis, Robert Gorham Davis, Peter Davison, Nicholas Demy, Margaret Dickie, Charles Doyle,

Paul Drake, Paul Engel, Enid Epstein, Father Bart, Ruth Fainlight, Allen Fesmire, Jack Folsom, David V. Forrest, Elinor Friedman, Philip Gardner, Joyce Garrett, Cay Gibian, George Gibian, Mick Gidley, James Gindin, Sarah Growe, Thom Gunn, Peter Hackett, S. J., Donald Hall, Pauline Hanson, Ildiko Hayes, Timothy S. Healy, S. J., Linda Heaton, Anthony Hecht, Elinor Herlands, Charles Hill, Michael Hollings, Joanne Hollingsworth, Eric Homberger, Patricia Hooper, John Horder, Daniel Huws, Helga Huws, Diane Johnson, Linda Johnson, Donald Junkins, Marlies Kallman, Carolyn Kizer, Annette Kolodny, Sylvia Koval, Dorothea Krook, Maxine Kumin, Gordon Lameyer, Philip Larkin, John Lehmann, Carol LeVarn, Christopher Levenson, Peter Levi, Eleanor T. Lincoln, Harold Littledale, Myron Lotz, George MacBeth, Julia Matcham, Madelyn Mathers, Jerome Mazzaro, J. D. McClatchy, Philip McCurdy, Nancy McGilliard, Elizabeth McQuat, W. S. Merwin, Gretchen Meyer, Diane Wood Middlebrook, Jill Modlin, Ruth Mortimer, Neva Nelson, Ken Neville-Davies, B. Z. Niditch, Perry Norton, Susan O'Neill-Roe, Aurelia Plath, Jennifer Platt, Patience Plummer, Annis Pratt, Robert Preyer, Sonia Raiziss, Helen Randall, Adrienne Rich, Robert Riedeman, Clarissa Roche, Paul Roche, Ned Rorem, Tom Rosenmeyer, Harriet Rosenstein, Jean Rossiter, Keith Sagar, Leonard Sanazaro, Stephen Sandy, Andre Schiffrin, Leonard Scigaj, Sallie Sears, Ann Shawber, Elizabeth Sigmund, Alan Sillitoe, Jane Sinauer, Robin Skelton, Carol Slade, Anthony Smith, Kathleen Spivack, Mary Sullivan, May Swenson, Stephen R. Tabor, Ron Tamplin, Constance Taylor, Trevor Thomas, Anthony Thwaite, Iris Tillman, Susan Toth, Laurie Totten, Mrs. A. Ventura, Elizabeth Von Klemperer, Janet Wagner, Aileen Ward, Mike Weaver, Hugh Webb, Sydney Webber, Sue Weller, Chou Wen-Chung, Leslie Westoff, James Whalen, Richard Wilbur, Bertram Wyatt-Brown, Edward Yarnold, Margaret York, Leah Zahler.

Index

INDEX

INDEX

INDEX

INDEX